EXODUS CHURCH AND CIVIL SOCIETY

This book investigates the intersection of theology and social theory in the work of Jürgen Moltmann. In particular, it examines the way in which his concept of the "Exodus Church" can illuminate the importance of the idea of civil society for a Christian public theology. The concept of civil society can aid in moving from the narrower category of "political theology," a term used frequently by Moltmann to emphasize the church's public commitment, to a broader understanding of theology's public task, which takes into account the plurality of ends and institutions within society. The idea of the Exodus Church enables deeper understanding of Christian ethical participation within a complex modern society.

ASHGATE NEW CRITICAL THINKING IN RELIGION, THEOLOGY AND BIBLICAL STUDIES

The *Ashgate New Critical Thinking in Religion, Theology and Biblical Studies* series brings high quality research monograph publishing back into focus for authors, international libraries, and student, academic and research leaders. Headed by an international editorial advisory board of acclaimed scholars, spanning the breadth of religious studies, theology and biblical studies, this open-ended monograph series presents cutting-edge research from both established and new authors in the field. With specialist focus yet clear contextual presentation of contemporary research, books in this series take research into important new directions and open the field to new critical debate within the discipline, in areas of related study, and in key areas for contemporary society.

Other Titles in the Series:

Wolfhart Pannenberg on Human Destiny
Kam Ming Wong

Revelation, Scripture and Church
Theological Hermeneutic Thought of James Barr, Paul Ricoeur and Hans Frei
Richard R. Topping

Postmodernism and the Ethics of Theological Knowledge
Justin Thacker

Pentecostal Theology for the Twenty-First Century
Engaging with Multi-Faith Singapore
May Ling Tan-Chow

Neopragmatism and Theological Reason
G.W. Kimura

Tantric Buddhism and Altered States of Consciousness
Durkheim, Emotional Energy and Visions of the Consort
Louise Child

Biblical Scholarship and the Church
A Sixteenth-Century Crisis of Authority
Allan K. Jenkins and Patrick Preston

EXODUS CHURCH AND CIVIL SOCIETY
Public Theology and Social Theory in the
Work of Jürgen Moltmann

SCOTT R. PAETH
DePaul University, USA

ASHGATE

© Scott R. Paeth 2008

All rights reserved. No part of this publication may be reproduced, stored in a retrieval system or transmitted in any form or by any means, electronic, mechanical, photocopying, recording or otherwise without the prior permission of the publisher.

Scott R. Paeth has asserted his moral right under the Copyright, Designs and Patents Act, 1988, to be identified as the author of this work.

Published by
Ashgate Publishing Limited
Gower House
Croft Road
Aldershot
Hampshire GU11 3HR
England

Ashgate Publishing Company
Suite 420
101 Cherry Street
Burlington, VT 05401-4405
USA

www.ashgate.com

British Library Cataloguing in Publication Data
Paeth, Scott
  Exodus church and civil society : public theology and social theory in the work of Jürgen Moltmann. – (Ashgate new critical thinking in religion, theology and biblical studies)
  1. Moltmann, Jürgen 2. Political theology 3. Civil society
  I. Title
  261.7'092

Library of Congress Cataloging-in-Publication Data
Paeth, Scott.
  Exodus church and civil society : public theology and social theory in the work of Jürgen Moltmann / Scott R. Paeth.
      p. cm. — (Ashgate new critical thinking in religion, theology, and biblical studies)
   ISBN 978-0-7546-6201-3 (hardcover : alk. paper) 1. Moltmann, Jürgen. 2. Religion and civil society. 3. Political theology. 4. Critical theory. I. Title.

BX4827.M6P34 2008
230'.044092—dc22

2008017010

ISBN 978-0-7546-6201-3

Mixed Sources
Product group from well-managed forests and other controlled sources
www.fsc.org Cert no. SA-COC-1565
© 1996 Forest Stewardship Council

Printed and bound in Great Britain by
MPG Books Ltd, Bodmin, Cornwall.

Contents

Acknowledgements — *vii*

Part I   Jürgen Moltmann's Public Theology

1 Moltmann, Modernity, and Public Theology — 3
2 The Development of Moltmann's Political Theology — 17
3 Promise, Covenant, and Human Rights — 37
4 Exodus Church and Civil Society — 49

Part II   Ethical Engagement and the Task of Public Theology

5 Public Theology and the Task of Theological Ethics — 61
6 Public Theology in the American Tradition — 77

Part III   Rationality, Civil Society, and The Role Of The Church

7 Theology, Reason, and Critical Theory — 101
8 The Evolution of the Theory of Civil Society — 113
9 Civil Society and the Church's Public Role — 127

Part IV Social Ethics and The Exodus Church

10 Public Theology, Critical Modernism, and the Kingdom of God — 153
11 The Theological and Social Character of the Church — 173
12 Conclusions and Prospects — 191

Bibliography — *201*

Index — *213*

Acknowledgements

This project is the end result of a 15-year journey with Jürgen Moltmann's theology. During college, when I first discovered a copy of *Theology of Hope* at a used bookstore, I had little acquaintance with Moltmann's theology or its antecedents. But the title of the book appealed to me, and so I bought it. Several months later, I encountered Ernst Bloch's *Principle of Hope*, and was moved by his vision of human hope. When I returned to Moltmann and connected the dots, the seeds of this project were sown.

Since then, I have been fortunate to have received encouragement, inspiration, and support from many sources. At Andover Newton Theological School, Princeton Theological Seminary, Albertson College, Quincy University, and DePaul University, I have been privileged to learn from and work among teachers and colleagues who have given advice and challenged me to push more deeply into not only Moltmann's work, but the connections that his work has with the broader themes I address in this volume, particularly the ideas of public theology and civil society.

This book is a revision of my doctoral dissertation, written under the direction of Max L. Stackhouse at Princeton Theological Seminary. Max is at the forefront of those who, over the years, have pressed me to consider issues at the intersection of religion and public life from different perspectives, and to consider the complexity and ambiguity of any attempts to understand the relationship between Christian ethics and social responsibility. Similarly, the other members of my dissertation committee, Daniel Migliore and Peter Paris, brought to my attention important resources for Christian ethical discernment that, not always obviously, have made their way into my own viewpoint.

Passages from this project have also appeared in my article "Jürgen Moltmann's Public Theology," in the journal *Political Theology*, volume 6, number 2 (2005), pages 215–34.

Since moving to DePaul University, I have been fortunate to have received considerable aid in bringing this project to completion. I was awarded a Summer Research Grant in 2005 to continue my revision work, as well as an Undergraduate Research Assistant grant to provide me with research help during the 2005–06 academic year. I was able to complete the final revisions during a research leave in the Fall of 2007. I am deeply grateful to Dean Charles Suchar and the administration of DePaul University for all of the aid that they have given me in bringing this project to fruition as well as my research assistant, T.J. Bigbee, whose aid throughout this project has been invaluable.

Finally, and most importantly, I must thank my family, particularly my wife Amy and our two daughters, Molly and Katelyn. For the many hours that I spent on this project, through which they patiently bore with me, I am deeply grateful.

PART I
JÜRGEN MOLTMANN'S PUBLIC THEOLOGY

Chapter 1

Moltmann, Modernity, and Public Theology

Introduction

Public theology strives to uncover the theological issues that underlie human culture, society, and experience.[1] It "points towards a wider and deeper strand of theological reflection rooted in the interaction of biblical insight, philosophical analysis, historical discernment and social formation."[2] As theology it is an interpretive and constructive project emerging from the experience and faith of particular religious communions in an attempt to reveal the general public relevance of the theological truth of which it speaks. It neither can nor should seek to separate itself from the larger social situation in which it finds itself, but has an obligation to seek those commonalities out of which human beings, as both religious and social creatures, may strive to recognize a larger set of meanings in economy, culture, politics and society.

My purpose in this volume is to examine the way in which public theology and theories of civil society engage one another around questions of institutional life, social obligation, and the moral formation of persons in the midst of a pluralistic society. In particular, I am interested in the question of how a public theology may advance and defend substantive moral values in the midst of an instrumentalized and secularized society. I am also interested in examining these issues through the lenses provided by the theology of Jürgen Moltmann, whose work ties together themes of ecclesiology, eschatology, ethics and public responsibility through a creative and critical engagement with the work of Ernst Bloch and the Frankfurt School of philosophy. In particular, I see Moltmann's conception of the "Exodus community," while underdeveloped, as providing a means through which the church's public responsibility within civil society may be clarified.

The fundamental problem that underlies this inquiry is the increasing dominance in public life of what Max Weber refers to as "instrumental" and "formal" modes of rationality that seek to categorize the rationality of human action on the basis

---

1 The term public theology has become extraordinarily prominent in recent literature, although its precise meaning is subject to considerable debate. Harold Breitenberg notes that "since 1974, when the term 'public theology' first appeared, seventeen books and over a hundred articles and essays have been published in which public theology(ies) or public theologian(s) appear in the title." E. Harold Breitenberg, Jr., "To Tell the Truth," *The Journal of the Society of Christian Ethics*, 23, no. 2 (fall/winter, 2003), 70.

2 Max L. Stackhouse, "Public Theology" in Nicholas Lossky, ed., *et al.*, *The Dictionary of the Ecumenical Movement* (Geneva: World Council of Churches, 2002).

of empirical and quantifiable measurements.³ This conception was picked up and developed by the Frankfurt School in their analysis of modernity.⁴ The dominance of such forms of rationality results in the marginalization of questions of substantive value, conviction and emotional attachment to the realm of the private, and to some degree "irrational," sphere of personal preference. What this means for Christian ethics is the relegation of its concrete claims about the nature of the human good, and the vision of society that correlates to that vision to, at best, a hypothetical and abstract human possibility, and at worst an unattainable "utopian" vision of the world to come.

This rise of instrumental rationality provokes grave questions about the relevance of Christian ethics to the modern condition. If Christianity really has nothing to say about the way in which modern life is lived, such as the values embodied in democracy, liberalism, and freedom that stand at the center of much of what the modern West embraces, then Christians must seriously reconsider their participation in such a way of life. If the trajectory of modern life is toward the mere negotiation of quantitative interest-values within a competitive system of private interest, then the idea that there might be such a thing as a constructive Christian social ethic is effectively refuted by its very irrelevance to life as it is actually lived. Religion would then become no more than an aesthetic escape valve, used by alienated consumers to render meaning to an essentially meaningless life.

There are no few Christians who would abandon constructive engagement with modernity. In particular, certain strands of narrative theology,[5] and the so-called "radical orthodoxy" of the school of John Milbank,[6] seek to divest themselves of the baggage of modernity in order to retrieve a sense of faith-based community in protest to such instrumentalization in society. Yet such abandonment is not the only

---

3 Weber's analysis of the various types of rationality identifies four different modes of reason in society: Instrumental rationality (*zweckrationalität*), Value rationality (*wertrationalität*), formal rationality, and substantive rationality. These modes of rationality are not exclusive of one another, however he identifies the rise of instrumental and formal modes of rationality as being indicative of the emergence of modern forms of economic life. See Max Weber, *Economy and Society* (Berkeley: University of California Press, 1978) 24–5, 85–6. Cf. Max Weber, "Politics as a Vocation" in *From Max Weber: Essays in Sociology* (New York: Oxford University Press, 1946), 77ff.

4 Max Horkheimer and Theodore Adorno, *Dialectic of Enlightenment* (New York: Continuum, 1972); Theodore Adorno, *Negative Dialectics* (New York: Continuum, 1973); Max Horkheimer, *Between Philosophy and Social Science: Selected Early Writings* (Cambridge: MIT Press, 1993); Max Horkheimer, *Critical Theory: Selected Essays* (New York: Continuum, 1972).

5 See Stanley Hauerwas, *The Peaceable Kingdom* (Notre Dame: Notre Dame University Press, 1983); *Resident Aliens* (with William Willimon) (Nashville: Abingdon, 1989); *Christian Existence Today* (Grand Rapids: Baker Books, 1995); *Truthfulness and Tragedy* (Notre Dame: University of Notre Dame Press, 1977); *Vision and Virtue* (Notre Dame: Notre Dame University Press, 1974); *Unleashing the Scripture* (Nashville: Abingdon, 1993); *Dispatches from the Front* (Durham, NC: Duke University Press, 1994).

6 John Milbank, *Theology and Social Theory* (Oxford: Basil Blackwell, 1991) and *The Word Made Strange* (Cambridge: Blackwell, 1997). See also John Milbank, Graham Ward and Catherine Pickstock, eds, *Radical Orthodoxy* (New York: Routledge, 1999).

course of action available. The possibility exists through an interpretation of the role of the church *in the midst* of society to show how Christian ethics can call modern instrumentalism into question.

In this chapter, I will consider what Moltmann's theology might contribute to such an analysis of the modern way of life.

Moltmann and Modernity

Jürgen Moltmann often speaks of his theology as being experimental, open to adjustment and revision. Theology, he states, is "an adventure of ideas. It is an open, inviting path" on which "*the road emerged only as I walked it.*"[7] Beginning with his attempts in *Theology of Hope*[8] to recover the eschatological basis of Christian theology, as well as his extension and expansion of those ideas in *The Crucified God*,[9] Moltmann has attempted to offer a way of doing theology that was both open to that which is culturally new and at the same time rooted in scripture and tradition. He has certainly not lacked for critics.[10] Yet he has maintained throughout the evolution of his thought both a commitment to his belief in the eschatological basis of Christian theology, and the obligation of Christian theology to remain open to the world and responsive to the ethical demands made of it by its social situation. As Richard Bauckham writes: "for Moltmann Christian political engagement is no substitute for Christian faith, but one of the forms which faith must take in action; and political theology is no substitute for dogmatic theology, but theology's critical reflection on its own political function."[11]

As his theology has developed, Moltmann has attempted to remain responsive to that political function with regard to how the church views its own public responsibility. In the 1960s this led Moltmann into movements for Christian–Marxist dialogue and to involvement with theologians in East Germany as well as

---

7 Jürgen Moltmann, *Experiences in Theology* (Philadelphia: Fortress Press, 2000), xv. Italics in original.

8 Jürgen Moltmann, *Theology of Hope: On the Ground and Implications of a Christian Eschatology* (New York: Harper & Row, 1967). Translation of *Theologie der Hoffnung: Untersuchungen zur Begründung und zu den Konsequenzen einer christlichen Eschatologie* (München: Chr. Kaiser, 1965).

9 Jürgen Moltmann, *The Crucified God: the Cross of Christ as the Foundation and Criticism of Christian Theology* (New York: Harper & Row, 1974). Translation of *Der gekreuzigte Gott; Das Kreuz Christi als Grund und Kritik christlicher Theologie* (München: Chr. Kaiser, 1972).

10 See, for example, Christopher Morse, *The Logic of Promise in Moltmann's Theology* (Philadelphia: Fortress Press, 1979) and Arne Rasmussen, *The Church as Polis: From Political Theology to Theological Politics as Exemplified by Jürgen Moltmann and Stanley Hauerwas* (Notre Dame: University of Notre Dame Press, 1995). For more appreciative, although critical, commentary on Moltmann's theology, see Douglas Meeks, *Origins of the Theology of Hope* (Philadelphia: Fortress Press, 1974); Richard Bauckham, *The Theology of Jürgen Moltmann* (Edinburgh: T&T Clark, 1995); Amatus Woi, *Trinitatslehre und Monotheismus: Die Problematik der Gottesrede und ihre social-politische Relevanz bei Jürgen Moltmann* (Frankfurt am Main: Peter Lang, 1998).

11 Bauckham, *The Theology of Jürgen Moltmann*, 99.

theologians in the West.¹² But as time has marched on and the social and political categories which were pressing have changed, Moltmann's theological project has also undergone change. The concerns that motivated him in 1964 have changed as the context in which they were formulated has shifted. The East Bloc vs. the West Bloc is no longer a category that calls for a Christian response, but other issues do, particularly issues of globalization, environmental destruction and human rights.¹³ But as the issues to which he is responding have changed, so has Moltmann's way of expressing his theological commitments.

Moltmann, along with J.B. Metz, was among the first to attempt to recover the social relevance of theology in terms of the category of "political" theology in Germany in the early 1970s.¹⁴ In that context, the use of the term "political" was a provocative plea to the church to become socially engaged and to take responsibility for speaking from its deepest commitments to the world of which it was a part. In the era of "*keine Experimenten!*"¹⁵ Moltmann and Metz expressed by their use of the phrase "political theology" precisely a desire to experiment with the categories by which the church could engage its social context. The cautious conservatism of post-war Germany set a tone in which any attempts to engage in major reforms were looked upon with suspicion.¹⁶ The goal was social stability, and the close proximity of communist rule in the DDR led to a deep mistrust of all things Left.¹⁷ Thus,

---

12 See Meeks, *Origins of the Theology of Hope*, 20; Bauckham, *The Theology of Jürgen Moltmann*, 103ff.

13 These concerns have been central to Moltmann's work since the late 1970s. His most developed reflection on globalization can be found in *The Coming of God* (Philadelphia: Fortress, 1996), *God for a Secular Society* (Philadelphia: Fortress Press, 1999), and *Experiences in Theology*. He dealt extensively with ecological issues in *God in Creation* (Philadelphia: Fortress Press, 1985), and with human rights in *On Human Dignity* (Philadelphia: Fortress Press, 1984). The details of his approach to these issues will be discussed throughout this book.

14 Whereas *Der gekreuzigte Gott* was first published in 1972, Jürgen Moltmann's exploration of the concept of political theology can be located somewhat earlier, to at least 1969, when he writes: "Political theology, in our opinion, no longer implies only theology and politics, church and state. Rather, responsible theology must become aware of an inherent political dimension in itself and in church life. On the other hand, political theology does not reduce everything to politics (C. Schmitt) nor does it submit theology and the church to the terms and requirements of state policy." "The Cross and Civil Religion" in *Religion and Political Society* (New York: Harper & Row, 1972), 18–19. A German version of this article appeared in J.B. Metz, Jürgen Moltmann, and Willi Olemüller, *Kirche im Prozess der Aufkarlung* (Munchen: C. Kaiser, 1970). Moltmann credits Metz with the recovery of the term, although it is as closely associated with him as it is with Metz.

15 Moltmann, "Preface: Twenty Five Years," in *Theology of Hope*, 8.

16 Geiko Müller-Fahrenholz, *The Kingdom and the Power* (Philadelphia: Fortress Press, 2000), 29–30. These themes are more broadly discussed in Gordon A. Craig, *The Germans* (New York: G.P. Putnam's Sons, 1982), 35ff.

17 As Douglas Meeks notes: "A largely externally imposed, no-risk politics and the German 'economic miracle' together played a large part in numbing the suffering and horror of the immediate past. In state and society it was a time of sober realism, of striving for social order without risk. The prevailing mood was marked by suspicion of all ideologies and utopias,

the way in which Moltmann and Metz framed their understanding of the political responsibility of the church in their alliance with movements for Christian–Marxist dialogue and the rapprochement with the East was deliberately confrontational. Moltmann's writings embody a spirit of resistance: "The *Sitz im Leben* of political theology today is the life of Christians who for the sake of their consciences suffer in the midst of the public misery of society and struggle against this misery."[18]

Having identified himself at this point as a "political theologian," Moltmann's theology did not however stop its development. In particular, his engagement in Christian–Marxist dialogue, his conversation with and critique of liberation theology,[19] and the changing of the socio-political context in which theological ethics was done post-1989 changed the categories with which Moltmann approached the questions of how Christians ought to respond in the midst of human social life. Today, when describing his theology, he is apt to use the term "public theology" rather than political theology.[20]

The Question of Public and Political Theology

One of Jürgen Moltmann's recent books asks in its subtitle about "the public relevance of theology."[21] But within liberal democratic societies today, including Germany and the United States, there often seems to be a sense that theology, in the sense of thoughtful, critical reflection on questions of faith, has no public relevance. At best, theology may serve in the background of a person's publicly declared (and publicly defensible) positions on issues, but, because it is deemed irrational and private, as the basis of public reason, it cannot become explicit. Theology, under such circumstances, cannot really be said to be "public" at all. It is shunted into the sphere of private opinions and dispositions, because social policy must be based upon principles, which are empirically and universally comprehensible. Religion as a mode of rational discourse is no more publicly viable than aesthetics.

However, it is not clear that, on the one hand, theological positions *are* in fact private matters, or even matters limited to the "language game" of the believing community. Nor is it clear that *non*-theological arguments in the public sphere are

---

out of which arose an ideology of maintenance and a utopia of the status quo and everywhere a penetrating sense of apathy for the future." *Origins of the Theology of Hope*, 4.

18 Jürgen Moltmann, "Political Theology" in *The Experiment Hope* (Philadelphia: Fortress Press, 1975), 101. The original article, "Political Theology," appears in *Theology Today* 28 no. 1 (April 1971) 6–23.

19 See, in particular, Moltmann's exchange with José Miguez-Boniño. Miguez-Boniño's contribution can be found in *Doing Theology in a Revolutionary Situation* (Philadelphia: Fortress, 1975) in which he offers a critique of European political theology, Moltmann's in particular, as buying into Bourgeois presuppositions about the nature of theology and society. Moltmann's reply can be found in his "Open Letter to José Miguez-Boniño," *Christianity and Crisis*, March 29, 1976, 57–63, reprinted in *Liberation Theology: A Documentary History* (Maryknoll: Orbis Books, 1992), 195–204.

20 Moltmann, *God for a Secular Society*, 1.

21 Moltmann, *God for a Secular Society*.

innately more rational than theological ones. Rather, the question of how theology may, and indeed must, articulate its social vision in the public sphere revolves precisely around the debunking of these assumptions and the recognition of that which is rational vis-à-vis the public realm is more complex than some liberal and post-liberal theories would lead one to believe.

Liberal democracy is frequently conceived of as entailing a certain set of agreed-upon presuppositions that all members must agree to if it is to exist and thrive. At the same time, what makes a *liberal* democracy is precisely the possibility that pluralism may exist within the boundaries of those agreed-upon presuppositions. Remove the presuppositions, and you lose the democracy. Remove the pluralism, and you remove the liberalism.

Moltmann's own interaction with liberal democracy is complex, and cannot be simply labeled and forgotten. The same is true of his attitude toward the themes of modernity out of which liberal democracy arises. On the one hand, he has been and remains quite critical of modern social and economic forms of life, seeing them as dehumanizing and alienating both from God and other human beings.[22] On the other hand, he is a strong supporter of democratic structures and, depending on the context in which the term is used, a pluralistic model of social life. What Moltmann does *not* address in his theology is the necessity for a well-developed model of society from which critique and affirmation might arise. Although he speaks in quite general terms about "society," it is frequently unclear what he means by the term, and he can sometimes appear to mean contradictory things. In order for the necessary clarification to take place, Moltmann's theology needs to be put into dialogue with the theory of civil society. The question of how civil society may aid in the clarification of Moltmann's relationship to modernity necessitates a clearer picture of both what Moltmann critiques in modernity, and the theological response he crafts. Let us now turn to that issue.

Modernity and the "Global Marketing of Everything"

There are two central features to Moltmann's critique of modernity under the general heading of "the global marketing of everything." These are, first, the critique of the autonomous self, and second, the critique of instrumentalism. For Moltmann, these are key elements in modern life that contribute to the isolation of questions of value and ethics from the public sphere.

The idea of the autonomous self is rooted in the principle that the nature of the self is not defined or determined by external forces, but develops through the rational exercise of consciousness and will in reflection upon self and world. The self can therefore be abstracted from particular social and communal situations for the purpose of defining universally binding descriptions of human rights and obligations.

Moltmann recognizes the value of individual human dignity as a precondition for human rights as well. However, he notes, "Human dignity lies in the fact that *each*

---

22 See Moltmann, *God for a Secular Society*, 71ff.

particular human being and *all human beings* are, in common, human."²³ Individual dignity cannot be separated for Moltmann from our essential inter-relatedness with humanity as a whole, beyond race, clan, or nation. Our individuality is possible only because we exist as members of a common human family. And, for Moltmann, that life-in-relationship is rooted in the *imago dei* and in God's claim upon human beings in covenant.²⁴ Individual humanity cannot be abstracted from its relatedness to God and other human beings. "Only in human fellowship with other people is the human person truly an image of God (Gen 1:28)."²⁵ Thus, Moltmann criticizes liberal political theory as "one-sided in emphasizing the individual rights of the human person over against economic, social, and political organizations of rule."²⁶

The ideology of the autonomy of the individual self allows modern society, in Moltmann's estimation, particularly in its liberal Western development, to ignore those fundamental social obligations that human beings share with one another and to glorify the image of the individual maker of his or her own destiny. He notes critically the view that "nothing must be 'just fate' not even a person's gender. We must be able to determine everything ourselves."²⁷ This is, in Moltmann's estimation, a pernicious and destructive tendency that divorces us from social structures, such as family and community, and obligations rooted in our capacity to promise:

> The liberty of persons cannot be maintained through progressive individualism of this kind. Nor can it be relinquished again in favour of membership of the traditional society. In my view, it can be preserved only through reliability and faithfulness. The free human being is the being who can promise, said Nietzsche – and who must keep that promise. Through the promises I give, I make myself in all my ambiguity unambiguous for others and for myself. In promising, we commit ourselves and become dependable. We acquire a firm configuration or Gestalt, and make ourselves people who can be addressed …. Those who forget their promises forget themselves; and those who remain true to their promises remain true to themselves. If we keep our promises, we come to be trusted; if we break our promises, people mistrust us. We lose our identity and no longer know ourselves.²⁸

---

23 Moltmann, *On Human Dignity*, 9. Italics mine. It should be noted that this echoes Kant's second formulation of the categorical imperative. The difference lies, however, not in the conclusion, but the derivation of the principle, as we shall see.

24 Thus, Moltmann writes: "Human beings in the fullness of their lives and in all life's relationships – economic, social, political, and person – are destined to live 'before the face of God,' to respond to the Word of God, and responsibly to carry out their task in the world implied in their being created in the image of God. They are persons before God and as such capable of acting on God's behalf and responsible to him. As a consequence of this, a person's rights and duties as a human being are inalienable and indivisible" (*On Human Dignity*, 23).

25 Moltmann, *On Human Dignity*, 25.

26 Moltmann, *On Human Dignity*, 25. Although not as central to his critique, he does go on to point out in opposition to those who would put these economic, social, and political organizations over human individuality that "in principle there is *no* priority of individual rights over social rights, just as conversely there is no priority of social rights over individual rights. Both stand in the genetic context of reciprocal conditioning just as historically the processes of the socialization and the individualization of people mutually condition each other." (25–6).

27 Moltmann, *God for a Secular Society*, 85.

28 Moltmann, *God for a Secular Society*, 87.

The emphasis on individual autonomy in the modern world, however, allows us to abandon a sense of the socially committed self and take refuge in the chaotic possibilities of an anchorless process of self-reinvention. Under those circumstances, we cease to be related to others and to God, and we cease to recognize our bondedness to others. In such circumstances, modernity can and does justify the objectification of human life and the refusal to acknowledge those "surplus people" who are the flotsam and jetsam of industrial society.[29]

This relates directly to the second aspect of Moltmann's critique of modernity, which is the rise of the positivistic conception of science, which objectifies the object of inquiry and seeks to "coerce" the natural world to comply with human ends.[30] Moltmann notes that the "will to dominate" motivates much of modernity's relationship with the natural world.[31] The experimental nature of modern rationality removes the subjective integrity of the target of the experiment. Moltmann sees the risks of this attitude playing out in the glorification of technological advance, with its accompanying acceleration of human existence,[32] as well as the cheapening of the value of human life and community and the "disenchantment" (Weber) of the world. He writes:

> All the taboos evoked by reverence for "Mother Earth" and the greatness of life were then swept away. The sciences "bring" (Bacon's word) "Mother Nature and her daughters" to the human being, who has to be a man, so that he can be nature's "lord and possessor," to use the sexist language of Francis Bacon and René Descartes. Here too, "discoveries" are made, are named after the discoverers, and rewarded with Nobel prizes. And here too, this scientific process of "discovery" does not just put an end to our ignorance. It also puts things in our power, and makes us their determining subjects. The *novum organon scientarium* is the *ars inveniendi*, as Bacon said: the new scientific instrument is the art of discovery. Scientific reason is instrumentalizing reason, reason whose epistemological drive is utilization and domination.[33]

Both of these trends are the result of the removal of questions of ultimate religious value from public life, and the replacement of the substantive claims of the faith community with questions of efficacy and utility. For Moltmann, this is the dark side of a modernity that has forgotten its roots, and for which its good has been subjected to perversion through a narrow focus on only one dimension of human existence. Only through the rediscovery of the innate and God-given value instilled in human beings, nature, and society is a salvation from the "end times" of modernity gone amok possible. The term that Moltmann uses to describe this process of instrumentalization and human isolationis "the global marketing of everything."[34] By this term, he intends to reflect the way in which these two dynamics of individual

---

29 Moltmann, *God for a Secular Society*, 13.
30 Moltmann, *God for a Secular Society*, 8. See Francis Bacon, *Novum Organon*, where he uses this metaphor to describe the role of the scientist vis-à-vis nature.
31 Moltmann, *God for a Secular Society*, 15. See also *The Coming of God*, 208ff.
32 Moltmann, *God for a Secular Society*, 88ff.
33 Moltmann, *God for a Secular Society*, 7.
34 Moltmann, *God for a Secular Society*, 68.

isolation and instrumentalization serve to commodify all dimensions of human life, and remove any sense of intrinsic value from it.

The role of Christian theology in modernity is not, however, the rejection of modernity *per se* in the attempt to recover that sense of intrinsic value. The twin problems of individualism and instrumentalism can only be solved through the theological reengagement of Christian theology with modernity. In fact, Moltmann speaks about the possibility of the "rebirth" of modernity through the "Spirit of Life."[35] The positive contributions of modernity are of enduring value, despite those negative trends. Moltmann claims what modernity adds to human life is in fact a "necessary" vision of human possibilities.

> There is only one alternative to the humanitarian ideas of human dignity and the universality of human rights, and that alternative is barbarism. There is only one alternative to the ideal of eternal peace, and that is a permanent state of war. There is only one alternative to faith in the One God and hope for his kingdom, and that is polytheism and chaos.[36]

It is only through the trust in the coming God, faith in the presence of God through his *Shekinah*, an acknowledgement of the enduring value of humanity through a reaffirmation of modernity's recognition of the innate dignity of all human beings, and the value of equality and justice, and an ecological reformation based upon a rediscovery of "God's hidden immanence in nature," that the "one-dimensional" (Marcuse) character of contemporary life may be combated.[37] Moltmann's development of both the ideas of "political" theology in his early career, and more recently "public" theology, are geared toward providing a theological grounding for these necessary reformations.

From Political to Public

There is a continuity and consistency that runs throughout Moltmann's approach to issues of Christianity and social concern, whether referred to as "political" or "public" theology. There is a method that remains in place throughout his theological evolution that brings together both a critical social theory and an optimistic utopian hope. By labeling his theology "political," Moltmann has always had a broader definition of the word in mind than simply "that having to do with state action." As a matter of fact, Moltmann has *always* been engaged in a larger project of "public theology" than he is often given credit for. A closer look at his earlier work demonstrates that what he meant by the label "political theology" was in fact identical to the intended usage of the term "public theology" in North America.

Moltmann's use of the term "political" is often imprecise, but most often when he identifies himself as a "political theologian" he seems to mean by that any theologian whose concerns extend to the social realm. Thus, for example, in

---

35 Moltmann, *God for a Secular Society*, 17ff.
36 Moltmann, *God for a Secular Society*, 17.
37 Moltmann, *God for a Secular Society*, 17ff. See also Herbert Marcuse, *One Dimensional Man* (Boston: Beacon Press, 1991).

discussing a "political hermeneutic of scripture," he writes: "This hermeneutic can therefore be called a political hermeneutic because it apprehends politics, in the Aristotelian sense of the word, as the inclusive horizon of the life of mankind."[38] Political, in this sense of the word, has to do with all aspects of human life, including not only the narrowly political sphere of the state, but also the spheres of economy, civil society, and family life.

Moltmann's central ethical concerns throughout his development have existed at the intersection of the spheres of state and civil society. The three areas of public life to which he has devoted the most attention during his career are the institution and establishment of social justice and human freedom as fulfillments of human potentialities, the struggle for world peace and the abolition of nuclear and other weapons of mass destruction, and a concern for ecological balance. Moltmann understands the "political" aspect of public responsibility to be broader than simply state action. It has always included the work done by small communities of interested persons in order to bring about social change. Thus, for example, labor unions, environmental groups, human rights committees and other organizations which lobbied, but were not members of, the state, and which also organized independently to work for greater peace and justice apart from the state, should also be understood as "political" from Moltmann's point of view. What is lacking in this view, however, is an analysis of how these institutions interweave into the larger fabric of civil society, such that Moltmann could provide the kind of general outlines necessary for a social ethic of hope.[39]

In this regard, Moltmann's work shares a strong affinity with Latin American liberation theology, in both a positive and a negative sense. Like liberation theology, Moltmann envisioned the need for Christians to work with others in the struggle to overcome oppression, political and otherwise. His understanding of politics both informed and was informed by the movement of basic Christian communities in Latin America.[40] In fact, it would probably be fair to say that Moltmann would agree with liberation theology that it is only through such small communities that any concrete social change can truly come about.[41] Such change must be bottom up and

---

38 Moltmann, *Religion, Revolution, and the Future*, M. Douglas Meeks, trans. (New York: Charles Scribner's Sons, 1969), 98.

39 Although, as Geiko Müller-Fahrenholz notes, given the scope of Moltmann's project, anything resembling a detailed social ethic would have been impossible. This should not have prevented Moltmann from offering a theological analysis of institutions based upon his overall project, thereby enabling the development of a broad outline for a social ethics. See *The Kingdom and the Power*, 107ff. At the same time, it must be said that one can find detailed discussions of ethical issues in a number of Moltmann's works, for example, *Politische Theologie – Politische Ethik* (München: Kaiser/Grünewald, 1984).

40 This can be seen most clearly in Moltmann's reflections on the idea of the "church of the poor." See, for example, *The Church in the Power of the Spirit* (New York: Harper & Row, 1977), 289ff., and *The Open Church* (London: SCM Press, 1978), 113ff. The church is called to be a "community of friendship" in which members act in common partnership with one another, rather than only an organization defined by casual membership. There is to be a "lifestyle" that corresponds to membership in the church as the community of Jesus Christ.

41 See, for example, Moltmann, *The Church in the Power of the Spirit*, 356.

democratic, rather than imposed upon the populace in any sense by a "vanguard party" or an authoritarian regime. This is reflected in Moltmann's criticism of those liberation theologians that seemed, as he thought was the case with Jose Miguez-Boniño, to be too uncritically Marxist, and who seemed committed to violent revolution.⁴²

At the same time, Moltmann also shares with liberation theology a lack of a deep sociological description of complex institutional life. To be sure, liberation theology developed its own sociological categories with which to understand the complex processes of social change. Additionally, it is not clear that the circumstances of social movements in Latin America during the 1960s, '70s, and '80s had the kind of openness to a complex and independent sphere of civil society which would make such an analysis meaningful. Nevertheless, such an analysis is missing in both liberation theology and in Moltmann's approach to political theology.

Another point of contact with liberation theology is their mutual critique of capitalism. Moltmann's work in Christian–Marxist dialogue, as well as his participation in and support for the student movements of 1968 aided in the development of his position that social justice and freedom from oppression for which the church hoped were inconsistent with a capitalist economic system.⁴³ He agreed with the Marxist humanist position that work in capitalist society is alienating and objectifying, and kept people from realizing their true humanity in Christ. Christian life, therefore, ought to be oriented toward liberating praxis.⁴⁴ This is a continuing concern in Moltmann's critique of modernity and the advance of globalization.

Central to Moltmann's understanding of political theology is the dialectic of cross and resurrection. The resurrection is the final act of a drama, the climax of which is the crucifixion. The authority of the cross is central to understanding Christian responsibility in the world, rooted as it is in the complexities of the problem of evil. Just as it is through the power of the resurrection that we are enabled to anticipate the coming kingdom, it is through the power of the cross that we are called always to heed the suffering of those left out by society, and to put their needs first in our calculation of social goods. No utilitarian calculus is permitted here. To say that a great number of people may be helped by a particular policy, which would nevertheless leave the poorest in misery, is to count as nothing the solidarity of God with those very poor in the life, ministry, and death of Jesus Christ (Matt. 25:31–46). It is therefore precisely

---

42 See Moltmann, "Open Letter to José Miguez-Boniño," in *Liberation Theology: A Documentary History*, 199.

43 See Moltmann, *Religion, Revolution, and the Future*, 74ff., and *God for a Secular Society*, 46ff.

44 However, Moltmann's understanding of the centrality of praxis does not mean that he accepted the content of the Marxist approach to praxis. Moltmann rejected the premise that a classless society, or the abolition of capitalism, in themselves, can lead to the realization of the utopia for which Marx hoped. As an outgrowth of modern, industrial society, the Marxist conception of human life lacks the "vitality to give it a peculiar rationality of its own" (*Theology of Hope*, 318). While human beings are certainly not less than the creative subjects who find their species-being in their productive activity, as Marx would have it, they are assuredly more than that, and Moltmann's understanding of praxis parts company with the Marxist approach at the point at which Marx failed to realize this.

for those poor that social reform is to take place. The marginal in society are to be brought to the center. Their needs are to be placed first, because the kingdom of God is for them, and it is the kingdom that we anticipate.[45] On the cross, and in the grave, Christ took on the burdens of the "godforsaken," and by taking on our sin and misery, he both freed us and obligated us to bear the burdens of the poor and outcast.[46] Therefore, a political theology properly conceived is one that operates out of a consciousness of the cross and its implications for society as a whole.

This trend has continued throughout Moltmann's work and remains central to his concerns. In his most recent work, though he has begun using the term "public theology" to describe his project more frequently, he has by no means abandoned the centrality of these themes from his political theology. At the same time, however, it is not immediately apparent what Moltmann intends by his use of "public theology." There is certainly no one definition on the basis of which we might understand what Moltmann is up to. However, a few points ought to be made at the outset, to be expanded upon throughout this book.

In the first place, I do not believe that the overall intent of Moltmann's theology has changed with the adoption of the term "public theology." By "political" he has always explicitly meant "social" in the broader sense of the word. His concern is with the entirety of social life, not just the narrowly political. Theology operates at every dimension of human social life and works toward the transformation of the entire public sphere. Christianity, as he has stressed at least since *The Open Church*, is rooted in a lifestyle that radiates out from the church and into the world. This is the church's missionary identity. Society is not subordinate to the state, as it was the earlier political theology of Carl Schmitt, but is oriented primarily toward the kingdom of God, which echoes throughout the common life of humanity.

With the fall of the Berlin wall in 1989, and the rather sudden and startling changes in global politics over the last two decades, the focus of any socially concerned theological project has also had to undergo a change. The fight is no longer between East and West, Soviet Union and the United States. In a literal sense, the social crises with which humanity is now faced are much more decentralized. Crises that threaten global peace, social justice, and ecological stability can no longer be dealt with by attempting to move one or two big pieces on the global chessboard (if they ever really could have been). The global truly has become local, and as a result, the social concerns of Christians have also become decentralized. Methods of organization have become more diffuse and strategies for public engagement have taken on new forms. Because of this, there is a potential in Moltmann's theology to address itself to the kind of pluralism that characterizes today's society, through a further development of the concept of the exodus church from his earlier writing, and understanding that approach to social pluralism through the articulation of a theological understanding of civil society; and by showing how other efforts in this general area can supplement and correct his work, Moltmann's theology may become more responsive to this decentralization of public life.

---

45 See Moltmann, *The Church in the Power of the Spirit*, 193ff.
46 See Moltmann, *The Crucified God*, 327ff.

The issue of public theology, however, must never be divorced from the issue of political theology, because the question of *who rules* is fundamental to Moltmann's conception of Christian responsibility. Regardless of governmental system, Christian hope is motivated by the insistence that Christ is the ruler of the social matrix, at every level, and as Christians, our allegiance is fundamentally to Christ's kingdom, and only provisionally to any earthly reign.

This is particularly important to Moltmann in light of the changes in the global social and political context of the last decade. In one essay, he asks, significantly, "what has happened to our utopias?"[47] In this essay, he points out that Christians run grave risks when they associate their hopes for Christ's reign with any of the particular and merely worldly utopias of which there seem to be an endless supply. Whether we are speaking of "socialism with a human face," or an "end of history"[48] in which free markets and democracy are now the only viable options for humanity, if we associate these visions of society with the coming reign of God, then we substitute a human-made idol for the real utopia to be brought about solely through God's work. The utopia toward which Christians are obligated to strive will be, Moltmann argues, "the utopia of justice," which exists to promote human rights and dignity, freedom and self-determination within society, and the principle that human beings cannot and should not ever be equated with commodities nor reduced to their cash value. This social vision ought to motivate the public theology of Christians, and empower them to fight against all social structures which degrade human worth, whether those social structures be found within a totalitarian government which pays no heed to the idea of human rights, or within a society that gives lip service to human rights, but is willing to trade away those rights for the sake of economic ideology or national interest. While it is important to weigh carefully the "problem of creating and maintaining tentative harmonies of life in the world"[49] in questions of social justice, we should never become complacent, nor conclude that because the present state of affairs isn't as bad as it could be, it is therefore as good as it gets. Moltmann notes: "Hope alone is to be called 'realistic,' because it alone takes seriously the possibilities with which all reality is fraught. It does not take things as

---

47 Jürgen Moltmann "What Has Happened to Our Utopias?" in Richard Bauckham, ed., *God Will Be All In All* (Edinburgh: T&T Clark, 1999).

48 See Francis Fukuyama, *The End of History and the Last Man* (New York: Avon Books, 1992). Moltmann's rejoinder to Fukuyama is telling: "As a Hegelian, Fukuyama must surely know that all earlier civilizations developed new systems for living once their inner contradictions had become unendurable. Left Hegelians such as Marx recognized this. But Fukuyama takes into account only the external alternatives, such as fascism, nationalism and socialism, thereby forgetting the inward contradictions inherent in the universal marketing of everything: the contradictions between market value and human dignity, between the First World and the Third, as well as between humanity and nature … . Fukuyama's 'end of history' is not a cause for messianic rejoicing over the best of all possible worlds; it is rather a reason for apocalyptic lamentations over the lack of any alternative to their misery" (Moltmann, *The Coming of God*, 225).

49 Reinhold Niebuhr, *An Interpretation of Christian Ethics* (New York: Harper & Row, 1963), 37.

they happen to stand or lie, but as progressing, moving things with possibilities of change."[50]

Conclusion

When Moltmann defines his theology as "public theology," he specifies that he means by this "kingdom of God theology." He then writes: "Kingdom-of-God theology intervenes critically and prophetically in the public affairs of a given society, and draws public attention, not to the church's own interests, but to 'God's kingdom, God's commandment, and his righteousness,' as Thesis 5 of the Barman Theological Declaration says."[51] Public theology, as Moltmann understands it, is not simply a description of the social function of the church in a pluralistic democracy, but a call to action to Christians to embody Christ's rule in their lives. It is public because it recognizes the sovereignty of God over every human venue and activity, and knows of no corner of human affairs where God is not active in bringing about his reign. And it is this understanding of the intersection of "public" with "theology" that can give good grounds for an understanding of society and a social ethic that is a true theology of hope.

---

50 Moltmann, *Theology of Hope*, 25.
51 Moltmann, *Experiences in Theology*, xx.

Chapter 2

The Development of Moltmann's Political Theology

Introduction

In this chapter, I will explore the broad outlines of the social perspective that has governed the development of Moltmann's public theology.[1] In the establishment of the main themes of Moltmann's political theology of the 1960s and 1970s, one can see a concern for understanding the role of Christian theology in a broadly construed public context, and with themes of institutional order and complexity that, while not fully developed, do provide a foundation for the linkage between this work and his latest work in public theology. In particular, the dialectical relationship between the cross and the resurrection stands at the center of Moltmann's understanding of the role of Christianity in public life.

Central to Moltmann's political theology is a dialectical understanding of Christianity's relation to its social setting. This dialectic moves between a moment of social criticism and a moment of transformative involvement. Political theology moves between these two interpretive poles in its attempt to formulate a moral stance vis-à-vis society and its demands.

Moltmann develops this dialectic of transformation and critique from a political hermeneutic grounded in the Christian hope and expectation of the coming kingdom

---

1   There is within German theology an emerging public theology movement which both intersects with and diverges from the path laid out by Moltmann and Metz. Wolfgang Huber has been a major motivating force for the growth of this movement. See in particular: Wolfgang Huber and Hans-Richard Reuter, *Friedensethik* (Stuttgart: W. Kohlhammer, 1990); Wolfgang Huber, *Protestanten in Der Demokratie: Positionen Und Profile Im Nachkriegsdeutschland* (München: Kaiser, 1990); *Die Tägliche Gewalt: Gegen Den Ausverkauf Der Menschenwürde* (Freiburg: Herder, 1993); *Gerechtigkeit Und Recht: Grundlinien Christlicher Rechtsethik* (Gütersloh: Chr. Kaiser, 1996); *Kirche in der Zeitenwende: Gesellschaftlicher Wandel und Erneuerung der Kirche* (Gütersloh: Gütersloher Verlaghaus, 1998); Wolfgang Huber and Stefan Berg, *Meine Hoffnung Ist Grösser Als Meine Angst: Ein Bischof Zu Glauben, Kirche Und Gesellschaft* (Berlin: Wichern-Verlag, 1996). See also Wolfgang Huber, ed., *Öffentliche Theologie*, 12 vols. (Gütersloh: Chr. Kaiser, 1991–2000) in particular Heinrich Bedford-Strohm, *Vorrang für die Armen: Auf dem Weg zu Einer Theologischen Theorie der Gerechtigkeit* (Gütersloh: Chr. Kaiser, 1993) and *Gemeinschaft aus kommunikativer Freiheit: Sozialer Zusammenhalt in der Modernen Gesellschaft: Ein Theologischer Beitrag* (Gütersloh: Chr. Kaiser, 1999). Other figures in this movement include Michael Welker. See Michael Welker, *Theologie und funktionale Systemtheorie: Luhmanns Religionssoziologie in theologischer Diskussion* (Frankfurt am Main: Suhrkamp, 1985).

of God. Of particular importance in the development of this hermeneutic was the influence of the German Marxist philosopher Ernst Bloch, whose *Das Prinzip Hoffnung* looms large over Moltmann's project.

The Idea of Political Theology

Political theology as Moltmann and his Catholic co-founder J.B. Metz[2] use the term needs to be distinguished at the outset from the political theology developed by Carl Schmitt in the 1930s.[3] The differences run far deeper than simply their respective locations on the political spectrum. Although it is true that Carl Schmitt's legacy is firmly and unfortunately cemented to the rise of National Socialism in Germany, whereas the sympathies of what came to be known as the "new" political theology of Moltmann and Metz have always run leftward, it is the theological grounds for their differences that are most significant for an understanding of how the political theology of the 1960s and 1970s is different from that of the 1930s.[4]

Central to Schmitt's political theology was a deep skepticism regarding democracy and the open character of liberal society. The "political" of Schmitt's "political theology" is defined, not by a public concern, but rather by an assumption of the inherent violence of the political realm. As in the philosophy of Thomas Hobbes, human society is a creation of political authority, developed out of the need for protection of human beings from one another. For the sake of that protection, power is asserted by the sovereign. Schmitt's political theology was thus defined by his emphasis on the dominant nature of the state as guardian and protector. In light of such a view of the state, however, the pluralism and representative character of Weimar liberalism was insufficient. Rather, what he demanded was a "qualitatively

---

2   The approach to political theology taken by Metz was deeply rooted in the Roman Catholic theological tradition, and in particular the theology of Karl Rahner. See Johann Baptist Metz, ed., *Faith and the World of Politics* (New York: The Paulist Press, 1968); *Theology of the World* (New York: The Seabury Press, 1973); Johann Baptist Metz and Jean-Pierre Jossua, eds, *Theology of Joy* (New York: Herder & Herder), 1974; *Christianity and Socialism* (New York: Seabury Press, 1977); Johann Baptist Metz, ed., *Christianity and the Bourgeoisie* (New York: Seabury Press, 1979); *A Passion for God: The Mystical-Political Dimension of Christianity* (New York: Paulist Press, 1998).

3   See Carl Schmitt, *Der Begriff des Politischen* (Berlin: Duncker & Humblot, 1963); *Der Leviathan in der Staatslehre des Thomas Hobbes* (Koln: Hoenheim, 1982) [English Edition: *The Leviathan in the State Theory of Thomas Hobbes*, trans., George Schwab, (Greenwood Press, 1996)], and *Politische Theologie: Vier Kapitel zur Lehre von der Soveranität* (München & Leipzig: Verlag von Dunker & Humbolt, 1934).

4   Recent discussions have highlighted the different interpretations of "political theology" on the part of Schmitt and Metz. In particular, Metz's own commentary on their differences can be found in the essay "The New Political Theology: The *Status Queaestionis*" in Metz, *A Passion for God*. See also Johann Baptist Metz, "Politische Theologie" in *Evangelische Kirchenlexicon* IV, 3rd ed. (Göttingen: Verdenhoek & Raprecht, 1986). Of additional interest is the analysis of Derek Simon, "The *New* Political Theology of Johann Baptist Metz: Confronting Schmitt's Decisionist Political Theology of Exclusion" *Horizons* 30, no. 2 (Fall, 2003).

total state."⁵ Whereas within the liberal state the plurality of spheres of human life were brought together and participated in the public life of society, Schmitt advocates the "privatization" of these other realms, in order to allow the state the proper sovereignty.⁶

Central to the sovereign's protective task is the distinction of friend from enemy.⁷ The enemy was the outsider, the one who did not belong to the unified social order represented by the state, and was therefore a threat to the stability of the society. The task of distinguishing the identity of the enemy falls to the sovereign. Only through the power of the sovereign might the proper protective role of the state be restored.

This leads to an endorsement of an authoritarian understanding of the state. The sovereign, as the one who may declare the state of emergency, and whose domination over the political sphere of life is absolute, may brook no dissent from the other spheres of human life. Democracy demonstrates its inherent weakness in its inability to distinguish friend from foe. By allowing for a diversity of social and political perspectives in society, and giving these perspectives, not only voice, but also the potential to wield power, democracy risked its own dissolution. The opposite of authoritarianism was ultimately anarchy.⁸ It is finally the dictator, properly understood, who can bring about the stability required for human life.⁹

The God-concept that is implied by Schmitt's version of political theology is based upon God's power and sovereignty as the root of human sovereignty. As God is toward the world, so is the dictator toward the nation. There is no room here for a weak, beaten or crucified God. God in this worldview is the Creator and Ruler of the World, but without the element of suffering that so characterizes the later political theologies of Metz and Moltmann. Coupled with his radical understanding of sin, without the concomitant faith in human possibilities, an authoritarian political philosophy develops in which the Other has no place except as an object of the nation's wrath.

While Moltmann and Metz were aware of Schmitt's approach to political theology at the time of the development of their own approach,¹⁰ their more

---

5 See Heinrich Meier, *Carl Schmitt and Leo Strauss: The Hidden Dialogue* (Chicago: University of Chicago Press, 1995), 22.

6 Meier, *Carl Schmitt and Leo Strauss*, 17.

7 Meier, *Carl Schmitt and Leo Strauss*, 4.

8 Schmitt, *Politische Theologie*, 67ff. For Schmitt, the final outcome of political theology is the creation of a "State Philosophy of Counterrevolution," as the title of his fourth of four chapters states.

9 And, despite his participation in NDSP politics, the properly understood dictator for Schmitt was not finally Hitler. That having been said, his support for the Reich and his heartfelt anti-Semitism did nothing to stem the tide of Nazi influence in Germany. To the time of his death, Schmitt never rejected either his authoritarian politics nor his anti-Semitism.

10 See Moltmann, "The Cross and Civil Religion." in *Religion and Political Society* (New York: Harper & Row, 1972), 9–47. It is rather telling that Moltmann's only extended discussion of Schmitt's political theology is found in a rather late piece. In "Covenant or Leviathan" in *God for a Secular Society*, he considers Schmitt's view of the state as a renewal and celebration of a pagan understanding of authority.

immediate precursors were the Christian social democrats of the previous generation, particularly Karl Barth and Paul Tillich. Additionally, the influence of Ernst Bloch on their thinking is crucial for understanding how their political theology developed.

The human experience of "longing" drives Bloch's analysis of human hope.[11] We recognize our existence as incomplete and unfulfilled. Our lives are consumed in the *noch nicht*, the "not yet" accomplished consummation of our desires and hopes.[12] Thus, we push these expectations into the realm of the future, the area of that which has not yet come to pass, or as Bloch writes: "the *discovery and unmistakable notion of the 'Not-Yet-Conscious.'*"[13] And we yearn for the coming of that future time.

Bloch sees human utopian longing as reaching its apex in the struggle for a communist society.[14] The Marxist worldview realizes the true character of human alienation as rooted within its social conditions, and by dispensing with those otherworldly dimensions of religious and philosophical utopianism, and focusing on the real liberation of human beings from alienating social conditions, seeks to achieve a real earthly utopia which reflects the truth of those desires for the kingdom of God that are reflected by religious utopianism.

This is not to say that Bloch refuses to take religious utopianism with utmost seriousness. Rather, he recognizes within it the core of that utopianism which finds its fulfillment in Marxist philosophy.[15] The final outcome of religious utopianism, however, is the removal of God from the equation. The God who establishes the kingdom of God finally becomes absorbed into the kingdom, as the kingdom itself becomes its own end. Thus, the theism which pursues the kingdom of God becomes, in the end, the atheism which seeks after the kingdom on earth, as it cannot be in heaven. As Bloch writes: "the religious kingdom-intention as such *involves atheism, at last properly understood atheism.*"[16]

Bloch's understanding of this godless coming of the kingdom of God is rooted in his expectation that after capitalism it will become possible for human beings to attempt a true realization of their inner natures as creating beings. It must, however, be understood that, even in such a context, the utopian possibility always opens out before humanity. It is never fully fulfilled. Even the classless society is an unfinished world, and even the fulfillment of the Marxist ideal leaves unfinished myriad human possibilities. Through the creative activity of people in society, human beings create their future out of the present moment. When human beings have finally been freed to begin this journey of utopian hope, says Bloch, they are finally able to strive for that which stands at the center of all human striving, from the earliest dreams of childhood to the most elaborate philosophical and theological systems – that "which shines into the childhood of all and in which no one has yet been: homeland."[17]

---

11 Ernst Bloch, *The Principle of Hope* (Cambridge: MIT Press, 1986), 6.
12 Bloch, *The Principle of Hope*, 9.
13 Bloch, *The Principle of Hope*, 11. Italics in original.
14 Bloch, *The Principle of Hope*, 1354ff.
15 Bloch, *The Principle of Hope*, 1196.
16 Bloch, *The Principle of Hope*, 1196.
17 Bloch, *The Principle of Hope*, 1376.

Both Metz and Moltmann were strongly influenced by this approach to philosophy and to reading the history of messianic movements, particularly Judaism and Christianity. They initiated an extended dialogue with Bloch in their own writings, and sought to appropriate some of his central themes for the Christian tradition. Yet their work was always self-consciously rooted in their respective theological influences. Although Bloch, with the Frankfurt School, directly affected their understanding of the theological task, they were not attempting to simply construct a religious edifice around materialist atheism. Rather, they began from their own theological agenda.

For Schmitt, this can be put more strongly: The themes of Schmitt's political theology ran directly contrary to the central themes of the "new" political theology of Moltmann and Metz. It was not simply that the new political theology was a mirror image or negation of Schmitt's approach. It was based upon and developed out of a completely different set of presuppositions. Schmitt's conceptualizations did not even enter the picture in the process of the development of this new political theology. The new political theology was rooted, not in a secularized and one-sided presumption about human nature, or upon a Manichean view of God and the world (either right wing or left wing), but based upon a set of theological presuppositions about who God is in Jesus Christ. For Moltmann, as for Metz, political theology was rooted, not in the sovereignty of God, but in the theology of the cross.

Jürgen Moltmann's Political Hermeneutic

The approach that governed the development of Moltmann's political theology, particularly in its early form, was a political hermeneutic grounded in Christian hope, expectation, and praxis.[18] This interpretive strategy emerges from Moltmann's conviction that Christian faith is rooted in the history of God's involvement with the world, and that this involvement levies concrete responsibilities on Christians. Moltmann writes:

> Political hermeneutics links up with the eschatological hermeneutic. Earlier hermeneutic usually remained at one level: from text to text, from understanding to understanding, from faith to faith. When hermeneutic, however, involves a promissory history, when the way of interpretation goes from promise to fulfillment. When it involves a history of hope, then interpretation goes from expectation to realization. When it involves the remembrance of liberation, then the way goes from oppression to freedom, that is, hermeneutic does not

---

18 The idea of political hermeneutics has been supplemented in Moltmann's writing since *The Trinity and the Kingdom* with a further concentration on a "Trinitarian hermeneutic," which stands in opposition to merely "monotheistic" approaches to interpretation. This hermeneutic presumes, in a way that expands on the premises of Moltmann's political hermeneutic, that the Trinity is not something deduced from scripture, but is rather the theological presupposition for the understanding of Christian interpretation of the Bible and life. "*The New Testament talks about God by proclaiming in narrative the relationships of the Father, the Son, and the Spirit which are relationships of fellowship and are open to the world.*" *The Trinity and the Kingdom*, 64 (italics in original). He expands this further in *Experiences in Theology*, noting that it is through the Spirit that proper interpretation takes place (145ff).

remain on the intellectual theoretical level, but wants to lead, by way of the experience of understanding hope, to a new praxis of hope.[19]

Moltmann opposes his approach to the hermeneutical methods of Dilthey and Marx, but the *bête noir* of his critique is Rudolf Bultmann's existentialist interpretive method.

Bultmann understood revelation as a matter of the individual's response to the "call to decision" embodied in Jesus Christ. This call to decision offers meaning and purpose to existence in "the search of the individual case for one's own being."[20] But this search for meaning is de-historicized in Bultmann's theology by his rejection of historicity in the content of the biblical story itself. The personal event of decision in the individual's life is valid irrespective of the historical content of the faith itself, though that content may be re-understood and appropriated in light of the decision. One may take on responsibility for the future in light of present decision, but Moltmann argues that, "for Bultmann ... this line of thought soon breaks down. For him, knowledge of the end of world history is 'presumptuous.' Therefore the question of the sense of the whole course of history is already meaningless."[21] What value there is in an existentialist hermeneutic can only be grasped when it is subjected to political hermeneutical critique. Then the existentialist approach "falls into the larger framework of the world historical-eschatological interpretation."[22]

But if the individualism of the existentialist hermeneutic is inadequate, so too is the Marxist and Feuerbachian critique of religion from the point of view of historical development. The virtue of the historical-revolutionary model of interpretation is its recognition of the logical of social transformation in the name of justice and against the present situation of human affliction and misery. Yet, it reads religion as "illusory" and an "opiate" when in fact in Christianity the very principles of protest against human misery are embodied in its founding events.[23] It is through the crucifixion and resurrection of Christ that the revolutionary possibilities sought in the Marxist critique of religion are to be found. Thus, "when we understand the cross of Christ in this connection as an 'expression' of real human affection, then, the resurrection of Christ acquires the significance of the true 'protest' against human affliction."[24] The recognition of this "protestant" core of the Christian message pushes, not toward passivity but toward proclamation. And the proclamation that is demanded is not one of acceptance of the world as it is but of expectation of the world as changed to the reflection of the crucified and resurrected one. This is not, it should be emphatically

---

19 Moltmann, *On Human Dignity*, 106–7.
20 Moltmann, *Religion, Revolution, and the Future*, 91.
21 Moltmann, *Religion, Revolution and the Future*, 91.
22 It should be noted that Moltmann's critique of existentialist hermeneutic is a critique based upon what he sees as an insufficient, not a wholly invalid, hermeneutical approach. He writes: "Today, the limitations of existentialist interpretation come into focus because the real unredeemed state of mankind looks different. Therefore, we must arrive at an ideological critique of this existentialist interpretation, while keeping in mind the concrete experiential content behind the outline of existence theology." *Religion, Revolution and the Future*, 101.
23 Moltmann, *Religion, Revolution and the Future*, 93ff.
24 Moltmann, *Religion, Revolution, and the Future*, 96.

noted, simply a future expectation, but an expectation that seeks present relevance. Interpretation is not simply about the reading of the texts, but also about the reading of the present moment.[25] The truly revolutionary historical hermeneutic is thus found in the hermeneutic of political theology.

As noted, a political hermeneutics of the gospel is rooted in Christian praxis and ethical commitment. Political hermeneutics interprets both the Bible and the present circumstances, and also recognizes that each puts the question to the other. "The church needs the Bible as its foundation and the public discussion as a check. Obedience and love need the discipleship and commitment to Jesus as their ground and the working out of present experience as a control."[26] This sets up a process of interpretation that recognizes the cross as the key hermeneutical symbol for Christian faith. "Content and manner of proclaimed and lived freedom must be legitimized by reflections on their ground in the crucified Christ."[27]

Yet, such an interpretation cannot solely be backward looking, or it loses its eschatological referent. The cross as the key to the interpretation of the gospel is coupled with an openness to the future of Christ and the kingdom. If "*God is the power of the future*"[28] as Moltmann has it, then the community of Christ's followers must understand their mission as oriented toward the coming of Christ's kingdom.

The question then becomes how these principles are to be applied to the particularities of a modern, pluralist society. Moltmann points to several key principles that he derives from this hermeneutic. In the first place, he writes, God's reign comes to the impoverished, "*to those who labor and are heavily laden*"[29] as well as to the "*humiliated and abused.*"[30] Moltmann understands this to mean the concretely poor and outcast of modern society, whose "poverty, hunger, and sickness rob a man of all dignity."[31] The kingdom of God is thus revolutionary in the sense that it calls people to a hope for the abolition of the unjust conditions of society, to the giving of rights to the rightless, and to the forgiveness of sins and the reestablishment of broken relationships.[32] As God incarnate, Jesus Christ alone possesses the capacity to bring this about. It is not a matter of believing in Christ as a moral exemplar or a political revolutionary, but rather a matter of believing in him as the *logos* of God. That recognition is what instills the hope of the public life of Christianity.[33]

This hermeneutical process cannot be merely about abstract theorization. Rather, it is a hermeneutic that is enacted in the concrete work of Christians in the world. A political hermeneutic is rooted in the apostolic life of Christians as they seek to make the message of the kingdom manifest in their proclamation. "The way of political hermeneutic cannot go one-sidedly from reflection to action …. Instead,

---

25 Moltmann, *Religion, Revolution, and the Future*, 96–7.
26 Moltmann, *Religion, Revolution, and the Future*, 102.
27 Moltmann, *Religion, Revolution, and the Future*, 102.
28 Moltmann, *On Human Dignity*, 106. Italics in original
29 Moltmann, *Religion, Revolution and the Future*, 103. Italics in original.
30 Moltmann, *Religion, Revolution, and the Future*, 104. Italics in original.
31 Moltmann, *Religion, Revolution, and the Future*, 103.
32 See Moltmann, *On Human Dignity*, 102.
33 Moltmann, *Religion, Revolution, and the Future*, 105.

this hermeneutic must bind reflection and action together, thus requiring reflection in the action as well as action in the reflection."[34]

Moltmann views the intellectual clarification of this political hermeneutic as a responsibility of theologians and religious leaders, yet it must be something more than simply the particular task of experts. Rather, it is a work that may take place throughout the life of the church. It is a "theology for active laypersons, not a specialized theology for priests and pastors."[35] The Christian ethics that Moltmann sees developing from these principles derive from the imperative to make the kingdom of God present in a sacramental way within the modern world.[36] This involves us in a process of anticipation of the coming kingdom about which Moltmann says this: "We must ... discover the unconditioned within the conditioned, the last in the next to last, and the eschatological in the ethical just as we believe that the blood and the body of Christ are present in the bread and wine of the Eucharist."[37]

In a broad sense, the ethics that Moltmann argues flow from the political hermeneutic of the gospel are rooted in the establishment of peace, justice and freedom, both in political and economic life, in solidarity with all those who suffer in society. This solidarity is rooted in the imperative of Christian love. This means that work must be done not only with the socio-economically poor, but also with those who struggle for human rights and against racism, sexism, and the degradation of the earth. This is possible only in the overcoming of personal apathy and complacency.[38]

I will turn now to consider in more detail the formal basis for Moltmann's project in his understanding of the dialectical relationship between the resurrection and crucifixion of Christ as reflecting a dialectic of social transformation and critique in modern society. Then I will look more closely at the basis for the positive material norm of Moltmann's political theology in his theological justification for human rights.

The Dialectic of Transformation and Critique

Moltmann's approach to political hermeneutics leads him to a consideration of the social dynamics of the cross and the resurrection. Moltmann recognizes that these are two interdependent dimensions of God's relation to the world, and that each cannot be understood without the other. The resurrection as the pledge of hope becomes meaningless without the cross as the guarantee of the solidarity of God with the suffering and marginalized. Moltmann notes that "hope without remembrance leads to illusion, just as, conversely, remembrance without hope can result in resignation."[39] Both aspects of the reality of Jesus Christ are necessary to a proper understanding of what God is doing in the world and what that entails for us. While *Theology of Hope*

---

34 Moltmann, *On Human Dignity*, 107.
35 Moltmann, *On Human Dignity*, 108.
36 Moltmann, *On Human Dignity*, 109.
37 Moltmann, *On Human Dignity*, 109.
38 Moltmann, *On Human Dignity*, passim.
39 Moltmann, *The Crucified God*, ix.

points to the positive moment in the dialectic of God's coming, *The Crucified God*, represents the negative moment.

Eschatology and the Coming Kingdom of God

If the resurrection of Jesus Christ is the pledge of the coming kingdom of God, how does Moltmann understand that kingdom as it relates to our present context? Central to Moltmann's understanding of the present relevance of faith is an idea we have already encountered – the idea of *anticipation*. The coming kingdom of God provides the anticipatory horizon against which we are obligated to judge our current context. At its most basic, the kingdom of God implies that God is in charge, and we are not. Human structures are therefore relativized to the structures implied in Christ's description of the kingdom, and human relations are determined, in principle, not according to the fallenness of our present circumstances, but according to the redemption of our future state. This anticipation becomes the governing norm of our action in the world, drawing us toward it as an ideal toward which we are commanded to strive, and against which we are to take the measure of the world around us.

The Easter appearances of Christ do more than simply testify to the reality of his physical resurrection, although they assuredly do at least that, but they also witness to the triumph of God's grace over the reality of death and decay, and announce the coming of the time when God's power, demonstrated in the resurrection, will be manifested throughout the cosmos: "The Easter appearances ... were recognized and proclaimed within a horizon of apocalyptic expectation: resurrection as an eschatological event – Jesus as the first fruits of the resurrection."[40]

Furthermore, this implies, argues Moltmann, not simply a *restitutio ad integrim* but rather a new creation.[41] The establishment of the kingdom of God implies the overturning of old structures and norms and their replacement by the reign of God, which will sweep away the old and inaugurate the *kairos* of God's peace and justice.[42]

---

40 Moltmann, *Theology of Hope*, 218.

41 The distinction between Moltmann's understanding of the idea of the future and Bloch's is instructive here, not least in that it points to a discontinuity in their respective thoughts. For Bloch, the category of the future that he used was *futurum*, whereas Moltmann uses the term *adventus*. Geiko Müller-Fahrenholz comments: "For [Bloch] the *futurum* was the 'actualization of primal potency.' What he meant was the power of *physis* (from which the word *futurum* is derived). Thus the ambivalence of *physis* or matter – it is *mater* and Moloch at the same time – also appears in the concept of *futurum*. In contrast to this, Moltmann develops his concept of the future from the concept of *adventus*. In the background is the Greek term *parousia*, which since Paul has been used as a designation for the coming of Christ in glory. The Risen One is the One who is to come. Consequently, Moltmann speaks of a 'god with *adventus* as the essence of his being.'" *The Kingdom and the Power* (Philadelphia: Fortress Press, 2000), 58. Thus for Moltmann, it is not the present reality that gives us the basis for the principle of hope, but the future of God, whose promises are made manifest in the resurrection of Christ.

42 This is an important distinction to be made between Moltmann and Pannenberg, and speaks to the differing ways in which they read Hegel. Pannenberg's understanding of

But what does that mean for the present? The coming kingdom exists today under the sign of the cross. It is a reality which is coming to be, and has not yet arrived. Thus, we struggle with sin, death, and evil in the light of Christ's cross, but we trust in God's triumph over these obstacles through our belief in Christ's resurrection. Moltmann writes:

> Thus the kingdom of God is present here as promise and hope for the future horizon of all things, which are then seen in their historical character because they do not yet contain their truth in themselves. If it is present as promise and hope, then this its presence is determined by the contradiction in which the future, the possible and the promised, stands to a corrupt reality. In the Reformers it was said that the kingdom of God is a *tectum sub cruce et sub contrario*. This was intended to mean that the kingdom of God is here hidden beneath its opposite: its freedom is hidden under trial, its happiness under suffering, its right under rightlessness, its omnipotence under weakness, its glory under unrecognizability. Here the kingdom of God was seen in the form of the lordship of the crucified one. This is a true insight, and one that cannot be relinquished. Only, the kingdom of God does not end in the paradoxical form of a presence of this kind. Its paradoxical hiddenness "under the contrary" is not its eternal form.[43]

Rather, it is because we know in Christ that the reality as it currently exists is "contrary" to the "eternal form" of the kingdom that we are empowered to strive for the kingdom. We recognize that things are not as they ought to be, and that sin and death still appear to have a hold on our reality: "The contradiction does not result automatically from man's experiences with history, with sin and death, but it results from the promise and the hope which contradict these experiences and make it no longer possible to put up with them."[44] Through our faith in God's faithfulness and our belief in the promise, we exist in a contradiction in which we find our present state of affairs intolerable, and we have no option but to seek to change it. Thus in the eschatological horizon of our history, we need to attempt to move toward the future that is of itself moving toward us. In this way we demonstrate our faithfulness to the promise made by God and reaffirmed in Jesus Christ.

However, because this reality takes place "*sub cruce*," we cannot anticipate the kingdom in a spirit of blithe optimism, but must be aware of the contradictory spirit of our world, and must be prepared for the suffering which this following in the way of the kingdom entails. Moltmann is not blind to the realities of sin and evil, but he does not see them as ultimate. He asserts that Christians must be willing to

---

eschatology is more organic and follows more closely the original Hegelian conception of the flow of history and the growth of the future out of the present moment. For Pannenberg, the future *grows out of* the present moment and tends toward the future. For Moltmann, on the other hand, the kingdom comes toward us from the future and in a revolutionary way establishes something genuinely new and unexpected. It is a more radical inbreaking of God's kingdom from the outside than Pannenberg's conception, in which the kingdom of God grows out from the inside. See Wolfhart Pannenberg, ed., *Revelation as History* (New York: Macmillan, 1968); Wolfhart Pannenberg, *Theology and the Kingdom of God* (Philadelphia: Westminster Press, 1969); *Systematic Theology*, 3 vols. (Grand Rapids: Eerdmans, 1991).

43 Moltmann, *Theology of Hope*, 223.
44 Moltmann, *Theology of Hope*, 224.

undergo struggle for the sake of the kingdom, that because it exists under the form of the cross, it is indeed the way *to* the kingdom. The person who follows Christ "is compelled to accept the world in all meekness, subject as it is to death and the powers of annihilation, and to guide all things toward their new being. He becomes homeless with the homeless, for the sake of the home of reconciliation. He becomes restless with the restless, for the sake of the peace of God. He becomes rightless with the rightless, for the sake of the divine right that is coming."[45]

But, in order to do this, it is necessary not only to be committed to the kingdom oneself, but to be committed within a community of the committed. The promise of Christ's coming reign leads to the growth of the community of faith, and its mission to spread the hope of this kingdom.[46]

The Identity and Relevance of Faith

In *The Crucified God*, Moltmann strives to be thoroughgoingly christocentric in his approach to understanding the significance of the cross. It cannot be taken as an abstraction or taken away from the reality of the one who was subjected to it: "A theology which did not speak of God in the sight of the one who was abandoned and crucified would have nothing to say to us."[47] But at the same time, precisely because the church must speak of it, the cross is not, for Moltmann, a matter of pure negativity. It is in speaking of the cross that the church can speak of Christ and "the freedom he offers," through which the church may become what it is called to be.[48]

Moltmann begins by considering what he terms the "identity and relevance of the Christian faith.[49] In the midst of a society in crisis, what exactly is it that can be said either about society from a Christian point of view, or about Christianity from a social point of view? In the first instance, the problem becomes one of whether the Christian faith can speak meaningfully in the midst of changed circumstances: "The reason for this lies less in theology than in the fact that in a pluralist society, what concerns everyone absolutely, and what society must absolutely desire, is more difficult to identify than in earlier and more homogeneous societies."[50] There can no longer be said to be any singular worldview under which the social order can be organized, and thus certainly no common religious perspective that can speak in the midst of this.

Christian identity has to be found in something more than simply social involvement, and it certainly cannot be found simply in the activism or the identification with particular social movements. Moltmann points out that what makes for *authentically* Christian identity is precisely Christianity's non-identity with other social movements – with its contrast to them: "When a Christian community feels obliged to empty itself in certain social and political actions, it must take care

---

45 Moltmann, *Theology of Hope*, 224.
46 Moltmann, *Theology of Hope*, 224.
47 Moltmann, *The Crucified God*, 1.
48 Moltmann, *The Crucified God*, 1.
49 Moltmann, *The Crucified God*, 7.
50 Moltmann, *The Crucified God*, 7.

that its traditional religious and political identity is not exchanged for a new religious and political identity, but must sustain its non-identity."[51] The root of Christian identity is found precisely in the following of Christ alone in the way that Christ has shown, which is to say, out of the realm of comfort and privilege and into the world of oppression and disadvantage. The Christian life is a life lived *"kenotically,"* just as Christ's own life was a process of *kenosis*. Without this movement, a self-conscious following of Christ into the world, says Moltmann, the result is a church that entrenches itself behind fortified walls. In doing so, it ceases to be an "open" church and retreats "into the apocalyptic situation of the closed church."[52]

Human community, according to Aristotle, is based upon the principle of the attraction of like to like. However, through the cross, this principle of identity is undermined and is no longer a matter of attraction of like to like, but is based upon an identification with the different – that is to say, the outcast and dispossessed: "The more this domain of external similarity, the 'Christian world,' collapses and society becomes 'different,' the more this analogical thinking and action loses its force. For both reasons, there then has to be a move towards dialectical thought and dialectical existence, and one's own identity has to be recognized and set forth in what is different and alien."[53]

The theology of the cross is about the identification with the alien. On the cross, God comes into the fullest possible identification with the depths of the human condition, and through that process is revealed, not according to a *theologia gloriae*, but in its opposite:

> God is revealed as "God" in his opposite: godlessness and abandonment by God. In concrete terms, God is revealed in the cross of Christ who was abandoned by God. His grace is revealed in sinners. His righteousness is revealed in the unrighteous and in those without rights, and his gracious election in the damned. The epistemological principle in the theology of the cross can only be this dialectic principle: the deity of God is revealed in the paradox of the cross. This makes it easier to understand what Jesus did. It was not the devout, but the sinners, and not the righteous but the unrighteous who recognized him, because to them he revealed the divine righteousness of grace, and the kingdom. He revealed his identity amongst those who had lost their identity, amongst the lepers, sick, rejected, and despised, and was recognized as the Son of Man amongst those who had been deprived of their humanity … . One must become godless oneself and abandon every kind of self-deification or likeness to God, in order to recognize the God who reveals himself in the crucified Christ.[54]

It is here, in the shadow of Christ's cross that Christian identity is affirmed, and Christian relevance is encapsulated. In a society that no longer assumes the normativity of the Christian message, it is in its identification with those who are pushed aside in society that Christians may discover the fullness of God. But if this is the case, how is it that the cross can accomplish this? How does the suffering man

---

51 Moltmann, *The Crucified God*, 17.
52 Moltmann, *The Crucified God*, 21.
53 Moltmann, *The Crucified God*, 26.
54 Moltmann, *The Crucified God*, 27.

on the cross free us from our identification with the world and for an identification with the outcast?

The Cross and the Crucified

The question of the cross is the question about Jesus Christ – who he is and how he died, as well as for what he died. To speak of a theology of the cross is thus to begin with a Christological understanding of theology. Moltmann spends a considerable amount of time looking into the theological and exegetical issues surrounding the identity of Jesus Christ and the significance of his death.

What does it mean to say that Jesus is God? Jesus is, according to Moltmann, "the eternal presence of God amongst men."[55] But what could it mean to say this? This is the core of many of the theological controversies that the early church attempted to resolve by speaking of Jesus Christ as "true God and true human." Yet Moltmann finds in the Christology of the early church a "mild docetism" that does not take wholly seriously what it means to speak of Christ's humanity.[56] A Christology that begins "from above" is one that loses its sense of the history of Jesus Christ in his "below-ness," and the human dimensions that this implies.[57]

Moltmann considers the question of Christ's crucifixion in the context of his life and preaching, arguing that "his preaching is tied to his person,"[58] and therefore the question of his life and his eschatological message of the kingdom is called radically into question through his death: "the true critique of the preaching of Jesus is the outcome of his life and his end upon the cross."[59] The hope embodied in Christ's incarnation and his proclamation of God's coming kingdom is contradicted by the historical fact of his death upon the cross. All that he said is nullified, and all that defined his mission is negated. In this context then, the negativity of the cross puts the question to the eschatological possibilities he embodied. The hope that he proclaimed could only be said to still be relevant in the face of the negation of this negation – in his resurrection from the dead. "This means either that his death represented the end of his eschatological message, or that his message must be proclaimed on a 'wholly other' basis, as the 'word of the cross.'"[60] Here he reaches back to the thrust of Luther's Heidelberg disputation in his emphasis on the contradiction of the cross to

---

55 Moltmann, *The Crucified God*, 88.
56 Moltmann, *The Crucified God*, 89.
57 Moltmann does acknowledge, however that the metaphor of "above" is important for a proper understanding of Jesus Christ. "It is true that the Christological answer starts 'above' and presents the mystery of Jesus on the pattern of the incarnation and resurrection, the humiliation and exaltation of the eternal Son of God. But the question about God which it assumes is that of finite being seeking the infinite being of God which imparts permanence. Thus it is not necessary 'to stand in the position of God [oneself] in order to follow the way of God's Son into the world.' Rather, one must accept the openness of one's own finite existence in order to recognize its fulfillment in one's own openness" (*The Crucified God*, 89). In this way, he sought to distance his own approach to Christology from that of Pannenberg, whom he is quoting.
58 Moltmann, *The Crucified God*, 121.
59 Moltmann, *The Crucified God*, 123.
60 Moltmann, *The Crucified God*, 123.

any theology that seeks to leap right to the resurrection. It *matters* that the resurrected is the crucified, and that the crucified is the incarnate One.

If the resurrection is taken away from the cross, both become mere abstraction. Yet in order to understand the full significance of the cross, we need to understand what it was that brought Christ to it. Thus, it matters to Moltmann that Jesus was viewed as a "blasphemer," as one who claimed an authority higher than the Law. "In his ministry Jesus placed himself with sovereign authority above the limits of the contemporary understanding of the law, and demonstrated God's eschatological law of grace towards those without the law and the transgressors of law, through his forgiveness of sins."[61]

It also matters that Jesus died as a rebel, crucified according to Roman law. "Crucifixion was a punishment for crimes against the state, not part of general criminal jurisdiction."[62] Jesus' death can therefore not be understood as divorced from the concrete social situation in which he found himself. Moltmann criticizes Bultmann on precisely this point, seeing in Bultmann's argument for Christ's "apolitical preaching" a "reading back" of later separations between religion and politics into the death of Christ.[63] And it also matters that Christ died as one "Godforsaken," for whom the pain of death was compounded by his experience on the cross of God-abandonment, as his cry of anguish on the cross signifies.[64]

Yet, in the person of Jesus, God is nonetheless present in the act of crucifixion. And God's presence in the crucifixion is essential for an understanding of the social dimensions of Moltmann's theology of the cross. God identifies on the cross with suffering humanity in every dimension of its suffering – not only in physical pain and social oppression, but also in the state of alienation from God.[65] In his death "for us," Christ brings God into the most intimate possible relationship to the human condition. And conversely, in his resurrection of the crucified Jesus, God overcomes all of these obstacles – the suffering, the evil, and the alienation of the world – and establishes the new order proleptically in Christ. But it is this proleptic aspect that needs to be considered in light of Moltmann's social theory. For while Moltmann argues that this proleptic experience of the kingdom in the Easter appearances of Jesus inaugurates God's kingdom, he also notes that this kingdom has not yet come, although it is nonetheless *anticipatorily* present in the resurrection: "In the crucified Jesus the 'end

---

61 Moltmann, *The Crucified God*, 128.
62 Moltmann, *The Crucified God*, 136.
63 Moltmann, *The Crucified God*, 137.
64 Moltmann, *The Crucified God*, 149. Unlike most martyrs, such as Socrates, Moltmann notes that Christ "clearly died with every expression of the most profound horror" (146). He goes on to note that this theological dimension is central to an understanding of the significance of Christ's death.

65 This controversial dimension of Moltmann's thought is not one that I can pursue at any length at this point. It will be given some attention at a later point in this chapter. I will note that in arguing that there is something that goes on *ad intra* in the Trinitarian life of God, which we can infer from Christ's death on the cross, Moltmann's theology has entered some difficulties. His doctrine of the Trinity is important in any discussion of public theology because of its explicitly social dimensions. Yet other aspects of this topic, while interesting and important, are less central to the case I am making here.

of history' is present in the midst of the relationships of history. Therefore in him can be found reconciliation in the midst of strife and hope for the overcoming of strife."[66] But both elements are essential. If we seek the resurrection hope without the cross, the result is triumphalism. But if we take the cross without resurrection, the result is despair. For Moltmann, the understanding of the resurrection of the crucified one is precisely what leads to the possibility of anticipation of the coming kingdom in the midst of circumstances of injustice and oppression.

The Cross as Critical Social Theory

The recognition that the hope of the kingdom is rooted in the raising of the crucified one is the foundation of Moltmann's understanding of the cross as "critical social theory."[67] Following the work particularly of Horkheimer, Adorno, and Benjamin, Moltmann attempts to understand the moment of Christ's death on the cross as the embodiment within Christian theology of the negative aspects of the dialectical process in history. This view is most fully sketched out in his section in *The Crucified God* on "The Theology of the Cross and Atheism," in which he looks at the issues underlying the cross in dialogue, not only with critical theory, but also the work of Dostoyevsky and Camus.

The issue of atheism stands at the center of the idea of the cross as critical social theory precisely because the cross calls into question the very existence and goodness of God. If Christ truly died in God-abandonment, what does this imply about who God is and what God's nature is? Contrary to the *theologia gloriae*, the *theologia crucis* journeys deep into the negativity of the cross to discover its significance. As Moltmann notes, the theology of glory shares a great deal in common with a rather bland "metaphysical" atheism, which seeks to determine the existence or non-existence of God *in abstracto*. The theology of the cross, however, while not taking seriously this rather casual intellectual atheism, *does* take with utmost seriousness the cry of *protest* atheism.[68] Protest atheism emerges from the recognition of the injustice and cruelty of the world, the dirty underbelly of modernist optimism, and declares the impossibility of divine reality in the face of abomination. To some degree the image of the crucified Christ on the cross is simply the confirmation of the senseless horror of human cruelty from the perspective of protest atheism.

Yet Moltmann argues that in the shadow of this negativity, the cross can also provide an answer to the atheism of protest precisely in its evocation of the suffering of God. Quite compellingly, Moltmann writes:

> What kind of a poor being is a God who cannot suffer and cannot even die? He is certainly superior to mortal man so long as this man allows suffering and death to come together as a doom over his head. But he is inferior to man if man grasps this suffering and death as his own possibilities and chooses them for himself. Where a man accepts and chooses his

---

66 Moltmann, *The Crucified God*, 185.

67 Moltmann writes: "Critical theology and critical theory meet in the framework of open questions, the question of suffering which cannot be answered and the question of righteousness which cannot be surrendered" (*The Crucified God*, 226).

68 Moltmann, *The Crucified God*, 221.

own death, he raises himself to a freedom which no animal and no god can have … . The peak of metaphysical rebellion against the God who cannot die is therefore freely chosen death, which is called suicide. It is the extreme possibility of protest atheism, because it is only this that makes man his own god, so that the gods become dispensable. But even apart from this extreme position, which Dostoevsky worked through again and again in *The Demons*, a God who cannot suffer is poorer than any man, for a God who is incapable of suffering is a being who cannot be involved. Suffering and injustice do not affect him. And because he is so completely insensitive, he cannot be affected or shaken by anything. He cannot weep, for he has no tears. But the one who cannot suffer cannot love either. So he is a loveless being.[69]

If the ability to love implies the ability to suffer, then the divine impassibility is finally a divine impossibility.[70] If God the Father underwent the loss of the Son on the cross as the Son underwent the experience of death, and if there was genuine suffering in the Godhead, then this implies two things: First, that God is not uninvolved in the workings of the world, but is, on the contrary, involved to the depths of his divine being; and two, that God too responds with genuine grief in the face of evil. Far from being a *Deus incurvatus in se*, God is turned outward to the problem of evil, and to overcoming it precisely at that point where he most fully experiences it.

In the light of protest atheism, of the kind embodied by Ivan Karamazov or Albert Camus, the theology of the cross can stand alongside them and declare its solidarity with their protest against human suffering. And as the theology of the cross can be seen as the taking of the protest directly into the heart of Christianity and transforming it, so can critical theory be seen as taking the theology of the cross into social criticism. Moltmann speaks approvingly of Max Horkheimer's understanding of critical theory as being essentially a "negative theology."[71] Moltmann writes:

> [Horkheimer] does not assert that there is an omnipotent, righteous, and gracious god, but he questions radically whether any immanent substitute could take his place. In his critical theory he challenges both traditional theism and its brother, traditional atheism. There is no theistic answer to the question of suffering and injustice, but far less is there any atheistic possibility of avoiding this question and being content with the world. It is impossible to be content with one's own possibilities, which are always limited. So Horkheimer uses the formula of "longing for the wholly other," which hovers between theism and atheism.[72]

---

69 Moltmann, *The Crucified God*, 222.

70 The question of the nature of divine love as *agape* might seem to call this statement into question. If, after all, the highest form of love is that love which regards the other irrespective of one's own good, then how can it follow that God's love need imply the possibility of suffering? But Moltmann's point here is different. Moltmann is objecting not to the idea that God's love is wholly other-regarding, but that God's love is *disinterested*. An apathetic God, from Moltmann's perspective, is one that exists as pure transcendence and cannot be said to be involved in the workings of the world. Moltmann, however, seems to overplay his hand here, due to an insufficient discussion of the principle of analogy, and through a lack of consideration for how it may be that divine suffering may be seen as akin to, rather than identical with, human suffering.

71 Moltmann, *The Crucified God*, 224.

72 Moltmann, *The Crucified God*, 224.

Just as critical theory can offer no answer to the problem of evil, so is the cross silent as well. Any rationalistic attempt to provide an answer for suffering simply "evacuates" the cross. Yet the theology of the cross cannot take refuge in atheism any more than critical theory can: "Were it to do so it would no longer be taking Jesus' dying cry to God seriously. The God of theism cannot have abandoned him, and in his forsakenness, he cannot have cried out to a non-existent God."[73] But if atheism is no solution, and if traditional theism is an unworthy rationalization, then we must turn once again to the possibility that it is precisely God who suffers on the cross. This possibility can overcome the objection of protest atheism because, according to Moltmann, "It takes the 'metaphysical rebellion' up into itself because it recognizes in the cross of Christ a rebellion in metaphysics, or better, a rebellion in God himself: God himself loves and suffers the death of Christ in his love."[74] If this is so, then God may no longer be seen as aloof from the concerns of society, but as the Father of the Son who was unjustly executed, God is deeply immersed in the cry for justice over evil. It is this that links the suffering of God to political theology.

Political Theology and the Theology of the Cross

In *The Crucified God*, Moltmann attempts to draw out the themes we have addressed thus far in order to make the case that a Christian political theology emerges out of Christ's experience of the cross. In formulating this theology, he rejects two potential models – the model of "unburdening," and the model of "correspondence." The unburdening model is based on the thesis that Christianity should be free from political involvement: "The church relieves the state of the burden of religion and in doing so relieves religion of the burden of the state. The more apolitical – in this critical sense – the church becomes, the more irreligious, secular, and rationalist becomes the state."[75] While such an approach is not without an element of truth, Moltmann argues that it provides no basis for achieving social reform. He notes that in such a view: "the freedom experienced in faith and practiced in the church can then coexist with any form of economic and social oppression. Furthermore, the freedom before God experienced in faith can be used as a substitute for the necessity of a real political liberation of the world."[76] This is unacceptable to Moltmann.

The correspondence model is an improvement. Rather than separating religion and political life, the correspondence model "seeks to build a bridge from the realm of free faith and the liberated church into the realm of politics by means of correspondences, reflections, and images"[77] Such a view seeks to maintain the God-world relation in the process of working to bring about greater political justice and equity. He puts this in the context of the "great hope" and the "little hopes" in which Christian faith believes. "This distinction is not a quantitative but a qualitative one. God is God and man is man. So the gap can only be bridged by analogies from

---

73 Moltmann, *The Crucified God*, 226.
74 Moltmann, *The Crucified God*, 227.
75 Moltmann, *The Crucified God*, 318.
76 Moltmann, *The Crucified God*, 319.
77 Moltmann, *The Crucified God*, 319.

the side of God, the church and faith."[78] The parables of the kingdom cannot ever approach the reality of the kingdom itself: "The kingdom of God can be socialism, but that does not mean that socialism is now the kingdom of God."[79]

Yet Moltmann qualifies his approval of this model. It is too much a one-way motion of God to the world. "If the difference is transferred to the relationship between 'Christian community and civil community,' the church is idealized so as to become the model of society. Its liberation is already presupposed, whereas in practice it only becomes free with the society in which it lives."[80]

The political theology endorsed by Moltmann is the political theology of the cross.[81] The political theology of the cross, contrary to the other models, seeks not an identification between church and society, nor their separation, nor even a correlation between the one and the other. The political theology of the cross is rooted in a deduction that what took place between God the Father and Jesus Christ on the cross carries with it very concrete political implications. Moltmann denies that such a theology necessarily links itself with left-wing or right-wing movements.[82] Rather, it is concerned with associating itself with those movements that most clearly reflect the reality of the freedom given in Jesus Christ. The fact that God has raised Jesus Christ from the cross, a political death reserved for the outcast, implies that it is with those outcast within society that God stands in the midst of their suffering: "The authority of God is then no longer represented directly by those in high positions, the powerful and the rich, but by the outcast Son of Man, who died between two wretches."[83]

An important element to note in this discussion is how Moltmann's understanding of the political implications of a theology of the cross does not simply begin and end with the cross, but reflects the dialectical relationship that Moltmann has frequently referred to – the idea that the resurrection of the crucified One is the mirror image of the crucifixion of the resurrected One, and that neither moment of the dialectic can be understood without the other. Hope in the resurrection without the cross is empty, and reflection on the cross of Christ without an acknowledgement of the resurrection is blind.[84] Both are needed for a full understanding of the political hermeneutic of the cross that Moltmann is proposing, and thus the confirmation of Christ's mission in his resurrection is a central element to an understanding of the event that takes place on the cross.

---

78 Moltmann, *The Crucified God*, 320.
79 Moltmann, *The Crucified God*, 320.
80 Moltmann, *The Crucified God*, 320.
81 Moltmann, *The Crucified God*, 324.
82 Moltmann, *The Crucified God*, 327.
83 Moltmann, *The Crucified God*, 327.
84 As Richard Bauckham notes: "The political importance of Moltmann's *dialectical* Christology and eschatology derives from the full recognition it gives to the negative, unredeemed character of objective present reality and therefore to the *difference*, even contradiction between what reality is presently like and what in the hoped-for divine transformation of reality can become." *The Theology of Jürgen Moltmann*, 102. Italics in original.

Conclusion

The political programme that emerges for Moltmann out of this dialectic of transformation and critique is one that seeks to combat what he refers to as the "vicious circles of death" in modern society.[85] He notes that there is not only one liberation theology that Christians should affirm, because there are myriad elements of a fallen society from which Christians must be liberated. Thus, liberation from the vicious circle of poverty must be met by a commitment to "the satisfaction of the material needs of men for health, nourishment, clothing, and somewhere to live. A further part of this is a social justice which can give all members of society a satisfying and just share in the products they produce."[86] This also means that political oppression must be met by a commitment to democracy and human rights. He notes: "If and to the degree that the democratic movement means the abolition of privilege and the establishment of political human rights, *democracy is the symbol for the liberation of men from the vicious circle of force.*"[87] Moltmann also refers to liberation in the cultural dimension of life, which he sees embodied in a growing regard of human beings for one another, and a growing respect reflected in their behavior. This is rooted in human fellowship and the overcoming of alienation.[88] And finally with regard to nature, Moltmann views liberation in the ending of human exploitation and pollution of the natural world. He notes that: "the relationship of working man to nature is not a master–servant relationship but a relationship of intercommunication which pays respect to the circumstances. Nature is not an object but man's environment, and in this has its own rights and equilibria."[89]

Moltmann's understanding of the theology of the cross thus leads him from the person of Jesus Christ, to the experience of God as Trinity in the event of the cross, to the social and political implications of this. Coupled with his focus on the expectation of the coming kingdom of God, as promised and sealed in the event of Christ's resurrection, this sets Moltmann a dialectical structure for his political theology, out of which he begins to develop those links to some of what we have already discussed. In particular, it leads him to a concern for the role of Christians in a pluralistic and technological modern society, and for a focus on the importance and priority of human dignity in the midst of a potentially dehumanizing world.

---

85 Moltmann, *The Crucified God*, 329.
86 Moltmann, *The Crucified God*, 332.
87 Moltmann, *The Crucified God*, 333. Italics in original.
88 Moltmann, *The Crucified God*, 333.
89 Moltmann, *The Crucified God*, 334.

Chapter 3

Promise, Covenant, and Human Rights

Introduction

In Chapter 2, I examined the central elements of Moltmann's theological programme, which I described as a dialectic of transformation and critique. The transformative element is rooted in the anticipatory consciousness that Christians possess on the basis of their eschatological expectation – that they follow a risen Christ. The critical dimension of his programme, on the other hand, is rooted in the knowledge that the risen Christ is also the crucified Christ. As he discusses at length in *Theology of Hope* and *The Crucified God*, it is the interplay of these two dimensions of Christian identity that create the impetus for Christian involvement in transformative social action, as Christians cannot be idle in the face of an unredeemed world.

Christian assurance of God's faithfulness, in turn, is rooted in two prominent themes in biblical and reformed theology, namely promise and covenant, which Moltmann uses to provide a foundation for a Christian conception of human rights. This emphasis on promise and covenant in turn deepens Moltmann's conception of the relations within the Trinity, which then becomes for him a model for human community.

Promise as Revelation

For Moltmann, God's revelation is intimately bound up in God's *promises* and God's *history*. God's revelation is not simply a transcendent principle, which can either be known through the independent exercise of the intellect or discovered through the direct self-revelation of God. Rather, it is discovered through God's relationship with God's people. Moltmann writes:

> Then the word of God – *Deus Dixit* – would not be the naked self-proof of the eternal present, but a promise which as such discloses and guarantees an outstanding future. Then the result of this revelation in promise would be a new perception of history's openness towards the future. Not all ages would have an equally immediate relation to God and an equal value in the light of eternity, but they would be perceived to be in a process determined by the promised *eschaton*. If the revelation of God in the resurrection of Christ contains within itself an eschatological differentiation, then it opens the way for history in the category of expectation, and remembrance, of assurance and imperilment, of promise and repentance.[1]

---

1 Moltmann, *Theology of Hope*, 59.

Rather than view theology from the perspective of human experience, Moltmann seeks to understand human existence in light of the eschatological horizon of God's revelation, that is, the yet-unfulfilled promise of God's reign.

Following Gerhard von Rad, Moltmann explores the history of the concept of promise in the Old Testament, considering how Israel understood itself in light of its covenant relationship with God. In Israel's history, Yahweh is manifested as the God who promises, who sends his people journeying. As a desert, nomadic people, they brought this God of promise with them when they settled in the land, and thus retained the promise motif in their religious practice, and in their understanding of their covenant with God.

Although Israel had moved away from a nomadic to an agricultural existence, they did not therefore abandon the promise character of their faith. Rather, the concomitant circumstances of epiphany actually take second place in Israel's faith to "the call and the pointer to the future. With that, the concept of revelation found in the epiphany religions is transformed. It is subordinated to the event of promise."[2] The future thus continues to be an operative religious category for Israel: "The whole force of promise, and of faith in terms of promise, is essentially to keep men on the move in a tense *inadequatio rei et intellectus* as long as the *promissio* which governs the *intellectus* has not yet found its answer in reality."[3] Thus, even when they have come to occupy the land, Israel continues to be under threat, and the promise of a peaceable kingdom remains in the future for them. Their continuing relationship of covenant with Yahweh requires that they continue to look forward to its absolute fulfillment in reality, and thus they are kept continually in a state of expectation.

What this means for Moltmann is that Israel begins to develop a taste for history – it understands itself as standing between the place where they once were, and the place for which they are destined. This can be seen, for example, in Deuteronomy, where the renewal of the covenant promise is intrinsically connected to the remembrance of the past slavery and divine liberation: "I am the LORD your God, who brought you out of the land of Egypt, out of the house of slavery; you shall have no other gods before me" (Deut. 5:6–7). Though the God of the covenant has liberated Israel, he has not yet completely fulfilled the promises of the covenant: "If the word is a word of promise, then that means that this word has not yet found a reality congruous with it, but that on the contrary it stands in contradiction to the reality open to experience now and heretofore … 'Future' is here a designation of that reality in which the word of promise finds its counterpart, its answer and fulfillment."[4]

But if revelation takes place through the experience of promise, who is the God who is revealed in these promises, and how is this God known? Moltmann answers that God is known as God in faithfulness to promises: "if the revelations of God are promises, then God 'himself' is revealed where 'he keeps covenant and faithfulness forever' (Ps. 146:6) … 'God himself' cannot then be understood as reflection on

---

2 Moltmann, *Theology of Hope*, 100.
3 Moltmann, *Theology of Hope*, 102.
4 Moltmann, *Theology of Hope*, 103–4.

his transcendent 'I-ness,' but must be understood as his self-same-ness in historic faithfulness to his promises."[5]

This requires us to understand our condition as an "in-between-ness" – in between the promise and fulfillment, past history and future history. Furthermore, this knowledge of God as the God of promise, and of ourselves as historically situated, means that we cannot take refuge in any type of a-historical transcendence, either within ourselves or with reference to our knowledge of God: "Knowledge of God is then an anticipatory knowledge of the future of God, a knowledge of the faithfulness of God which is upheld by the hopes that are called to life by his promises. Knowledge of God is then a knowledge that draws us onwards – not upwards – into situations that are not yet finalized but still outstanding."[6]

This is the central theme that Moltmann finds in the Old Testament narratives, reflected not only in the Pentateuch, but also in the prophetic and apocalyptic literature. God's promises constantly propel the people of Israel forward at the same time they remind them from where they have come. Thus, the people of Israel are firmly historically situated as a community that looks forward to the completion of God's pledges. During those periods when they deviate from this linear historical view, seeking to take refuge in the cyclical view of history represented by the pagan religions surrounding them, God calls them back with reminders of their unique relationship and their calling as a people.

Yet, as Moltmann points out, the early materials and the prophetic materials cannot overcome the problem of death, which stands as the boundary condition for the fulfillment or disappointment of all promises.[7] The apocalyptic literature seeks to extend beyond this boundary, toward a universalization of the promises, and a cosmic horizon of their fulfillment, yet in doing so, it also accepts certain dualistic premises about the nature of good and evil and the cosmic struggle between them. As Moltmann writes: "The apocalyptic expectation is no longer directed towards a consummation of the creation through the overcoming of evil by good, but towards the separation of good and evil, and hence the replacement of the 'world that lies under the power of evil' by the coming 'world of righteousness.'"[8] Apocalyptic thus augments the particularity of Israel's history with God and its horizon of death with a universal and cosmic horizon of fulfillment, in such a way that it seeks to escape from the boundary conditions brought on it by human finitude.

The Resurrection and the Fulfillment of the Promise

It is against the horizon of human finitude and death that Moltmann considers the promissory character of the resurrection of Jesus Christ. Indeed, it is the resurrection of Christ that provides the context for all Christian eschatological thinking, as it is the guarantee and the foretaste of the fulfillment of God's promises.

---

5   Moltmann, *Theology of Hope*, 116.
6   Moltmann, *Theology of Hope*, 118.
7   Moltmann, *Theology of Hope*, 131.
8   Moltmann, *Theology of Hope*, 134.

Central to Moltmann's claim is the insistence that there is continuity between the God of the Old Testament covenant, and the God who raises Jesus Christ from the dead. The resurrection is thus not a complete historical novelty, but is in fact the extension of the same history of promise that Yahweh inaugurated with Israel:

> The God who reveals himself in Jesus must be thought of as the God of the Old Testament, as the God of the exodus and the promise, as the God with "future as his essential nature," and therefore must not be identified with the Greek view of God, with Parmenides' "eternal present of Being," with Plato's highest Idea and with the unmoved Mover of Aristotle, not even in his attributes. Who he is, is not declared by the world as a whole, but is declared by Israel's history of Promise. His attributes cannot be expressed by negation of the sphere of the earthly, human, mortal and transient, but only in recalling and recounting the history of his promise. In Jesus Christ, however, the God of Israel has revealed himself as the God of all mankind.[9]

Hope in the promises of God has thus, through the resurrection of Jesus Christ, become a universal hope for all humanity and the cosmos. Furthermore, this hope extends, not only to the possibility of its fulfillment within the context of one or even a hundred thousand human lifetimes, but has as its horizon the possibility of fulfillment beyond death, since death itself is overcome in Jesus Christ.

At the same time, Moltmann is careful to point out that God's history is indivisibly connected with the covenant with Israel, and it is therefore of central importance to emphasize that Christ was a Jew. The Jews are the carriers of the covenant, and the primary witnesses to God's action in history: "If ... theology takes seriously the fact that Jesus was a Jew, then this means that he is not to be understood as a particular case of human being in general, but only in connection with the Old Testament history of promise and in conflict with it."[10] With the resurrection, the promise is reaffirmed and extended, but still not yet fulfilled. While Jesus' resurrection demonstrates the reality of this future for all humanity, that reality remains a "not yet." Our present circumstances still contradict it.

And so, from Moltmann's perspective, it is not simply Jesus' reality as the reaffirmation of the promise of redemption that is significant, but precisely Jesus' *future* as the one who will come again to establish God's reign throughout the cosmos. But in order for this to be so, we need to have a proper understanding of a future eschatology, in the sense of the actual expectation of the definitive in-breaking of God in history. Such an eschatology must be a horizontal, and not only a vertical, expectation of communion with God. If it is to be in continuity with the fulfillment expectation of Israel, then both the promise and its fulfillment need to be rooted in the historical reality of those to whom the promise is made. To remove them from history is not to fulfill the promise, but rather to substitute a heavenly state for the embodied presence of God's kingdom on earth, and it is this trend in the history of theology that Moltmann vigorously rejects.[11]

---

9 Moltmann, *Theology of Hope*, 141.
10 Moltmann *Theology of Hope*, 142.
11 See Moltmann, *Theology of Hope*, 164.

Christ's history is then connected explicitly with his bodily resurrection from the dead, which roots his history in the history of a suffering and redeemed humanity. His resurrection is an affirmation of human life and a reassertion of the connection between the covenant promises and the possibility of those who keep faith with it may survive to enjoy its fulfillment. To put it in Hegelian terms, the resurrection is the negation of the negation of human life in death.

The promise that is embodied in the covenant, both with Israel and pledged in the resurrection of Jesus Christ, has a concrete ethical implication in Moltmann's description of the nature of human rights, which emerges, not only from our creation in the image of God, but also (and primarily), in the nature of God's promises to us.

Human Nature, Covenant, and Human Rights

Moltmann's theology of human rights is rooted in God's claim upon human beings.[12] This claim has a three-fold grounding in 1) the image of God in human beings, 2) the incarnation of Jesus Christ, and 3) the coming kingdom of God.[13]

The central element of God's claim upon human beings, however, is the promissory history of God's relations to human beings. Moltmann insists that "liberation, covenant, and the claim of God are the basic content of the biblical witness of the Old Testament" and that "the human rights to freedom, to community, to dominion, and to the future are inseparable constituents of God's claim upon human beings and the whole creation."[14] In other words, the rights that give human beings their innate and inalienable dignity in the world are rooted in the rights of God over humanity.[15]

This is not to suggest that the *imago Dei* does not play an important function in Moltmann's approach to human rights. But it is to stress that human rights are not innately a matter of the doctrine of creation *per se*, but rather are rooted in the dignity granted by God to those whom God has redeemed.[16] The *imago Dei* is important for outlining the basis for particular fundamental human rights. "By *fundamental* human

---

12 Moltmann, *On Human Dignity*, 21. See also Jürgen Moltmann, "A Theological Declaration on Human Rights," in World Alliance of Reformed Churches, *Theological Basis for Human Rights* (Geneva: W.A.R.C., 1976), 8. For earlier reflection on issues of human rights, see "The Theological Basis of Human Rights and of the Liberation of Human Beings," in *The Experiment Hope*, 147ff.

13 Moltmann, *On Human Dignity*, 20.

14 Moltmann, *On Human Dignity*, 21. This is confirmed and strengthened in the New Testament, in which the basis of human rights is established on the ground of the revelation of God in Christ. "According to the New Testament, Christian theology reflects the liberation of human beings from sin, law, and death through the coming, the sacrifice, and the resurrection of Jesus Christ ... Liberation through the vicarious death of Christ, the new covenant in his blood, and the new rights and duties of the fellowship which is composed of slaves and free persons, Jews and Gentiles, men and women (Gal. 3:28) are the basic content of the biblical witness of the New Testament" (21).

15 See Douglas Meeks, "Introduction," *On Human Dignity*, xi.

16 For an in-depth discussion of the *imago Dei* in Moltmann's theology, see Moltmann, *God in Creation*, 215ff.

rights we mean those rights and duties which belong essentially to what it means to be truly human."[17] This has three dimensions for Moltmann.

First, the *imago Dei* establishes human rights, not only in matters of individual and political rights, but "in the fullness of their lives and in all life's relationships – economic, social, political, and personal."[18] The direct implication of this for Moltmann is that no sphere of human activity may deprive us of our basic humanity. Human rights are prior to the claims of particular nations, economic systems, or societies. "Respect for freedom of conscience is the foundation of a free society."[19] The political principle that flows from this is the priority of democracy in political organization.[20]

Moltmann goes on to note, however, that God's claim on human beings does not only grant us rights. This would result in far too individualist a conception of human rights. The rights we are granted by God's claim come at the cost of concomitant duties according to which we are obligated. Moltmann specifically points out that we are obligated to resist efforts to dehumanize and violate the rights of our neighbors.[21]

Second, the *imago Dei* establishes the rights of human beings, not only as individuals, but also in community with others.[22] As with his first principle, this both seeks to move away from the individualist biases of liberalism and root the *imago Dei* in a set of covenantal relations within a social context. Moltmann writes:

> In fellowship before God and in covenant with others, the human being is capable of acting for God and being fully responsible to God. As a consequence of this, the social rights and duties of the human community are just as inalienable and indivisible as persons' individual rights and duties. Human beings have to heed the dignity and the responsibility of community in economy, society, and state, just as the latter has to heed those of the former … . Thus the rights of human beings to life, freedom, and self-determination always arise together with the human community's claim upon people.[23]

Human rights are necessarily human rights *in community*. To the degree that an emphasis on individual rights becomes a justification for the violation or abuse of

---

17 Moltmann, *On Human Dignity*, 23.
18 Moltmann, *On Human Dignity*, 23.
19 Moltmann, *On Human Dignity*, 23.
20 Moltmann, *On Human Dignity*, 24.
21 Moltmann, *On Human Dignity*, 24. Of interest in connection with this is Moltmann's discussion of the right to use violence in revolutionary situations, which he discussed in *Religion, Revolution, and the Future*. At this stage of his career, he seems to have argued for the right to use force in the name of protection of the innocent. He writes that "the problem of violence and nonviolence is an illusory problem. There is only the question of the justified and unjustified use of force and the question of whether the means are proportionate to the ends" (143). While in the intervening years he has moved to an explicit affirmation of the non-violent option as being central to the discipleship of Christ, it is unfortunate that he has not offered a sustained meditation on the ambiguity of violence, or the question of whether, in the protection of the neighbor, it might ever be justified.
22 Moltmann, *On Human Dignity*, 25.
23 Moltmann, *On Human Dignity*, 25.

human rights in the social life, human beings are not honoring the full implications of their creation in the image of God.[24] Furthermore, they are not cognizant of the full implications of the covenantal basis of human life under God. Full appreciation of human rights needs to take the maximum possible account of both individual and social rights.[25]

Finally, human rights are rooted in the justification and renewal of human relationships. In anticipation of the coming of God's reign, human rights embody the expectation of how human beings are intended to be with one another and act toward one another. In liberation from sin and evil, human beings are freed to recognize and honor one another's dignity and freedom to be for God and for one another. "Human rights can only be realized when and insofar as the justification of unjust human beings and the renewal of their humanness takes place."[26] In the resurrection as the pledge of the coming kingdom, the rights of humanity are affirmed as the anticipation of properly conceived human relationships under God and God's kingdom. "Through the outpouring of his Spirit on all flesh (Acts 2), God renews his likeness on earth, unites a divided humanity and liberates his creation from the shadow of evil. In the coming of his kingdom, God will ultimately glorify his right, justify human beings, and transfigure creation."[27]

The Trinity and Human Community

The foundation of human rights that exists within the context of covenantal relationships has another dimension as well. For Moltmann, the doctrine of the Trinity is essential for an understanding of the way in which human social relationships are rightly ordered. The kingdom of God is realized through the Trinitarian relations of the Father, the Son, and the Spirit. Moltmann writes:

> The kingdoms of the Father, the Son, and the Spirit mean continually present strata and transitions in the kingdom's history. Just as the kingdom of the Son presupposes and absorbs the kingdom of the Father, so the kingdom of the Spirit presupposes the kingdom of the Son and absorbs that. In developing a doctrine of the kingdom of God, which is differentiated in a Trinitarian sense, we are also searching for a theology of the history of human freedom.[28]

---

24 Moltmann also considers the question of the responsibility of human beings, not only for the rights of themselves and their contemporaries, but also of the rights of the earth and of future generations. Moltmann asserts that human beings cannot assume a kind of tempocentric concern with their own good while ignoring the rights of the future generations to the goods given by God. At the same time, the earth itself that is created by God is given to human dominion, not for exploitation, but for care. Cf. Moltmann, *On Human Dignity* 28–9 and *God in Creation*, passim.
25 See Moltmann, *On Human Dignity*, 33ff.
26 Moltmann, *On Human Dignity*, 31.
27 Moltmann, *On Human Dignity*, 31.
28 Moltmann, *The Trinity and the Kingdom*, 209.

Through the Trinitarian life of God, and in the power of the Holy Spirit, the possibility of a renewed relationality is opened up within human life that allows us to live in proper relationship to one another.

Moltmann wants to restore an understanding of the Trinity that begins with *persons-in-communion*, rather than an approach that begins with a single divine essence. His criticism of what he sees in Western Trinitarian theology as an over-emphasis on the unity of God is motivated by the social importance that he places on the doctrine of the Trinity, seeing it as the key to human relationality. Without an emphasis on the fundamental relationality of the three persons, we have no real sense of the innate relationality of human beings with one another. Barth's approach to the Trinity reserves the realm of freedom and sovereignty for God alone, while leaving no sense of a model for human relationship and action.[29] Karl Rahner's approach, on the other hand, leads to a solitary mysticism.[30]

By contrast, Moltmann wants to emphasize the *perichoretic* union of the three persons of the Trinity. He notes: "If we search for a concept of unity corresponding to the biblical testimony of the triune God, the God who unites others with himself, then we must dispense with both the concept of the one substance and the concept of the identical subject. All that remains is: unitedness, the at-oneness of the triune God."[31]

The interrelations of the three persons of the Trinity become manifest in history through "their dispensation of salvation, which is to say in their opening themselves for the reception and unification of the whole creation."[32] Through this dispensation, God "draws us into and includes us in his eternal triune life with all the fullness of its relationships."[33] On this basis, human beings cannot be understood to have their essential humanity in a solitary subjectivity, any more than God can. Rather, the divine *perichoresis* "corresponds to human fellowship of people without privileges and without subordinances. The perichoretic at-oneness of the triune God corresponds to the experiences of the community of Christ, the community which the Spirit united through respect, affection and love."[34] It is this understanding that is behind Moltmann's claim that "the trinity is our social program," as he declares in *Experiences in Theology*.[35] The relational nature of human beings speaks against the rise of individualism and the privatization of social relations in modern society.

This has implications as well for the nature of the church. If the church is based in a Trinitarian faith, then it takes on the characteristics of the Trinitarian life. Thus, "a Christian doctrine of the Trinity which is bound to the history of Christ and the history of the Spirit must conceive the Trinity as the Trinity of the sending and seeking love of God which is open from its very origin. The triune God is the God who is open to

---

29 Moltmann, *The Trinity and the Kingdom*, 144.
30 Moltmann, *The Trinity and the Kingdom*, 148.
31 Moltmann, *The Trinity and the Kingdom*, 150.
32 Moltmann, *The Trinity and the Kingdom*, 157.
33 Moltmann, *The Trinity and the Kingdom*, 157.
34 Moltmann, *The Trinity and the Kingdom*, 158.
35 Moltmann, *Experiences in Theology*, 332ff.

man, open to the world, and open to time."[36] The church is a community of persons, reflecting the communion of persons in the Trinitarian life. But just as the Trinitarian life of God is not closed off and insular, so the church is a *public* church in light of the Trinity. It is a church that is open to the world and engaged in the world, giving of itself as God gives from the divine life of the Trinity.

The question arises, however, as to how far we can take the relationship between the Trinity and the social nature of human beings, either in the church or in the larger social context. One cannot presume that it is within the realm of human possibility to completely attain the kind of perichoretic union within human communities that exists in the godhead. However, as Miroslav Volf points out, the doctrine of the Trinity creates a "socioethical principle" in which "although the triune God cannot bestow legitimacy on political power, there must in created reality still be broken creaturely correspondences to this mystery of triunity."[37] But the question is, how deep do these correspondences run, and what can we conclude from them? On the one hand, the Trinity provides a negative critical principle upon which we can evaluate practical life in human society.[38] But there is also a positive dimension, since the Trinity provides a principle of love and mutuality which is germane to all human relationships, including social and political relationships.

Miroslav Volf, with regard to his own project, which seeks to draw relationships between the doctrine of the Trinity and types of human community (specifically, the church), notes some of the difficulties with this approach. He writes:

> Although trinitarian ideas can undeniably be converted into ecclesiological ideas, and indeed are so converted, it is equally undeniable that this process of conversion must have its limits, unless one reduces theology to anthropology or, in reverse fashion, elevates anthropology to theology. The reasons for this are obvious. Our notions of the triune God are not the triune God, even if God is accessible to us only in these notions. A certain doctrine of the Trinity is a model acquired from salvation history and formulated by analogy to our own experience, a model with which we seek to approach the mystery of the triune God, not in order to comprehend God completely, but rather in order to worship God as the unfathomable and to imitate God in our own, creaturely way. Trinitarian models bring God to expression in the same way all language about God does, namely as a God who is revealed anthropomorphically, but who always remains hidden "*in the light of his own being*" because God dwells "in unapproachable light" (1 Tim. 6:16). As Erik Peterson has emphasized, the *mystery* of triunity is indeed found only in the deity itself.[39]

We cannot speak univocally about the divine being. Our language about God must always be equivocal and analogical. As a result, we can make no completely confident statements about the nature of God's immanent being, and as a result any social model we build upon this basis is by necessity provisional.

Volf goes on to note an additional issue: "'Person' and 'communion' in ecclesiology cannot be identical with 'person' and 'communion' in the doctrine

---

36 Moltmann, *The Church in the Power of the Spirit*, 56.
37 Volf, *After Our Likeness* (Grand Rapids: Eerdmans, 1998), 192.
38 See Thomas Thompson, *Imitatio Trinitatis* (Princeton Theological Seminary, Diss., 1994), 165.
39 Volf, *After Our Likeness*, 198. Italics in original.

of the Trinity; they can only be understood as *analogous* to them."[40] Whatever may be true about our knowledge of God, we know it only through our *creaturely* understanding of God.[41] We cannot presume to establish a social model on the basis of such knowledge without qualification.

This is a problem rooted in Moltmann's confidence in his ability to divine the workings of the immanent Trinity. Moltmann often seems to move beyond an analogical understanding of the Trinitarian interrelationships, opting instead to read the theological tradition rather literally in its description of how the Father, the Son, and the Spirit exist with regard to one another. This leads him to conclusions such as that the Son must have been *born* and not merely *begotten* of the Father, so that "he is a motherly Father too."[42] The difficulty here is not the feminine language for God, but rather the literalization of the creedal statements about God in order to draw that theological conclusion. It may be possible, with a more circumspect approach to the issue, to make a case using an explicitly analogical understanding of the Trinitarian relations and human society, and draw much the same conclusion, particularly in light of an understanding of human relationality rooted in the *imago Dei*.

What is valuable in Moltmann's analysis of the nature of the Trinity and its social implications are precisely the insistence that human beings, through their creation in God's image, exist innately in relationship with one another. The Trinity can very well be a social programme, in an analogical sense, if it provides a careful consideration of the way in which the divine nature creates a model toward which human beings are to strive, but recognizes that model to be provisional, and subject to revision. However, Moltmann's insistence on the equality and interrelationality of the three persons of the Trinity does indeed provide a basis for an understanding of human relationships in society as rooted in democratic and equitable relationships, rooted in love and mutual respect.

Conclusion

In developing his conception of a political theology, Moltmann sought to root a humanistic concern with questions of basic rights in a just society in the foundational theological categories of the Christian faith. Just as the transformative potential of Christianity is rooted in its faith in the Resurrected One, and its commitment to critique is rooted in the theology of the cross, so is the Christian conception of community rooted in the Trinitarian interrelationships of Father, Son, and Holy Spirit. The promissory character of God's covenantal relationship with his people is a reflection of the relationship that exists within the Godhead itself. And this in turn provides the foundation for a Christian community that seeks to create something

---

40 Volf, *After Our Likeness*, 199. Italics in original.
41 Volf, *After Our Likeness*, 199.
42 Moltmann, *The Trinity and the Kingdom*, 164. There is in this comment and the argument that Moltmann makes in its favor, a trace of Arianism, which Moltmann avoids by his repeated insistence on the coeternity of the Father and the Son, and by an emphasis on their perichoretic union. But the hint still remains, and is not completely eliminated by these other factors.

new within society, while at the same time dwelling within and participating in the larger social reality of which it is a part.

In rejecting the privatization of Christian life in modern society, Moltmann sets himself the task of interpreting the importance of the gospel in the midst of a cultural situation to which it often seems to be irrelevant. Yet, Moltmann's way of doing this is rooted neither in an embrace of a civil religion which is wholly affirmative of society, nor in a retreat to the church as an enclave. The church is a "contrast society" for Moltmann, but the contrast society that the church embodies is, in Moltmann's view, a society in contrast to the contradiction of modern society to its own proper form – the kingdom of God. Thus, Moltmann can argue, "the modern world with its potentialities and its limitations can be in accord with the kingdom of God or in contradiction to it. Those who hope for God's kingdom will contradict the contradictions of the modern world and will welcome those points in which it corresponds to the kingdom."[43] This principle embodies the core of Moltmann's public theology. His approach operates through a dialectic of critique and transformation, through which the "contradictions of the modern world" are "contradicted." Theology and ethics, therefore, cannot be a matter of "Christian self-description" as some approaches would have it. Rather, they must take the questions of modernity seriously enough to engage it in constructive conversation about its own proper ends.

In doing this, as I will demonstrate, Moltmann must deal with the nuances of social life, and consider the complex relationship of the church with the modern context. If the church is called to represent the gospel in the midst of modern society, then how the church relates to the complex intersections of institutional life in society needs to be considered, and considered in ways that Moltmann has not adequately dealt with. The church as the body of Christ is a formational community through which Christians come to understand who they are in the midst of a world that seeks to define them according to the modern standards of autonomy and productivity. Yet, Moltmann argues, the church needs to be an "exodus community," which is to say a community that exists within the modern world, but has the kingdom of God as its destination. Such a community has a responsibility to live within the world as it is, but in anticipation of the world as it is coming to be.

---

43 Moltmann, *God for a Secular Society*, 220.

Chapter 4

Exodus Church and Civil Society

Introduction

In the previous chapters I have attempted to lay out the theological foundations for Moltmann's political theology, particularly as they touch upon the foundational questions of the cross, resurrection, covenant, and the Trinity. Moltmann's conception of the church, as I alluded at the end of the last chapter, emerges from his analysis of these themes. What the church is and how its vocation connects to the larger social reality that Moltmann is attempting to describe is a function of the church's commitment to and reflection of these other theological themes.

In this chapter, I will examine how Moltmann understands the role of the church within society, in particular with regard to the question of "civil religion." His conception of the church as an "exodus community" is central to the case that I propose to make in subsequent chapters about the dual identity of the church as civic institution and as theological entity. It is *because* the church exists as an entity within civil society and also as a community set apart through its faith in the promises of God, that it can act in anticipation of the coming Kingdom of God in ways that have the potential to make genuine political and social progress in modern society.

Modern Society and the Church

What is most significant for Moltmann about the church is not its institutional character *per se*, but its calling as witness to the promises of God, embodied in Christ's life, death and resurrection, and in the expectation of the kingdom. As a called community, the church has its identity in its faith in Jesus Christ. Thus, before one can consider the role of the church as an entity within society, one must consider its role as an *ekklesia*, as a community of those "called out" for a specific task in, to and for the world. This means that one must be clear in the first instance about the nature of that task.

Moltmann sees the identity of the church primarily as a *missionary* identity. What the church does is determined by its commission to spread the gospel. Furthermore, the church is not simply a static entity but is a church "on the move." It is, as Moltmann terms it, an "exodus church." By this, he means that it is a church that may never rest content with either its own position in the social structure, nor with the world in which it finds itself. Rather, the church is the ever-expectant community. Its gaze is always directed forward to its coming future, and thus its object is never the comfort of things as they are, but the anticipation of things as they are yet to be. Thus, it is a community that embodies what Bloch referred to as the "not-yet-conscious" world of hope.[1]

The mission of the church, then, is to bring this not-yet-conscious expectation to consciousness, by proclaiming its inauguration in the resurrection of Jesus Christ. In order to accomplish this, the church must be engaged in a critical dialogue with its context, in our case, what Moltmann refers to as "modern society." The central question he raises is whether it is possible, in light of its eschatological expectation, for the church to become an accommodating element in society, or if it must at its heart be a critical force in society.

The development of modern society coincided with an increasing privatization of religious life. Whereas once the church existed as a *cultus publicus*, in the modern era, it has become a *cultus privitas*.[2] From its status as a public voice, religion has fallen into the status of a subjective opinion, useful for motivating one in one's public dealings, but in itself irrelevant to the system of social needs.[3] "'Religion' ceases to be a public social duty and becomes a voluntary private activity."[4]

Coinciding with this is the "disenchantment" of the natural world and the rationalization of all human activities. Modern society claims to be governed not by superstition or fantasy, but by a calculus of efficiency and instrumental reason, which by definition must exclude religious concerns from its purview. As religion has become a purely internal state, the external world has become more and more secularized: "The world is surrendered to the reason of man."[5] In this context, modern society expects religion to fulfill certain functions – to meet human beings' subjective needs for religion, their associative needs for community, and their institutional needs for an official embodiment of faith.

This, in its turn, leads to an increasing romanticization of the religious. The focus becomes the individual and his or her belief, understood primarily emotionally, rather than on the objective workings of God in history: "Faith is the receiving of one's self from God. This places it in a position for radical loneliness, makes it 'individual,' desecularizes it in the midst of an organized society."[6] It is a reaction to the rationalization and modernization of the world, and an attempt to preserve a place for the divine in a de-divinized culture.

Additionally, religion is supposed by modernity to embody community. Not only is the individual human being the locus of religious thought, but also humanity in its

---

1 Bloch, *The Principle of Hope*, 114.
2 Moltmann, *Theology of Hope*, 310.
3 See *Theology of Hope*, 305. In this regard, Moltmann is echoing points which had already been made by Hegel and Weber, both of whom saw the declining public role of religion as expanding the emancipatory interests of society, but both of whom also recognized the continuing importance of religion's person-forming and opinion-forming influence on one's private life. In some sense, this parallels the argument made by Neuhaus in *The Naked Public Square*, and the somewhat different approach taken by Stephen Carter in *The Culture of Disbelief* (New York: Basic Books, 1993). On the other hand, see Peter Berger, ed., *The Desecularization of the World* (Grand Rapids: Eerdmans, 1999).
4 Moltmann, *Theology of Hope*, 310.
5 Moltmann, *Theology of Hope*, 312.
6 Moltmann, *Theology of Hope*, 314.

species-being. This mode of operation also embodies a romanticist reaction to modern culture, which can be detected for example in leftist revolutionary movements, as well as in the moderate socialist world of Emile Durkheim and the conservative communitarianism of Ferdinand Tönnies. The central concept in this approach is that of "community" as, using Moltmann's words, the "cult of co-humanity,"[7] which is itself rooted in the romantic movement, and carries its anti-modernist agenda forward into a social critique.

Finally, society expects the church to function as an institution, embodying in some sense an official status in society. It provides a formality and an authority that relieves individuals of the pressures contained in modern society. "Stereotyped patterns of conduct give them an enduring, stable, and communal character. Thus there emerges a new store of unvarying customs and axioms at work, consumption, and intercourse."[8]

Moltmann's point in this section of *Theology of Hope* is not to completely renounce these social roles, but to point out that they do not exhaust the church's mission, and become constraints out of which the church must break:

> If Christianity, according to the will of him in whom it believes and in whom it hopes, is to be different and to serve a different purpose, then it must address itself to no less a task than that of breaking out of these its socially fixed roles. It must then display a kind of conduct which is not in accordance with these. That is the conflict which is imposed on every Christian and every Christian minister. If the God who called them to life should expect of them something other than what modern industrial society expects and requires of them, then Christians must venture an exodus and regard their social roles as a new Babylonian exile. Only where they appear in society as a group which is not wholly adaptable and in the case of which the modern integration of everything with everything else fails to succeed, do they enter into a conflict-laden, but fruitful partnership with this society.[9]

As can be seen from this passage, Moltmann views the church's critical role in society, not as a separation from society's fallenness, but as a partnership, in which the church calls the society to a recognition of what it is destined to be in the fullness of time. Just as the church in its life and proclamation strives to anticipate the coming kingdom and live into its reality, so too does the church work within society to bring it to a greater realization of its own tasks in this regard.

However, this is only possible because the church at the same time does not seek to identify itself with society, but seeks to be in some sense an indigestible lump, a reminder to its society that the gospel cannot be assimilated to a context that is something less than the kingdom of God, and that instead the whole of society has to be seen as toward, in, and under the larger picture of God's reign. In this regard, the church is to be an "exodus church," always on the way to the destination toward which it is called. It is a pilgrim church, which has its journey as part of its fundamental character. When it takes part in society, its participation is always both

---

7 Moltmann, *Theology of Hope*, 316.
8 Moltmann, *Theology of Hope*, 322.
9 Moltmann, *Theology of Hope*, 231.

an affirmation and a critique of that society. An affirmation of its identity as called by God to a vocation of justice and peace-making, and a critique of its insufficiency on precisely these points. The risk that faces a church that allows itself to become too comfortable is stultification. Moltmann writes: "Here the task of Christianity today is not so much to oppose the ideological glorification of things, but rather to resist the institutional stabilizing of things, and by 'raising the question of meaning' to make things uncertain and keep them moving and elastic in the process of history."[10]

Thus, the church is called into solidarity with those who are kept on the outside of structures of power and authority in society – the poor, weak, sick and marginalized, whoever they may be. In solidarity with the "least" in society, the church witnesses to those yet-unfulfilled promises that stand at the center of its mission. It witnesses to the reality of the kingdom which is yet to come, and declares specifically that it is for these outcast and marginalized in particular that the kingdom is coming. Thus, it proclaims the continuing hope of the poor for justice, the weak for a protector, the sick for healing and the victims of war for peace. It declares through its solidarity with these that the kingdom is on the way, and has already been realized in the resurrection of Christ: "Hope alone keeps life – including public, social life – flowing free," declares Moltmann.[11]

The Gospel and Civil Religion

In articulating the relationship of the exodus church to modern society, Moltmann hastens to distinguish his own understanding of political theology from civil religion. Whereas his own approach is rooted in the church's status as a critical and transformative force in society, with an independent norm from society, the church's role in society has commonly been that of the justification of, and in some cases the glorification of, the society.

Moltmann points specifically to the situation of the church under the Third Reich as an example of the danger inherent in civil religion. Lacking that critical component from which it could have resisted the incursions of National Socialism, much of the church in the 1930s became complicit in the glorification of Hitler and his policies. Moltmann notes: "Politics will never again become our religion, neither political nor civil. Without the deadly horror and the unbearable guilt of such a political religion we would probably not be so critical. Without Auschwitz the national flag would perhaps still hang in the Christian churches in Germany."[12]

At root, the civil religion Moltmann is resisting is a return to the French tradition of civil religion, especially as articulated in the work of Rousseau and Durkheim.[13]

---

10 Moltmann, *Theology of Hope*, 324.

11 Moltmann, *Theology of Hope*, 324.

12 Jürgen Moltmann, "Christian Theology and Political Religion," in *Civil Religion and Political Theology*, ed., Leroy Rouner (Notre Dame: University of Notre Dame Press, 1986), 42.

13 And the roots go farther back than that. The kind of civil religion of which Moltmann speaks can be found in the Roman cult of the emperor that attempted to force Christians to proclaim the lordship of Caesar. "The public practice of religion is therefore the primary civic

In the case of the former, the civil religion was the embodiment of the General Will, an expression of the unity of social life and what Daniel Elazar calls a "secularized divinity."[14] In the case of the latter, religion was the symbolic representation of society's self-worship.[15] In both cases, they represent a form of idolatry that Moltmann sees as lying underneath all civil religions.[16]

The chief exemplar of the kind of civil religion that Moltmann is criticizing is Carl Schmitt. It is instructive to view the way Moltmann criticizes his understanding of "political religion" and distinguishes his own viewpoint from it. Schmitt's political theology was oriented towards a justification of the state and categorizing of the entirety of human rights under the sphere of the political. It was not, however, a Christian theology in any meaningful sense. Schmitt's political theology was, according to Moltmann, "nothing more than the theory of a political religion necessary for the support of the state."[17] The diabolical elements of Schmitt's political theology lie behind any civil religion, which is based upon the schema of friend versus enemy and insider against outsider. In determination of particular national or cultural symbols as carrying a divine import, civil religions reinforce the identification of individuals with the narrow horizons of particular interest groups. Christian theology, however, must have a universal horizon. Moltmann notes that "the ecumenical solidarity of the Christian church is for me higher than national loyalty or cultural, class or racial associations."[18]

Moltmann makes five points regarding the way civil religion functions in modern society. In the first instance, Moltmann argues, civil religion "provides self-esteem, self-justification, and a collective public feeling of dignity."[19] It also creates harmony in society through a process of symbolic integration of citizens with their surrounding culture. Third, civil religion serves the friend/foe dichotomy that Schmitt wrote about. "The external enemy and the internal enemy strengthen collective legitimation and integration," he writes.[20] Moltmann also notes that civil religion in modern society, unlike the kind advocated by Schmitt, is most effective when it does not attempt to control the entirety of life but "leaves open the private sphere and only deals with proper public behavior and prescribed public expression."[21] Finally, and related to this, Moltmann notes that because of this civil religion does not have the capacity

---

duty. In Rome the *crimen laesae religionis* as given not yet through theoretical denial of the state religion but only through the practical neglect of the requisite observance of the cultus. *Godless* was only used to blame those who refused publicly to honor the state gods." Moltmann, "Christian Theology and Political Religion," 46.

14 Daniel Elazar, *Covenant and Civil Society: The Constitutional Matrix of Modern Democracy* (New Brunswick, N.J.: Transaction Publishers, 1998), 50. Cf. Jean Jacques Rousseau, "Second Discourse on the Origins of Inequality," in *Basic Political Writings*.

15 See, for one example, Emile Durkheim, *Selected Writings* (Cambridge: Cambridge University Press, 1972), 220.

16 Moltmann, "The Cross and Civil Religion," 35.

17 Moltmann, "Christian Theology and Political Religion," 43.

18 Moltmann, "Christian Theology and Political Religion," 41.

19 Moltmann, "Christian Theology and Political Religion," 47.

20 Moltmann, "Christian Theology and Political Religion," 47.

21 Moltmann, "Christian Theology and Political Religion," 47.

to speak meaningfully to spheres other than the public sphere. He notes, "modern political religion remains in the grip of ideology and is only a pseudoreligiosity."[22] It is thus neither a transformative nor a critical theological stance vis-à-vis society.

It is interesting to dwell for a moment on the different ways in which Moltmann is using the term "political" here. In his criticism of Schmitt, he understands "political religion" as equivalent to the civil religion that glorifies particular cultural or national aspirations. Yet "political" has a different connotation when addressed to his own understanding of "political theology," which is political on the basis of the particular dynamics implied by the cross and resurrection of Jesus Christ. This distinction, as Leroy Rouner points out, is rooted in a Barthian suspicion of the substitution of "any human program of thought for the biblical kerygma."[23] The question is not, for Moltmann, politics or no politics, but rather, politics based on the cross and the expectation of the kingdom, or politics based on tribalism and self-interest.

Civil religion in this sense is not compatible with the church's mission in society as an exodus church because it is first and foremost the theological justification of the *civitas teranna* rather than the kingdom of God. Christians have a concrete public responsibility within the modern world as agents of change within the multiple spheres of responsibility that they are given within a complex civil society.

Exodus Church and Civil Society

Moltmann finally grounds his understanding of the social responsibility of this "church on the move" in a doctrine of vocation borne of Christian expectation. As Christian theology is inescapably a missionary theology, it is called to go out into the world in proclamation of the coming kingdom. In attesting to Jesus Christ and his future in the world, the church calls the world to acknowledge the latencies and tendencies existing in the world that lead it toward the anticipation of the kingdom. "The risen Christ calls, sends, justifies, and sanctifies men, and in so doing gathers, calls, and sends them into his eschatological future for the world. The risen Lord is always the Lord expected by the Church – the Lord, moreover, expected by the church for the world and not merely for itself."[24]

It is important to note that the *gathering* of Christians into the church is, for Moltmann, the precondition for the *sending* of Christians into the world. Both aspects of this are necessary. The church as the community of the called provides the critical and expectant center of the Christian life, from which Christians are nourished for their being in the world and in service for others.[25] That service that Christians are called upon to render to the world is rooted in its eschatological expectation. "The Christian Church," Moltmann writes, "has not to serve mankind in order that this world may remain what it is, or may be preserved in that state which it is, but in order that it may transform itself and become what it is promised to be."[26]

---

22 Moltmann, "Christian Theology and Political Religion," 47.
23 Leroy Rouner, introduction to *Civil Religion and Political Theology*, 9.
24 Moltmann, *Theology of Hope*, 325.
25 Moltmann, *Theology of Hope*, 327.
26 Moltmann, *Theology of Hope*, 327.

This commitment to service is finally a vocation to serve God in the world in the various social roles we are to play. It means that we must be involved in the institutional life of civil society, and not merely stand aloof as "resident aliens." Although it may be, as Moltmann quotes, that "To Christians every home is foreign," it is also true, as the quote continues, that "every foreign place is home."[27]

Yet Christian vocation is not intended to be understood as a static category in Moltmann's view. He recognizes that society is complex, and that the social relations that are formed therein are multiplicitous and dynamic.[28] Yet the vocation of Christians within civil society is to engage in the transformation of society from within these various social roles. "The Reformers' identification of call and 'calling' was never intended to dissolve the call into the calling, but *vice versa* to integrate and transform the 'callings' in the call."[29] This requires, according to Moltmann, a "creative discipleship" that is oriented toward the creation of community and restoring relations of justice within the world, as well as a critical and transformative hope that Moltmann speaks of as "creative expectation."

But the character of this creative expectation needs to be understood in the context of a proper understanding of the variety of social roles inhabited by the Christian within society. Moltmann's understanding of the missionary character of the church, while crucial for an understanding of how Christians can be formed to embody anticipatory consciousness within society, is not well developed in the context of the theory of civil society proper. It is necessary to consider more closely how institutions in general, and the church in particular, operate within society to form values and create particular visions of integrity out of which people may act in complex moral situations. Moltmann offers no such analysis in his work, and thus his understanding of the exodus church remains somewhat abstract. In Part Four, however, I will return to Moltmann's understanding of the role of the church in modern society, after having considered the idea of civil society more closely.

From Political to Public Theology

Moltmann's intent from the publication of *Theology of Hope* to the present has been to discern the public calling of Christians, and their responsibility for the world in which they find themselves. To this end, he has developed a political hermeneutic of the gospel with which both to interpret the gospel in light of the current questions of society, and to interpret society through the lens of the promissory history of God revealed in the Bible. This political hermeneutic, from Moltmann's perspective, must emerge from the praxis of Christians engaged in the struggle of living in a modern, technological society, and must lead Christians to understand that society both critically and in light of the tendencies and latencies that suggest the possibility of social transformation.

The key interpretive element in Moltmann's political hermeneutic has been the dialectical relationship between the promises of God as manifested in the history of

---

27 Moltmann, "Christian Theology and Political Religion," 41.
28 Moltmann, *Theology of Hope*, 333.
29 Moltmann, *Theology of Hope*, 333.

Israel, and confirmed and validated for the entire world in the resurrection of Jesus Christ, and the reality of the contradiction of the Christian hope in the suffering and death of Christ in God abandonment. Both of these elements are necessary for an effective Christian political hermeneutic. Without the realization of the reality of suffering and the contradiction of the actual state of human affairs in the gospel, Christian hope becomes a utopian illusion. But without the recognition of the reality and the concrete possibility of that hope, the recognition of suffering and evil in the world leads only to despair.

Kept alive within the Christian church, this dialectical interpretation of the world serves as an inspiration and impetus for Christians to anticipate the coming kingdom of God in the midst of the yet-uncompleted world. Christians are called upon to grapple with social and political problems, and not to stand apart from them. At the core of such an ethic stands Moltmann's understanding of the church as an exodus community, that exists within the world, but as a community of faith on the way to the kingdom of God and working within the various worldly callings to realize the possibilities inherent in the Christian call.

And yet, one serious charge must be lodged against the broader social application of Moltmann's understanding of the relationship between theology and social life. In his concern for the exodus character of the church, Moltmann has not developed a theological understanding of institutional identity which would enable him to articulate how the church, not only as a movement of the faithful in the world, but as an institution that participates with other institutions within society, may contribute to the constructive development of those human possibilities which may anticipate the coming kingdom of God. As it stands, the church possesses no institutional identity for Moltmann. It is a social movement that may pervade institutional life, but he has offered no theological or sociological understanding of how the church may do this. What is needed, then, is a conception of the church among institutions within civil society that would allow a clearer understanding of the possibility that the spirit of anticipation may develop and move out beyond the church's walls.

Moltmann's language has shifted more and more in the direction of speaking about "public" rather than "political" theology. The general shape of his theology has not changed along with his language, and it has not become clear how he understands theology as a public process to be distinguished from a political theology. If the political hermeneutic of the gospel is to become a public hermeneutic, then it must include a fuller set of tools for the analysis and description of the way in which Christians interact with and within civil society. Moltmann's concept of the exodus church may provide the kind of model that is necessary for the creation of such a public theology. But if so, it must include a wider use of the idea of civil society as a theory of institutions and a means of understanding how Christian theology may utilize these theories.

Conclusion

In these first chapters, I have sought to sketch the main contours of Moltmann's theology as a resource for Christian public engagement with modern society, as, in other words, a "public theology." In Part II I will examine the nature of public theology as it has emerged in the American context. The public role of religion in the United States has been influenced, to a great extent, by the differing role that religion takes, as compared with Germany. Nevertheless, the interplay of Moltmann's theology with American public theology can offer resources for Christian reflection on public life that each on its own might lack. The crucial third component of my analysis, the theory of civil society, with be the subject of Part Three.

PART II

ETHICAL ENGAGEMENT AND THE TASK OF PUBLIC THEOLOGY

Chapter 5

Public Theology and the Task of Theological Ethics

Introduction

In Part I, I examined the structure and the main themes of Jürgen Moltmann's theological project, particularly as they bear on the question of what came to be known as his "political theology." Yet, in recent years, as the concept of the political has come to be understood more fully as a function of a larger social setting, the idea of a political theology has begun to be subsumed under the larger category of "public theology." Moltmann has joined in this move, often utilizing "public" and "political" theology interchangeably in his work. In order to examine the significance of this move on Moltmann's part, I want to turn the question of just what is meant by "public" theology, broadly conceived. In this chapter, I will examine some key characteristics of public theology, both as a descriptive and a normative category. I will then examine the development of the idea of public theology in the United States. In the next chapter, I will look more closely at the contemporary articulation of public theology as it has developed its own particular identity as a theological movement, before turning to a comparison of Moltmann's project with several of the key figures in American public theology.

The following themes are not intended to be exhaustive or determinative for public theology as a field of endeavor. They are, however, themes that recur in the literature of public theology on a consistent basis, and that aid in a fuller understanding of what draws public theologians together under one banner (as we will see in the next chapter).

The Need for a Christian Account of Public Life

Public theology as a mode of inquiry relates to the intersection of Christian theology with the entirety of human life. As such, there is no dimension of human existence that is beyond its scope.[1] The purpose of public theology is to give a Christian account of public life in all of its complexity.

This entails that public theology be engaged in discussion and analysis across a broad spectrum of disciplinary outlooks. Theology as a public endeavor needs to take account of the work that is done in sociology, economics, environmental studies, and the natural sciences in order to be able to claim applicability and relevance

---

1   See David Tracy, *The Analogical Imagination* (New York: Crossroad, 1981), 31.

outside of the walls of the church. It must consider the "resources of rationality" that are shared across disciplinary boundaries for public discourse to take place.[2] An approach to economics, for example, that seeks to construct a Christian approach to economic life without taking constructive account of the work of economic theories from Aristotle to Smith, Marx to Keynes, would not only be incapable of dealing with many of the relevant economic questions with which Christians must deal, but would also be deemed laughably irrelevant in discussion with economists.[3]

Yet, theology is not bound to such disciplines in terms of its own goals or its own understanding of what is necessary in terms of social critique. Theology needs to engage in a constructive dialogue across disciplinary boundaries in order to be an effective public advocate for a Christian view of society. Before proceeding I will provide a preliminary sketch of the tasks that public theology needs to undertake in engaging in such interdisciplinary conversation.

Three Tasks of Public Theology

The typology that I am summarizing in this section should not be taken to be definitive or exhaustive of the nature of public theology, but simply a useful heuristic for understanding how public theology interacts with its social setting. Dimensions of this typology can be seen in various approaches to public theology, some approaches emphasizing one aspect, some another, but in most cases all three of these aspects can be seen in those theologies that can be considered to be "public" theologies.

These three factors, the analytic, interpretive, and constructive, describe the interaction of theology with broader questions of public concern. A theological approach that neglects an analysis of the social situation in which it finds itself will suffer a crisis of relevance, while one that provides no interpretation based upon its own reflective resources suffers a crisis of identity. Finally, one that offers no constructive proposal for a Christian approach to the world will suffer a crisis of responsibility.

The Analytical Task of Public Theology

Analysis can take a number of different forms, depending on the way in which theology is engaging in public discourse. I do not intend analysis to be understood as an attempt to out-do those disciplines with which theology is in dialogue in their

---

2   See J. Wentzel van Huyssteen, *The Shaping of Rationality* (Grand Rapids: Eerdmans, 1999), 3; also Calvin Schrag, *The Resources of Rationality* (Bloomington: Indiana University Press, 1992).

3   This is one of several flaws in D. Stephen Long's *Divine Economy* (New York: Routledge, 2000), which seeks to offer a theological interpretation of economics without dealing in any depth with the details of economic theory, or with any careful description of how contemporary capitalism actually works. An appropriate Christian response to economics would demonstrate a concern with the way economics is actually done and interpreted by professionals in the field, and bring Christian principles to bear on such a discipline, rather than attempt to reconstruct the discipline out of one reading of the gospel.

own methods. Rather, by analysis I mean an attempt by theology to understand the context, setting, and application of another discipline according to criteria relevant for a fruitful discourse. In a sense, this is simply a reiteration of H. Richard Niebuhr's dictum that the first question the theologian must ask is "what's going on?"[4]

Analysis is the process by which theology asks what's going on. In asking this question, theology makes itself accountable for a reasonable understanding of those methods used by its disciplinary partner, and for seeking to see how those methods are applied. It is an open question as to how much of an expert one needs to become in another discipline in order to engage it in discourse. Certainly, the more one knows about, say, chemistry, the better able one is to engage in a discussion with chemists about the nature of their work. The depth of dialogue is aided by an understanding of other disciplines, but it is not necessary as a basis of interdisciplinary discussion.[5]

Additionally, analysis means seeking to gather empirical data relevant to the process of understanding. Again, the depth of data is dependent on the depth of analysis one wishes to undertake. An in-depth theological analysis of the phenomenon of globalization, for example, would require a very broad and deep consideration of a great deal of empirical data,[6] as would a consideration of the theological implications of the U.S. prison system.[7] But this does not mean that an exhaustive survey of evidence is always necessary for a theological analysis of an aspect of public life. What is required is the willingness to look at the situation in terms of the facts available.

It must also be said that theology is not merely passive or receptive in this interchange. Inasmuch as theology may learn from such interdisciplinary conversation, it also has something to teach. What theology adds to social, economic, political and psycho-cultural analysis is the specific attention to ultimate values that are, sometimes in distorted forms, operational in the midst of the "facts." By drawing attention to the ultimate objective of human knowing in general and in the particular case, public theology adds a crucial element to the discussion.

Analysis means being both willing to be subjected to the questions of other disciplines, and being willing to subject those other disciplines themselves to scrutiny. David Tracy speaks of this under the heading of "critical correlation," by which church and world critique one another.[8] He writes: "On the one hand, meanings discovered as adequate to our common human experience must be compared to the meanings disclosed as appropriate to the Christian tradition in order to discover how similar, different, or identical the former meanings are in relationship to the latter."[9]

---

4   H. Richard Niebuhr, *The Responsible Self* (New York: HarperCollins, 1963), 60.

5   See Paul Tillich, *Systematic Theology*, vol. 1 (Chicago, University of Chicago Press, 1951), 12.

6   See Max Stackhouse, ed., *God and Globalization* 4 vols. (Trinity Press International, 2000-2007). Also Hans Küng, *A Global Ethic for Global Politics and Economics* (New York: Oxford University Press, 1998) and *Global Responsibility* (New York: Continuum, 1993).

7   As, for example, Mark L. Taylor, *The Executed God* (Minneapolis: Fortress Press, 2001).

8   See Tracy, *The Analogical Imagination*, 24ff; *Blessed Rage for Order* (Chicago: University of Chicago Press, 1975), 79ff.

9   Tracy, *Blessed Rage for Order*, 79.

The critical correlation about which Tracy speaks provides a means for disciplines to cross-pollinate in a creative way, so that each discipline supports and sustains the findings and insights of the other. This aspect of analysis in particular leads directly into the task of interpretation, to which I will turn presently.

Finally, analysis means being able to formulate the problem both from a theological point of view, and in a way that takes account of what other disciplines have to contribute to the discussion. This is a theme to which I will return throughout this book. It is embodied in what I am calling the dialectic of critique and transformation in Moltmann's approach to public theology, and reflected in the way in which I attempt to understand the church as both a theological and sociological entity in light of the theory of civil society. It is crucial to public theology that it strives to make itself understandable in dialogue with those with whom it is in conversation. If it cannot present its outlook in a way that makes sense in terms of sociology, economics, physical sciences, or whatever other disciplines it is in dialogue with, then it cannot be understood to be properly public. At the same time, not every theological concept needs to be translatable to be relevant. It is sufficient for public theology to be "multi-lingual" in the sense of being able to speak conceptually both in terms of its own concepts and at the same time relate those concepts to the approaches of other disciplines. This means that, descriptively, theology may develop a way of thinking that is comprehensible by those who accept the theological presuppositions of the Christian faith, but at the same time develop a different but related approach that is relevant to those who do not.

With these elements of analysis in hand, it is still necessary to make sense of what it is that is going on. Simply having "the facts," as it were, does not provide a sufficient basis for doing theology in a public way. It is necessary to bring the data and concepts from the analytical realm into the hermeneutical realm, and begin a process of interpretation through which the concepts are subjected to theological scrutiny. All of this leads us to a consideration of the interpretative task of public theology.

The Interpretive Task of Public Theology

Analysis is an attempt to discover the nature of the problem or problems being dealt with in a dialogical situation between theology and other disciplines. Interpretation involves going beyond the description of a situation or problem, and attempting to understand it in light of the gospel. This means that theology has to bring to bear the traditions, resources, and authorities of its own worldview on the question at hand, in order to discern to some extent what Christian faith has to say that is relevant to this situation.

Different elements of the Christian tradition will be relevant to public discussion of different issues in differing contexts. The importance of a particular doctrine or theological approach is discovered through the comparison of the issue at hand with questions of Christian responsibility and a discernment of what is true about the world from the Christian perspective. However, there are several touchstones of Christian theology that are important resources to any useful hermeneutical discussion of public issues. The relevance of these doctrines will be discussed in the context of

Moltmann's theology and the theory of civil society throughout this project. At this point, I simply want to point in a more general way to their importance.

First and foremost, the centrality of Jesus Christ to any Christian interpretation of public life is essential to a genuinely Christian public theology.[10] There are of course theological approaches from other faith traditions in which Jesus Christ is either non-essential or irrelevant,[11] but for a public theology rooted within the truth of the world as understood from the perspective of Christianity, it is impossible to be truly engaged in a theology of public life without a relation of everything, either directly or indirectly, to the person and work of Jesus Christ.

The second interpretive keystone for any Christian public theology is the doctrine of the Trinity.[12] This doctrine and the doctrine of the incarnation represent perhaps the two most unique religious contributions of Christianity to the world. A public theology inconsiderate of the importance of these two doctrines deprives Christianity of the uniqueness of its public voice and the importance of its own interpretative angle on the world.

Theology as God-talk must take seriously the question of who God is and how God relates to the world. Christianity's contribution of the doctrine of the Trinity to the discussion of this matter gives it resources out of which it can offer a unique perspective to questions of public importance, particularly around subsidiary questions such as the doctrine of creation and anthropology, each of which benefits from a self-consciously Trinitarian theological perspective.

---

10 It is important to note here, however, that the *way* in which Jesus Christ is central may vary from one approach to public theology to another. Not every Christocentric public theology has to be rooted in a Barthian interpretation of Christ, though Barth's monumental importance on this subject cannot be gainsaid. However, the public theology of David Tracy deals with Jesus Christ very differently than Ronald Thiemann does, owing respectively to their revisionist and narrativist inclinations. Both, however, seek to demonstrate in different ways the importance of Christ to a Christian public theology.

11 Jewish reflection on public life, for example, is as richly textured in its own way as Christian public theology, but forms its public concern out of a different set of issues, to which Jesus Christ is quite reasonably marginal at best. Daniel Elazar's 4-volume work, *The Covenant Tradition in Politics*, for example, focuses on the evolution of the covenantal polity through ancient Judaism to the modern world. The intersection of Judaism and Christianity is vital to his presentation, but Jesus Christ *per se* is not central to his argument, nor does he develop any sort of Christology. This is similarly true of the faith-based activism of Michael Learner's *Tikkun*, which roots its understanding of reconciliation in Jewish resources. See Daniel Elazar, *Covenant & Polity in Biblical Israel: Biblical Foundations & Jewish Expressions* (New Brunswick, N.J., U.S.A.: Transaction Publishers, 1995); *Covenant and Commonwealth: From Christian Separation through the Protestant Reformation* (New Brunswick, N.J.: Transaction Publishers, 1996); *Covenant & Constitutionalism: The Great Frontier and the Matrix of Federal Democracy* (New Brunswick, N.J., U.S.A.: Transaction Publishers, 1998); *Covenant and Civil Society: The Constitutional Matrix of Modern Democracy* (New Brunswick, N.J.: Transaction Publishers, 1998).

12 See Max L. Stackhouse, *Public Theology and Political Economy* and S. Mark Heim *The Depth of the Riches: A Trinitarian Theology of Religious Ends* (Grand Rapids: Eerdmans, 2001).

This is of particular importance for a theology rooted in a pluralistic understanding of society, as we will see throughout our examination of Moltmann's public theology. His self-conscious rooting of Christian social responsibility in the doctrine of the Trinity, while not without problems, forms the basis of a theory of human relationality and communicativity that is particularly relevant in considering the theological dimensions of civil society.

Also connected to the relation of Christian theology to social pluralism is the third feature on which I wish to focus – the understanding of the church. The character of the church as the "body of Christ" (1 Cor. 12:12ff.) and as "ministers of the new covenant" (2 Cor. 3:6ff.) and those to whom the "ministry of reconciliation" has been given (2 Cor. 5:16ff.) is central to the connection of Christian ethical principles to the larger social context in which the church dwells. The relationship between ecclesiology, ethics and public life reflects our theological presuppositions about the nature of the church.[13]

The church exists in a precarious situation in modern society. On the one hand, both its message and its history demand that it be engaged in the multiplicity of issues concerning public life, but if modernity insists on creating an instrumentalized set of social conditions, is there really any role that the church can play? The possibility exists, as Durkheim suggested a century ago, that the church might simply become the realm in which the structures and institutions of modern society are symbolically affirmed and raised to the level of religious veneration.[14] But the church as a particular community of faith, as the body of Christ, has a responsibility to the gospel it preaches that cannot finally be reduced to a reflection of social relations. This being the case, it is important to ask just how it is that the church can be relevant in the context of a pluralistic public life.

Different doctrines may provide lenses through which to perceive questions of public theology, depending on the issues at stake. Questions of the doctrine of creation are of central importance (although not without the three mentioned above) to issues of science and ecology.[15] For a consideration of questions of society, however, these three, together with subsidiary theological issues that arise from

---

13 See Miroslav Volf, *After Our Likeness: The Church as the Image of the Trinity* (Grand Rapids: Eerdmans, 1998); David S. Cunningham, *These Three Are One: The Practice of Trinitarian Theology* (Oxford: Blackwell Publishers, 1998); Gary Simpson, *Critical Social Theory* (Philadelphia: Fortress, 2002). From the point of view of the relationship of religious language, liturgy, and ethics, William Everett's *The Politics of Worship: Reforming the Language and Symbols of Liturgy* (Cleveland: United Church Press, 1999) offers a provocative consideration of the way that changes in liturgical language alter perceptions about public life, and vice-versa.

14 As in the work of Emile Durkheim, for example. See *The Elementary Forms of Religious Life* (New York: Free Press, 1995); "Concerning the Definition of Religious Phenomena" in *Durkheim on Religion* (Atlanta: Scholars Press, 1994), 74ff.

15 See, for example, Jürgen Moltmann, *God in Creation* (Philadelphia: Fortress Press, 1980) and *Science and Wisdom* (Philadelphia: Fortress Press, 2003); Deiter Hessel, ed., *Theology for Earth Community* (Maryknoll, NY: Orbis Books, 1996); Sallie McFague, *The Body of God* (Minneapolis: Fortress Press, 1993); Rosemary Radford Reuther, *God and Gaia* (San Francisco: HarperSanFrancisco, 1992).

them, are of primary importance to any interpretative approach to the development of a theology of public life.

The Constructive Task of Public Theology

The process of analysis and interpretation is essential to coming to a clear understanding of the issues at stake and the appropriate resources available for the formulation of a Christian response to public issues. However, neither element is of much use without the subsequent task of formulating a practical response to the issue in question. Once more, depending on the realm of public life at issue, the character of the constructive task might change. What the constructive task of formulating a Christian response to a new scientific discovery is will be different from the task of formulating a response to issues of law, or medicine, or the character of the family. Each of these spheres of human relationality and institutional life requires that the process of analysis and interpretation take place, leading to a constructive response, but there is no single response appropriate to all such questions.[16]

A constructive response that simply seeks to lay a theological template over a particular issue, failing to consider the complexities that arise from the analytical task, will quickly become irrelevant to the issues at stake in the particular situation. The constructive task of public theology must arise out of a genuine consideration of the facts at issue in dialogue with the relevant disciplines. In a certain sense, we can paraphrase Kant and say that interpretation without analysis is empty.

But the corollary to this is that analysis without interpretation is blind. What distinguishes public theology from philosophy or sociology is precisely that its commitments rise out of theological convictions. If an attempt to do public theology without an appropriate consideration of the facts is insufficiently *public*, then an attempt to do so without the process of interpretation is insufficiently *theological*. How these two elements are brought together is precisely what public theology does in its constructive moment. What issues rise to the fore in any particular presentation of a public theology depends on the interpretive choices of the theologian in confrontation with the facts at hand, but cannot avoid an attempt to come to terms with both dimensions.

In Part IV of this book I will attempt to engage in a constructive public theological project in dialogue with Moltmann's conception of the "exodus church." Before doing so, however, it is important that we gain a fuller picture of the discipline of public theology as it has emerged in the American context over the last century.

---

16 Hans Küng speaks of this in his *A Global Ethic for Global Politics and Economics* in reference to political ethics this way: "political ethics implies an obligation to conscience which is not focused on what is good or right in the abstract, but on what is good or right in the concrete situation. Here a universal norm as a constant is combined with specific variables determined by the situation" (73). This, for Küng, represents the middle way between the unsavory alternatives of a machiavellian *realpolitik* on the one hand and a fuzzy-headed moralism on the other. The alternatives that he lays out with regard to political ethics could be said to be more broadly applied in my description of the necessity for both analysis and interpretation, and Küng's book is an exemplary case of a highly nuanced ethic rooted in a public theology.

Precursors to Public Theology

There are any number of examples that one could give for precursors to American public theology. One could speak of the Puritan divines, both English and American, and the close affinity they sought between religious and civil obligation.[17] One could also look at the public implications of Jonathan Edwards' theology as one author has recently done.[18] One could consider the theology of Lyman Beecher or William Ellery Channing, Shailer Matthews or Washington Gladden. All of these represent in their own ways precursors to the kind of public theology that has come to be represented on the American scene by David Tracy, Max Stackhouse, Cornel West and others. In the following pages, I want to explore the influence of some important early 20th-century figures as precursors to the contemporary forms of public theology in which Moltmann's theology partakes. Each of these theologians exemplifies in a different way the key themes of the previous section, while paving the way for the later theologies I will turn to in the next chapter.

Walter Rauschenbusch: The Ethics of the Kingdom of God

The ethical normativity of the kingdom of God was central to Walter Rauschenbusch's theology.[19] It provides the moral basis for Christian action in the social sphere, and a guideline for the means by which Christians seek to "Christianize" the social order. Rauschenbusch's understanding of the kingdom is rooted in the synoptic Jesus' sayings and parables.[20] Rauschenbusch's goal is to create a society that acts according to the imperative described by those sayings.

Rauschenbusch's experiences as a pastor in the Hell's Kitchen section of New York City solidified his commitment to address the plight of the working poor at the turn of the century and mobilized him to formulate a theology that was responsive to his perception of social need. He saw the treatment of workers under capitalism as the chief cause of social misery, alcoholism, and demoralization of workers and the repression of their aspirations. His analysis of the situation led him to conclude that a revolution of sorts was needed to overcome the situation created by capitalism, that capitalism would not of its own accord overcome.[21] Yet Rauschenbusch did not advocate the violent overthrow of capitalism, but rather the moral reformation

---

17 See A.S.P. Woodhouse, *Puritanism and Liberty* (London: J.M. Dent & Sons, 1992).

18 Gerald R. McDermott, *One Holy and Happy Society: The Public Theology of Jonathan Edwards* (University Park, PA: Pennsylvania State University, 1992).

19 Walter Rauschenbusch, *The Righteousness of the Kingdom* (Lewiston: Edward Mellen Press, 1999); *A Theology for the Social Gospel* (Nashville: Abingdon Press, 1978); *Christianity and the Social Crisis* (Louisville, KY: Westminster/John Knox, 1991); *Christianizing the Social Order* (New York: Macmillan Company, 1926).

20 Rauschenbusch, *A Theology for the Social Gospel*, 133. Cf. *Christianity and the Social Crisis*, 54ff.

21 Donald Meyer points out that the later vision of Rauschenbusch as utopian and unrealistic with regard to human sin is mistaken. To the contrary, "Rauschenbusch defended a doctrine that liberalism had generally been eager to mute, that of original sin. Original sin, he observed, was one of the few tenets of the old individualistic religion that pointed toward a solidaristic,

of society by the Spirit of Christ, who is "immanent in humanity and is slowly disciplining the nations and lifting them to share his spirit."[22] The social misery of life under the new form of capitalism of that period called for Christians to work, not only for the salvation of individuals but for the transformation of the entire society. Sin was not only a matter of individual infirmity, but of societal malaise. Just as the Spirit of Christ worked within the individual to bring about personal redemption, so Christ was working to bring about the redemption of the social life as well.

How was the social order to be Christianized? From Rauschenbusch's perspective, certain sectors of the social order were already Christianized. The family in particular is an example of a sector of society that, to Rauschenbusch, is more reflective of the Spirit of the kingdom. He notes that: "The simplest and most familiar social organization is the family. It is also the most Christian."[23] He finds the process of Christianization also taking place within the church and educational institutions as well.[24] Moreover, democratic political institutions are making progress compared to royal and imperial structures of the past.

For those sectors of society that have not been so Christianized, it is the task of Christians to bring the principles central to their religious faith to these institutions. Rauschenbusch is explicit that by "Christianization" he does not mean making Christianity into the official or even semi-official state religion of the United States. Rather, "Christianizing the social order means bringing it into harmony with the ethical convictions which we identify with Christ."[25] These ethical convictions are embodied in principles of freedom, equality, and sharing for Rauschenbusch.

Thus, Rauschenbusch seeks to provide a theological basis for particular social reforms. For example, he seeks an economic democracy in which the workers have a voice in the use of the means of production, and in which their humanity is recognized as of value: "men can have no fraternal relations until they face one another with a sense of freedom and equal humanity."[26] Although Rauschenbusch does not go as far as the communists (or even the socialists), he does advocate a kind of communitarian cooperativism in which property is held to some extent in common, by employers *and* employees, and life is seen as being of greater value than property.[27] The social and personal aspects of renewal in Rauschenbusch are interrelated, as it is precisely

---

social view of the Christian task." Donald Meyer, *The Protestant Search for Political Realism: 1919–1941*, 2nd edn (Middletown CT: Wesleyan University Press, 1988), 130–31.

22 Rauschenbusch, *Christianity and the Social Crisis*, 209.
23 Rauschenbusch, *Christianizing the Social Order*, 128.
24 Rauschenbusch, *Christianizing the Social Order*, 145.
25 Rauschenbusch, *Christianizing the Social Order*, 125.
26 Rauschenbusch, *Christianizing the Social Order*, 353.
27 Rauschenbusch, *Christianizing the Social Order*, 412ff. His final section of this book, on "Methods of Advance" summarizes the salient points of these principles. Harlan Beckley, analyzing Rauschenbusch from a Roman Catholic perspective, writes: "Advancing justice, according to Rauschenbusch's understanding of the kingdom, requires that the social order maximize opportunities for individuals to integrate their natural interests through self-development in solidarity with others." *Passion for Justice* (Louisville, KY: Westminster/John Knox Press, 1992), 346.

through the trust of the individual in Christ and the influence of the church in society, that such transformation is possible.

> True love, that is, could precede equality. It was this true love that inspired the ideal of equality in the first place. But how could it get into human nature, prior to equality? How could it survive, once implanted? On this, Rauschenbusch had only pure religious answers. The origin of true love was clear enough: it was revealed in Jesus Christ. The basis for its persistence in the face of inequality was clear enough. Those bore it who believed in Jesus Christ.[28]

The impetus for social reform was found in the action of the love of Jesus Christ upon individuals committed to following his way. Under such circumstances, social inequality, poverty, disease and starvation were evils to be eradicated if possible, and at the very least mitigated.

It should be noted that this overall social program involved a transference to the entirety of social and political life what is already embodied with the family, church, and educational institutions. These are the launching platforms for the project of Christianization. Rauschenbusch's theory thus depends both on the pluralism of social institutions and the ability for such institutions to exercise influence on the larger social context.

Reinhold Niebuhr: Religion and Realism in Public Life

In the case of Reinhold Niebuhr, the public import of theology is precisely in its realism about the concrete possibilities for society.[29] This realism was rooted in Niebuhr's perception of the intractability of human sin, and our inability to completely overcome it in human social relations.[30] For Rauschenbusch, justice was a positive moral principle, whereas for Niebuhr, it was a negative regulative principle. Whereas Rauschenbusch's push for social reform was based on an optimistic appraisal of human potential to overcome the evil of the social situation, Niebuhr's was based upon a belief that social reform was a necessary constraint on human vice.[31] Love, in the Christian sense of *agape* was for Niebuhr an "impossible

---

28 Meyer, *The Protestant Search for Political Realism* 132.

29 Analyses of Niebuhr's thought are legion. Among the recent efforts are Langdon Gilkey, *On Niebuhr: A Theological Study* (Chicago: University of Chicago Press, 2001); Charles C. Brown, *Niebuhr and His Age* (Philadelphia: Trinity Press International, 1992); Richard Whiteman Fox, *Reinhold Niebuhr: A Biography* (San Francisco: Harper & Row, 1987); Ronald Stone, *Professor Reinhold Niebuhr* (Louisville, KY: Westminster/John Knox Press, 1992); Robin Lovin, *Reinhold Niebuhr and Christian Realism* (New York: Cambridge University Press, 1995). The collection of essays, edited by Charles W. Kegley and Robert W. Bretall, *Reinhold Niebuhr: His Religious, Social, and Political Thought* (New York: Macmillan, 1956) is a classic set of analyses.

30 This is the theme of a great many of Reinhold Niebuhr's books, but central to this theory is *The Nature and Destiny of Man*, 2 vols. (New York: Macmillan, 1964), particularly the first volume on human nature.

31 On this point, Donald Meyer is instructive: "Rauschenbusch wrote in a season of pragmatic hope and confidence, certainly: socialism was to be the extension of progressivism.

possibility," against which human beings must measure their striving, but which they will never reach.³² While grim about the potential for the success of such human striving, Niebuhr nevertheless believed that it is necessary for the sake of arriving at a worldly approximation of the ideal of love.³³

Human pride and arrogance believe that such a possibility is realizable within history, but Christianity recognizes the tragic aspect of historical existence – that we are called and condemned to strive for that which we cannot achieve. Nevertheless, our hope comes from our knowledge that in the cross of Jesus Christ, sacrificial love has in fact triumphed over the reality of sin. Jesus Christ as the embodiment of God's grace testifies to the reality of that impossible possibility. Niebuhr writes:

> Christianity is a faith which takes us through tragedy to beyond tragedy, by way of the cross to a victory in the cross. The God whom we worship takes the contradictions of human existence into Himself. This knowledge is a stumbling block to the Jews, and to the Gentiles foolishness, but to them that are called it is the power and the wisdom of God. This is a wisdom beyond human knowledge, but not contrary to human experience. Once known, the truth of the gospel explains our experiences which remain inexplicable on any other level. Through it we are able to understand life in all of its beauty and its terror, without being beguiled by its beauty or driven to despair by its terror.³⁴

This theological backdrop allows Niebuhr to approach questions of public moment in the spirit of free responsibility, recognizing the necessity for making hard decisions in ambiguous situations, without shying away from the tragic implications of such decisions.³⁵ Thus, in his earlier work, such as *Moral Man and Immoral Society*, Niebuhr could stand unabashedly on the side of socialism and acknowledge the

---

Niebuhr wrote in a context of pessimism: socialism was to be a rescue from disaster. But the fact remained that Rauschenbusch's conception of political strategy was not an appropriate windmill for Niebuhr's tilting … . Rauschenbusch did not, as did Niebuhr, radically distinguish equality – justice – from perfect mutuality, or the Kingdom; he identified it with the Kingdom. Rauschenbusch, with his synthesis of religion and politics, differed from Niebuhr more on the side of religion than on the side of politics." *The Protestant Search for Political Realism*, 260.

32 Reinhold Niebuhr, *An Interpretation of Christian Ethics* (New York: Harper & Row, 1963).

33 See Reinhold Niebuhr, *The Nature and Destiny of Man*, I:88.

34 Reinhold Niebuhr, "The Christian Church in a Secular Age," in *The Essential Reinhold Niebuhr* (New Haven: Yale University Press, 1986), 85.

35 This aspect of Niebuhr's thought was one reason why he was admired outside of theological circles as well as in. It is noteworthy that his popularity extended to a group of political theorists who dubbed themselves "atheists for Niebuhr." See Meyer, *The Protestant Search for Political Realism*, xx. At the same time, this attitude has contributed to the "disputed legacy" that Niebuhr left behind. Harlan Beckley notes: "it is hard to imagine right- and left-wing disciples of Rauschenbusch or Ryan, such as we have experienced among Niebuhr's students. This aspect of Niebuhr's thought does not render his theory and conception of justice useless to someone trying to apply it … . Right wing Niebuhrians distort the thinking of their mentor. Doctrinaire socialism is also ruled out by Niebuhr's realism, even in its thirties version. Nevertheless, Niebuhr as an agent acting for justice, exceeded an analysis of his theory of justice and is nearly impossible for even his most loyal students to emulate." Beckley, *Passion for Justice*, 341.

centrality of the class struggle, while at the same time recognizing that even in a situation of pure political justice, human society would still be infinitely far from the realization of its highest ethical ideals.[36] This remains a continuous concern throughout Niebuhr's career. Even in later life when he had moved past socialism to a more moderate liberalism, this spirit can be seen, for example, in *The Irony of American History*.[37]

What remains consistent with Niebuhr above all is his commitment to understanding the Christian faith in a way that is publicly meaningful and responsible. His chief complaint against a certain branch of the social gospel movement was, as Niebuhr saw it, its refusal to engage in serious contemplation of public questions and answers. Christians have an obligation to seek relative justice and equality under the conditions of a fallen human situation. This can be done neither by a refusal to see things as they are, nor by a refusal to acknowledge the importance of ideals. The paradoxical situation of Christian public life is in its tension between *is* and *ought*, and in the eternal and often futile struggle to reconcile the two.[38]

This paradox can be see throughout Niebuhr's writings, particularly with regard to controversial questions such as desegregation[39] and nuclear war.[40] His moral stand always sought to recognize the tragic necessity of the moment, while at the same time acknowledging a higher moral responsibility, which remains beyond human capacity until human capacities move beyond history.[41]

H. Richard Niebuhr: Theology and Social Responsibility

H. Richard Niebuhr makes an interesting companion to his brother's approach to theology and public life, both for what they shared in common and for what they did not. Like Reinhold, H. Richard Niebuhr took seriously the participation of Christians in the larger public life of society. He devoted a great deal of his work to describing the dynamics of Christian public participation. Like his brother, he was concerned with public life not only in its political dimension, but also in all of its manifestations. And like his brother, he was also deeply concerned with questions of justice in complex social situations. However, H. Richard took a more subtle approach than Reinhold, and sought to apply his insights with less bravado.

---

36 Reinhold Niebuhr, *Moral Man and Immoral Society* (New York: Charles Scribner's Sons, 1960).
37 Reinhold Niebuhr, *The Irony of American History* (New York: Scribner, 1952).
38 Niebuhr's recognition of the paradoxical nature of public life shows the deep influence that Max Weber's sociological approach had on him. Weber recognized that to enter into the realm of the political was a soul-endangering journey into ambiguity, yet he recognized that an ethic of responsibility demanded it, as well as its methods. Niebuhr recognizes this as well. Yet, also like Weber, Niebuhr recognizes that it is our ideals that motivate us to seek those relative forms of justice that are possible within history as a reflection of a higher obligation to an ultimate end.
39 See Brown, *Niebuhr and His Age*, 222–3.
40 See Brown, *Niebuhr and His Age*, 217ff.
41 This theme is central to the second volume of *The Nature and Destiny of Man*.

In considering the relationship between theology and public life, in his earliest work Niebuhr considered questions of social status as it related to denomination selection.[42] Denominationalism was not a virtue but a vice for H. Richard. The fact of social division in the church was an example of its failure to realize its own stated aim in cultural terms, which Niebuhr called "an unacknowledged hypocrisy."[43] Exploring the social dynamics that exist among the different forms of congregational life in the United States, H. Richard sees them as being connected to economic and social dynamics that have little to no relationship to basic theological or liturgical positions:

> What is true of ethics and polity is true of theology. Less directly, but none the less effectively, theological opinions have their roots in the relationship of the religious life to the cultural and political conditions prevailing in any group of Christians. This does not mean that an economic or purely political interpretation of theology is justified, but it does mean that the religious life is so interwoven with social circumstances that the formulation of theology is necessarily conditioned by these. ... Back of the divergences of doctrine one must look for the conditions which make now the one, now the other interpretation appear more reasonable or, at least, more desirable. Regarding theology from this point of view one will discover how the exigencies of church discipline, the demands of the national psychology, the effect of social tradition, the influence of cultural heritage, and the weight of economic interest play their role in the definition of religious truth.[44]

Theology has an obligation to pay attention to these social dynamics, not only because of its social responsibility, but also because of its intra-ecclesial responsibilities. Consciousness of the vicissitudes and complexities of public life will allow Christians to exercise these responsibilities in such a way as to solidify structures of community within the world, with the goal of "the building up of an organic whole in which the various interests and the separate nations and classes will be integrated into a harmonious, interacting society, serving one common end in diverse manners."[45]

In *The Kingdom of God in America*, Niebuhr analyses the way in which religious symbols had the cultural effect of both forming and critiquing the social formation of the United States. On the one hand, they provide resources for the development of a positive construal of the interaction of religion and society in America. On the other hand, these symbols have the effect of creating in the United States a sense of its own providential chosen-ness.[46] This sense pervades American culture in such a way as to lead to an unwarranted sense of our own righteousness and the purity of our motives. At the same time, the principles of the kingdom of God, for better or worse, have become "secularized" in the broader culture of the United States:

---

42 H. Richard Niebuhr, *The Social Sources of Denominationalism* (New York: Meridian Books, 1957).
43 H.R. Niebuhr, *The Social Sources of Denominationalism*, 6.
44 H.R. Niebuhr, *The Social Sources of Denominationalism*, 16–17.
45 H.R. Niebuhr, *The Social Sources of Denominationalism*, 266.
46 H. Richard Niebuhr, *The Kingdom of God in America* (Middletown, CT: Wesleyan University Press, 1988).

As the nineteenth century went on the note of divine favoritism was increasingly sounded. Christianity, democracy, Americanism, the English language and culture, the growth of industry and science, American institutions – these are all confounded and confused. The contemplation of their own righteousness filled Americans with such lofty and enthusiastic sentiments that they readily identified it with the righteousness of God. The crisis of the kingdom of the Christ was passed; it occurred in the democratic revolution, or in the birth of modern science, or in the evangelical revival, or in the Protestant Reformation. Henceforth the kingdom of the Lord was a human possession, not a permanent revolution. It is in particular the kingdom of the Anglo-Saxon race, which is destined to bring light to the gentiles by means of lamps manufactured in America. Thus institutionalism and imperialism, ecclesiastical and political, go hand in hand.[47]

Niebuhr's discomfiture with such an identification of Christ with culture extends to his skepticism about the social gospel as well. Whereas Reinhold Niebuhr's criticism centered on what he viewed to be its insufficient understanding of sin, H. Richard noted its identification of Christ with cultural trends.[48]

At the same time, H. Richard agrees both with his brother and with Rauschenbusch that Christianity cannot be based on a retreat from public responsibility, even if public involvement exposes Christianity to certain risks. Thus, for example, while striving to make fine distinctions as to the relations between Christian principles and democratic ones, Niebuhr nonetheless writes: "Government by the people is not a stage on the way to the Kingdom of God, but realization of the actuality of divine rule does lead to government by the people. Democracy is a gift which is added to men who seek first the Kingdom and its righteousness."[49] He continues:

> When government is regarded dispassionately, when men abandon the religious interest they have in defending certain political traditions and forms as though their salvation depended on these, when they understand that no government can either imperil or hasten the Kingdom of God, then they have freedom to work out rationally those political devices which are best suited to serve the limited ends of the human state. In politics as in every other sphere faith in the Father of Jesus Christ frees men from that jealous regard for their particular social idols which they must have so long as they see these as centers of meaning and worth. Released from the necessity of defending institutions because they are ours and because we think we can justify ourselves by them, our minds are set free to consider the forms of government critically and to work for the establishment of the best form possible under the circumstances. A Christian citizen, statesman, or political scientist is like Paul, free to give up the traditional law and to devise in liberty those measures which, according to reason and experience, best serve the limited, temporal ends of a limited political society.[50]

---

47 H.R. Niebuhr, *The Kingdom of God in America*, 179.

48 H. Richard Niebuhr, *Christ and Culture* (New York: Harper & Row, 1951), 100–101. See "The Kingdom of God and Eschatology in the Social Gospel and Barthianism" in *H. Richard Niebuhr: Theology, History, and Culture* (New Haven: Yale University Press, 1996), 117–22.

49 H. Richard Niebuhr, "The Relation of Christianity and Democracy," in *H. Richard Niebuhr: Theology, History, and Culture*, 149.

50 H.R. Niebuhr, "The Relation of Christianity and Democracy," 150.

There can be no direct inference of a particular political system from Christianity, from H. Richard's perspective, but democracy can be justified precisely through the freedom of the Christian before the social system.

H. Richard Niebuhr nonetheless insists on Christian social responsibility, for example, around questions of war. Where there are no easy answers, Christians may not simply opt out, but must enter into the ambiguities of the situation in good faith. Thus, Niebuhr writes: "Knowing that war is crucifixion, the church prays for all men, for its enemies, and the enemies of the nation in which it carries out its work, as well as for itself and these nations."[51] It is the theological concepts that govern the social stance in the final analysis, not the social analysis that governs the theological stance.[52]

What the three outlooks discussed in this section share in common with one another, and with the other figures to be discussed in the next chapter, is a commitment to a "theologically informed public discourse about public issues," as Harold Breitenberg has defined public theology.[53] They are each rooted in the belief that theology has something meaningful to say to its larger social context, which is comprehensible within that context. It "seeks to offer an interpretation of the common life and to provide the moral and spiritual vision to guide it."[54] Like Moltmann, they believe that theology has something to say to the world, which the world needs to hear, and that it is only through hearing it that the world may move

---

51 H. Richard Niebuhr, "A Christian Interpretation of War," in *H. Richard Niebuhr: Theology, History, and Culture*, 173.

52 It is interesting to compare H. Richard's approach in the above-cited essay with his arguments in "The Grace of Doing Nothing." There we also see Niebuhr attempting to develop a social stance out of theological precepts. Christians may not be able to do anything constructive in the case of the Sino-Japanese war, he argued, but Christians may be able to do nothing in a constructive way: "This way of doing nothing the old Christians called repentance ... What is suggested is that the only effective approach to the problem of China and Japan lies in the sphere of an American self-analysis which is likely to result in some surprising discoveries as to the amount of renunciation of self-interest necessary on the part of this country and of individual Christians before anything effective can be done in the East." Reinhold was offered an opportunity to reply to his brother's essay, noting that H. Richard seeks to build an ethic of Christian perfectionism. Yet, "the highest ideals which the individual may project are ideals which he can never realize in social and collective terms." Reinhold argues that human beings have an obligation to act in love for the establishment of justice for "love may qualify the social struggle of history but it will never abolish it, and those who make the attempt to bring society under the dominion of perfect love will die on the cross." H. Richard's reply points to an interesting distinction in their theological outlooks. According to H. Richard, "for my brother, God is outside the historical process" and thus history is a tragedy. His own perspective, on the contrary, is "eschatological" and therefore "tragedy is only the prelude to fulfillment, and a prelude which is necessary because of human nature; the kingdom of God comes inevitably though whether we shall see it or not depends on our recognition of its presence and our acceptance of the only kind of life which will enable us to enter it, the life of repentance and forgiveness." This debate is reprinted in Richard B. Miller, *War in the Twentieth Century: Sources in Theological Ethics* (Louisville: Westminster/John Knox Press, 1992), 3-24.

53 Breitenberg, "To Tell the Truth," 13.

54 Stackhouse, "Public Theology," *The Dictionary of the Ecumenical Movement*.

toward more fully becoming its true self. Although each theologian understands this in his own way, Rauschenbusch, Niebuhr, and Niebuhr each contribute to a fuller understanding of how theology may be done publicly.[55] In the next chapter, I will turn to examine how several more contemporary theologians attempt the same task.

Conclusion

The key question raised by public theology, namely, how religion can engage meaningfully with society, encompasses all dimensions of human action in the world. As such, it must deal in an intelligible manner with those realms of inquiry with which it comes into contact. To do so requires an analytic, an interpretive, and a constructive move in the process of public engagement.

The idea of public theology emerged from the struggle of Christians to participate within integrity in public life in the midst of a society that is manifestly contrary in many ways to the Christian understanding of the ideals of human community. The question that the central figures in this chapter attempted to answer is what the Christian response to this fact ought to be. Whether it is Rauschenbusch's call to "Christianize" the social order, or Reinhold Niebuhr's brand of Christian Realism, or his brother's more perfectionistic and tentative engagement with the social realm, each contributed to the subsequent development of what became public theology proper. The theologians whom we will examine in the next chapter benefited from the contributions that these figures, in addition to many others which time and space do not permit me to examine, made to the struggle to articulate a pragmatic form of Christian social engagement. Moltmann's theology also benefited from these contributions, as I will demonstrate. His work intersects in interesting ways with American public theology, reiterating and building upon themes of Christian public responsibility which are important waypoints toward a constructive Christian understanding of the church's place in civil society.

---

55 And indeed it should be pointed out that Martin Marty coined the term "public theology" precisely to describe the way Reinhold Niebuhr worked (mentioning Rauschenbusch in passing as another example). See Martin Marty, "Reinhold Niebuhr: Public Theology and the American Experience," *Journal of Religion* 54, no. 4 (Oct. 1974) 332–59.

Chapter 6

Public Theology in the American Tradition

Introduction

Although the term "public theology" has gained global currency in recent years, its development as a distinctive approach to reflection on the Christian responsibility in public life has its roots in American theological soil. In some sense, American theology has always had a "public" dimension, extending back to the colonial period. Movements for social reform have often been based in religious communities, whether it is the Quaker origins of abolitionism, the Methodist roots of the Temperance movement, or the Civil Rights movement, rooted as it was in the Black church tradition. It is no accident that, far more than we see in modern European history, mass movements in the United States have a religious foundation.

In recent decades, Christianity has maintained its public persona, even as debate about the proper place of religious faith in public life has become more hotly contested. The further question of what "publicness" means in a pluralistic society is raised by a number of prominent public theologians, some of whom I will examine in this chapter. The figures that I will explore in this chapter by no mean represent an exhaustive accounting of the possibilities for public theology, but they are representative of important trends in the public theology movement in the United States. Furthermore, they provide interesting points of contrast with Moltmann's emerging public theology, allowing us to shed light on the public possibilities that his own approach provides.

In the last chapter, I considered some of the main aspects of public theology, particularly the analytic, interpretive, and constructive dimensions of its task. I also looked at some of the precursors of the movement as it developed in the second half of the 20th century. In this chapter, I will attempt to further clarify the nature of public theology as a discipline by considering three prominent public theologians: David Tracy, Ronald Thiemann, and James Skillen. I will then turn to compare their approaches to public theology with Moltmann's project in an attempt to demonstrate the great degree of overlap among their approaches.

Public Theology in the United States

David Tracy: The Three "Publics" of Public Theology

In *The Analogical Imagination*, David Tracy outlines a proposal for a public theology grounded in three complementary "publics" – the public of the church, the public of the academy, and the public of society.[1] Theology is, as Tracy argues, "public discourse."[2] To each of these publics, Tracy argues, theology has a specific and distinct contribution to make, and must speak in such a way as to make itself understood to each of these publics. Theological language must thus be able to move freely among these publics while at the same time not losing its distinctive message to them.

Tracy first considers the public of society, as the widest public to which theology must address itself. Society, as Tracy uses the term, is "the broadest term available to encompass three realms: the technoeconomic realm, the realm of polity, and the realm of culture."[3] That is to say, society is concerned with economic issues, political issues, and that broad array of symbolic expressions that help to make up our common life.

The technoeconomic realm is concerned with "the organization and allocation of goods and services."[4] In other words, it has to do with questions of how the economy should be ordered and how technology should be utilized. As such, its primary form of rationality is an "instrumental" or "means-ends" rationality. That is to say, it is a rationality that determines what ends it is pursuing (for example, social prosperity) and then determines the means appropriate to achieve them. It is thus driven a pure calculation of instrumental costs and benefits without regard to non-instrumental or substantive questions of the good. Once a goal has been set, the question becomes: what is the most efficient way to meet that goal? As such, this realm cannot exist on its own terms or for itself, for it does not within itself have the capacity to determine on the basis of what ends ought to be valued and pursued by the means to be determined.[5] It does not have the internal capacity to determine whether a particular end is worthwhile to pursue, or, alternatively, if a particular means to an end ought to be pursued. As pure instrumentality, it is value-neutral. As Tracy notes: "The major problem of instrumental reason is also obvious: Its relative inability to define *ends* for the polity and culture on other than either an instrumental or merely intuitive basis."[6] Thus, it needs the other two realms.

The realm of polity has to do with the communal discourse about what means and ends ought to be valued. In a democracy, it has to do with the public debate around policy and the social good. In some sense, it has to do with the widest shared values of a community. Due to this, it presumes that, despite the various value-systems

---

1 Tracy, *The Analogical Imagination* (New York: Crossroad, 1981).
2 Tracy, *The Analogical Imagination*, 3.
3 Tracy, *The Analogical Imagination*, 6.
4 Tracy, *The Analogical Imagination*, 7.
5 Tracy is here echoing the argument's we have seen earlier, made by Weber and Horkheimer, as well as in modified form by Habermas.
6 Tracy, *The Analogical Imagination*, 8. Italics in original.

with which we come to the common discourse, we have a fundamental capacity to understand and evaluate a variety of points of view without undue prejudice: "A public discussion of polity issues appealing to all intelligent, reasonable, and responsible persons is a necessity, not a luxury, for any humane polity."[7] Whatever point of view one attempts to advocate in this realm, it must be "in principle open to all reasonable and responsible persons."[8]

The realm of culture has to do, in a very broad definition of the term, with "art and religion." Tracy quotes Clifford Geertz's definition of culture as "a system of symbols which acts to establish powerful, pervasive, and long lasting moods and motivations."[9] This is the realm of society through which theologians act on the other realms. Through the use of its own symbol systems, theology can attempt to create or influence the modes which affect the values that percolate to the other two realms: "The artist, the religious personality, the philosopher, the social scientist, the literary critic, devote major energy to interpreting participatory symbols, including their relevance to the needs of the whole society."[10] Whatever else theology may be, as *public* discourse, it is in the business of the interpreting of the social significance of its own religious symbols. The fact that we live in a culturally pluralistic society means that the kinds of symbol systems, which attempt to influence the public discourse, will be necessarily diverse, and thus there will be combinations of cultural moods operating within the polity and the technoeconomic spheres at any one time.

Let us pause here to consider the social significance of theology as Tracy understands it. As we have seen, the purpose of theology, while not exclusively a matter of public symbolic interpretation, nevertheless includes this. Furthermore, it does this interpretation in the context of an irreducible social pluralism. That is to say, from the point of view of cultures, theology is not the only game in town, and there are other symbolic discourses to which people may (and do) turn for the purpose of bringing meaningfulness to existence. Theology must do its work while being constantly aware of its own public credibility and its need to speak in a relevant way in its context.

Were society homogeneous, either culturally or politically (or economically, for that matter), it would be potentially easier for theology to perform its task without reference to those other cultural forces with which it must be in conversation and disputation. At the same time, however, the fact that our context demands an awareness of a plurality of intellectual and cultural currents only highlights the necessity of theology to be aware of the problem of pluralism. As a dweller in multiple publics, the fact of pluralism is already a phenomenon with which theology must reckon.

---

7 Tracy, *The Analogical Imagination*, 9.
8 Tracy, *The Analogical Imagination*, 9. The notion of public reason Tracy is using here bears some similarities to John Rawls' notion of overlapping consensus. The difference, I believe, lies in Tracy's confidence that religious points of view can be comprehensible in a public situation without having to appeal to some outside neutral principle of inquiry. See Rawls, *Political Liberalism* (New York: Columbia University Press, 1996).
9 Tracy, *The Analogical Imagination*, 7.
10 Tracy, *The Analogical Imagination*, 11.

Turning to Tracy's second public, we begin to get an idea of the way in which theology must contend with other cultural forces, for in the academic realm, theology is required to justify its existence as, in some sense, a "science" worthy of academic study. If theology is to be "public" in the context of the academic community, then it needs to take seriously the question of its own internal grounds of justification, not simply with regard to its internal norms, but also with regard to the demands of other academic disciplines. It cannot "retreat to commitment,"[11] but must rather engage with the resources offered by the philosophical and social-scientific disciplines with which it is engaged.

The question arises in this public as to the scientific status of theology as opposed to religious studies. Among many in academia, the necessity for a faith commitment in theology robs it of its status as an "objective" science. For many, the preference for "religious studies" indicates this distinction: "'Religious studies,' therefore indicates an objective, non-normative scholarly study of religion as distinct from what is viewed as, at best, the theologian's use of special 'confessional' criteria, or, at worst, special pleading for traditional norms."[12]

Tracy considers Stephen Toulmin's distinction between "compact," "diffuse," and "would-be" scientific disciplines. The model for the "compact" disciplines is the hard sciences. One major element of these sciences as opposed to the "diffuse" and "would-be" sciences is "a specific and realistic set of agreed collective ideals."[13] The diffuse sciences, by contrast, "first, lack a clear sense of disciplinary direction and thereby a host of unresolved problems; second of professional organization for the discussion of new results."[14] As a consequence, there is no cohesion within the discipline and thus a difficulty in locating its significance as an academic discipline. While there are some for whom this may or may not be tolerable and who thus will attempt to retreat to some particular faith perspective to try to make a compact discipline out of theology, unless it retains its commitment to a public perspective, and a willingness to engage with the other scientific and philosophical perspectives, it will betray its commitment to its responsibility in the academic realm. "Theology aids the public value of both academy and society when it remains faithful to its own internal demand – publicness. Without that demand for publicness – for criteria, evidence, warrants, disciplinary status – serious academic theology is dead."

The third public to which theology addresses itself is the church. The church exists in Tracy's analysis as both a sociological and a theological reality. Both of these elements need to be included for an adequate understanding of theology's "public" nature.

The theologian encounters the church as a theological reality as he or she experiences it as a "'gift,' more exactly, as participating in the grace of God disclosed in the divine self-manifestation in Jesus Christ."[15] As such, the church stands under the grace and judgment of God, as does the theologian who exists as part of that

---

11 W.W. Bartley, *The Retreat to Commitment* (La Salle, IL: Open Court Publishers, 2003).
12 Tracy, *The Analogical Imagination*, 16.
13 Tracy, *The Analogical Imagination*, 17.
14 Tracy, *The Analogical Imagination*, 18.
15 Tracy, *The Analogical Imagination*, 23.

community. The theological reality of the church is a concrete determinant of those things that the theologian will consider in constructing a theology, for the theologian has internalized the values and truth assertions of that religious community. The theologian is thus always in no small way accountable to this public, just as he or she is to the other two publics: "For all theologians, however, including those who are primarily either academic or cultural theologians, the church functions as a genuine public – at least in the minimal sense of a concerned body of critical readership for theological proposals. Usually in the fuller sense of one voluntary association to which one is responsibly committed and whose traditions and authentic demands one has internalized."[16]

This ought not be construed as an argument that theologians are simply mouthpieces for their traditions. Rather, one can relate to one's ecclesial tradition in a number of different ways. One can be an ardent supporter of the ecclesiastical structures to which one is committed, and to its governing ideas. But one can also be a loyal critic of one's tradition, bound to it and committed to it, but also willing to critique it on those points at which it is perceived to have left the realm of truth.

The church also exists as a sociological reality, and the theologian needs to be aware of the church in this reality also. This is as much as to say that the theologian has to be aware of the way in which the church also functions with regard to these two other publics. The church, according to Tracy, functions for the theologians as a "generalized other."[17] That is to say, it is the theoretical community of discourse to whom his or her ideas are addressed. The theologian does his or her work with this community in mind.

The church is also a voluntary association, and as such differs from a family unit.[18] It has a particular function in society, and in some ways stands as a mediating institution between the individual and family units and the larger socioeconomic, political, and cultural spheres.[19] But the church as voluntary association implies that one can move from one church or other religious institution to another whenever one chooses. The effect that the churches have on the larger social whole is thus often indirect.[20]

As an interpreter of the church to the other two publics that he or she addresses, the theologian has a responsibility to be cognizant of and able to use the sociological tools put at his or her disposal. In addressing these publics, the theologian is bound to come into conflicts and infelicities which will be difficult to overcome. Tracy argues that attention to the sociological reality of the church will aid the theologian in negotiating these channels. As such, the theologian must be willing to use the method of correlation, bringing sociological and theological understandings of reality into conversation with one another. "To account theologically for the full spectrum of

---

16 Tracy, *The Analogical Imagination*, 22–3.
17 Tracy, *The Analogical Imagination*, 21.
18 Tracy, *The Analogical Imagination*, 21.
19 Tracy, *The Analogical Imagination*, 22.
20 Tracy, *The Analogical Imagination*, 22.

possible relationships between church as a theological and as a sociological reality, the most relatively adequate model is the correlational model."[21]

The question is the way in which the church and society interact with one another. Tracy argues that "in general, the church is always influenced by society; sometimes it is even determined by it. In other instances strictly theological religious considerations determine the church's relationship to society. The latter is especially so when the church acts as prophetic critic of society or as transformative sacrament of the 'world.'"[22]

The theologian thus stands in a complex relationship to these three publics and especially to the church, for "the church is always one public as addressee for the theologian and usually also an internalized public as an object of moral, religious, and theological loyalty."[23] The theologian addresses the other two publics of society and academy from within the public of the church, and is thus responsible for interpreting the reality of the church to these other two publics insofar as its reality affects and is affected by them. The church cannot help being engaged with these two publics, and the chief question for a public theology is the way in which these publics will interact.

Every theologian, Tracy argues, implicitly addresses all three publics mentioned. Different theologians may primarily address one or another of these publics, and as such may have certain "elective affinities"[24] for the particular emphases of the public to which they primarily belong, but no theologian exists in one public to the exclusion of the others. "Every theologian must face squarely the claim to meaning and truth in the church tradition, the paradigms for rational enterprises in the academy, the models for rationality in the three overlapping realms of contemporary society."[25] The theologian must be clear about his or her own self-understanding in order to determine the way in which they approach theology, but regardless, the particular claims of the theologian within a particular church tradition have a generalized public significance, for as Tracy writes: "if any religious thinker or theologian produces some classical expression of the human spirit on a particular journey in a particular tradition, that person discloses permanent possibilities for human existence both personal and communal."[26]

Ronald Thiemann: The Public Role of the Church

The second option I want to consider is illustrated by Ronald Thiemann's understanding of the particular role the church plays in social discourse. Thiemann's approach is rooted in a "narrative understanding" of Christian theology that bears some similarities

---

21 Tracy, *The Analogical Imagination*, 24.
22 Tracy, *The Analogical Imagination*, 24–5.
23 Tracy, *The Analogical Imagination*, 25.
24 Tracy, *The Analogical Imagination*, 5.
25 Tracy, *The Analogical Imagination*, 29.
26 Tracy, *The Analogical Imagination*, 14.

to the perspective of Stanley Hauerwas.[27] Basing his approach on the work of George Lindbeck and Hans Frei,[28] Thiemann's approach emphasizes the centrality of theology understood as, to use Frei's term, "Christian self-description,"[29] rather than as in some way correlated with cultural questions in the way that Tracy intends. Thus, its role is "to 're-describe' the internal logic of Christian faith,"[30] rather than to place that faith in a larger philosophical or cultural framework.

Rejecting approaches that he sees as advocating an "eternal covenant" between God and particular cultural, social, or philosophical expressions, Thiemann emphasizes nonetheless that Christian faith has a responsibility to interact creatively with its surrounding culture. He notes that "a careful description of the fabric of Christian thought and practice requires attention to the broader social and cultural setting within which Christians seek to live lives shaped by the gospel."[31] Yet he does not believe that such an interaction can be methodologically specified ahead of time. Rather, it is based on the particular ways in which Christianity finds itself interacting with society at a given time that it chooses how, *ad hoc*, it should engage it.[32] Christian theology is finally accountable to only one "public" – that of the Christian community. It may, on an *ad hoc* basis, engage in conversation or coordination with the spheres of society or the academy, or other institutions in a pluralistic society, but its first job is to explicate the meaning of the Christian narrative for the sake of the church. "Theology," says Thiemann, "like all activities within the Christian community, has a single ultimate goal, namely, to sustain and nurture Christian identity."[33] That Christian identity is rooted in its tradition. He goes on to say:

> Theology must then presuppose tradition because tradition *is* the living, developing Christian community. In the same sense, theology presupposes faith and seeks through critical reflection to understand that faith more fully. Anselm's description of theology as "faith seeking understanding" continues to provide an apt account of the theologian's task. The theologian speaks from within the community of believers and thus speaks from the commitment of faith. The theologian cannot adopt a standpoint of radical doubt or assume a hypothetical position of neutrality vis-à-vis the Christian faith. The theologian is seeking neither to justify nor disconfirm that complex phenomenon we call faith. The theologian strives simply to *understand* through critical reflection. The process of understanding

---

27 There is in fact a great deal more space between them than common ground. Although they both emphasize the role of the church and both base their theologies on a type of "Yale School" approach, Thiemann is positively, if critically, disposed toward liberal democracy, whereas Hauerwas rejects it.

28 George Lindbeck, *The Nature of Doctrine* (Philadelphia: Westminster Press, 1984) and Hans Frei, *The Eclipse of Biblical Narrative* (New Haven: Yale University Press, 1974).

29 Hans Frei, "Eberhard Busch's Biography of Karl Barth," in, *Karl Barth in Review*, H. Martin Rumscheidt, ed. (Pittsburgh: Pickwick Press, 1981), 103.

30 Thiemann, *Constructing a Public Theology* (Louisville, KY: John Knox/Westminster Press, 1991), 23.

31 Thiemann, *Constructing a Public Theology*, 65.

32 This notion of *ad hoc* correlation was coined by Paul Werpehowski to describe his method of "briccolage" in the interaction between church and culture. See "*Ad Hoc* Apologetics," *Journal of Religion* 66 (1986): 202–301. Thiemann uses it in several places in his work.

33 Thiemann, *Constructing a Public Theology*, 133.

may yield a radical criticism and reinterpretation of the tradition, or it may result in a confirmation of many ancient formulas. The outcomes of theological investigation cannot be predicted in advance precisely because the theologian operates within the temporal ebb and flow of history and community. But the goal of theology remains constant, namely, to understand more fully and more critically the Christian faith in order that the community might better exemplify the Christian identity to which it has been called.[34]

While this is certainly a part of Christian theology, Thiemann never articulates in a convincing manner just why this must be the *whole* of Christian theology. Surely *communication* of the Christian faith is an equally important element of theological discourse in addition to self-description. Furthermore, it is unclear just exactly *how* critical reflection may work within the Christian faith if part of that critical reflection does not involve at least to some degree a correlation of the tradition's answers to contemporary questions, and to the human condition generally.

Thiemann works from the perspective of what he refers to as a "nonfoundationalist" point of view, arguing that Christian theology should consider itself "thick description" as opposed to "explanation" in the sense of making Christian faith plausible on non-Christian grounds. "The goal is not to provide an overarching theory that explains how 'church and world' or 'fundamental question and answer' are related to one another. Rather, the goal is to identify the particular places where Christian convictions intersect with the practices that characterize contemporary public life."[35] Not basing its self-understanding on a self-contained and all encompassing "method," Christian theology is instead based on an understanding of the truth of the Christian narrative. One reason why this is an important step is that it serves to aid the Christian faith, which is in danger of being co-opted by civil religion and secularization.[36] The heart is taken out of Christian faith when it is turned to abstraction and distracted from its narrative core.

The church's first function, according to Thiemann, is to clean its own theological house. In those ways in which it has accommodated itself to the dominant cultural forces of the modern era, it has ignored that which is its most attractive element – its message of the good news. Thus, Christian theology needs to turn back to its own internal resources to discover the ways in which it might be relevant to the contemporary society.[37]

Then, Christian faith may indeed work within its pluralistic context to actualize its public voice. But it will do this not by "correlating," in Tracy's sense, its message with sociological and philosophical trends, but rather by making "*ad hoc*" alliances with groups and organizations with which it can find some common ground at the present moment. Thiemann compares his approach to Karl Barth's, arguing that Barth used philosophy and other disciplines as "simply a temporary borrowing of a tool to help us better understand the complex meaning of the Christian gospel."[38]

---

34 Thiemann, *Constructing a Public Theology*, 135.
35 Thiemann, *Constructing a Public Theology*, 22.
36 Thiemann, *Constructing a Public Theology*, 38.
37 It is important to note that Tracy is also cognizant of this danger, as the first paragraph of *The Analogical Imagination* indicates.
38 Thiemann, *Constructing a Public Theology*, 82.

In order to discern the ways in which we ought to make such alliances, Thiemann argues, we need "a concerted educational effort to link theological training to empirically grounded policy studies."[39] Thus, Christian theology cannot pretend that the external world does not exist, or that Christian ethicists do not need to be aware of the premises and consequences of particular policy decisions. Rather, in order for the church to exercise its prophetic role in society, it needs to be fully engaged with those topics on their own terms.

How does Thiemann view the kind of policy studies that Christians should be engaged in? It is unclear. Although he speaks in general terms of "a meeting of faith and empirical science" and "a concerned educational effort to link theological training with empirically grounded policy studies,"[40] he never offers concrete proposals to suggest what such an approach might look like. What exactly is the role of empirical data, for example, on welfare reform, in the construction of a Christian point of view on the proper role of the government or private institutions in the provision for the poor?[41] Thiemann offers no proposals. He argues that "the church can no longer be content to focus its public ministry primarily on the issuance of social statements and public proclamations" but must rather "devise new models for the development of public policy."[42] Fair enough, but what *kind* of policies? And furthermore, apart from issuing public statements and proclamations, in just what kind of public activity should the church partake? The most that could be said on the basis of Thiemann's argument in *Constructing a Public Theology* is that the Christian narrative, as self-description, forms persons who can then enter into public life. But this is a far cry from determining what the church *qua* church ought to do. Individuals formed by their participation in the community of faith may no doubt form opinions and positions on the basis of their faith commitments, but how those faith commitments ought to translate into a set of public criteria for social action is left out of Thiemann's equation.

This is part of a larger conceptual problem with Thiemann's approach to public theology. One the one hand, theology ought to prepare us for participation in a larger and pluralistic public life. But pure self-description cannot do this. Unless the point of self-description is to make oneself understood to one who does not share one's theological preconceptions, no possible public discourse can take place. The problem is particularly stark when Thiemann argues that he rejects David Tracy's approach to "correlation," although he still affirms the aspects of "mutual criticism" in Tracy's theory.[43] But Thiemann fails to illuminate how mutual criticism is possible when neither partner speaks of anything but themselves. Simply speaking of how I am different from my dialogue partner does not allow for any degree of criticism, unless it is of the type that amounts to "you are wrong because you are not me."

---

39 Thiemann, *Constructing a Public Theology*, 42.
40 Thiemann, *Constructing a Public Theology*, 42.
41 As for example, was done in Stanley W. Carlson-Thies and James Skillen, eds, *Welfare in America: Christian Perspectives on a Policy in Crisis* (Grand Rapids: Eerdmans, 1996).
42 Thiemann, *Constructing a Public Theology*, 41.
43 Thiemann, *Constructing a Public Theology*, 23.

There needs to be a broader epistemological framework upon which to base a public theology than a narrative approach can give.

This point is well made by Wentzel van Huyssteen in *The Shaping of Rationality*, in which he engages in a critique of Thiemann on precisely these points. Van Huyssteen notes that, by beginning from a standpoint of faith that is shielded from any possibility of criticism, Thiemann puts himself outside of the realm of rational discourse about the very premises of his public involvement. Although "the goal is to identify the particular places where Christian convictions intersect with the practices that characterize contemporary public life," a theology rooted in an incommensurable faith stance lacks the grounding to engage in such identification.[44] This is due to the tendency among narrativist theologians in general to confuse the grounds on which they hold particular positions with the fundamental faith commitments out of which those positions arise.[45] "To completely collapse a faith commitment into the conceptual structure in which we hold that commitment, epistemically transforms faith into fideism, and the conceptual structure of our religious and theological beliefs into a sophisticated, but nevertheless still crypto-foundationalist belief system."[46]

The result of this is the failure of a means of addressing broad theological principles to the realm of public policy. By advocating a merely *ad hoc* approach to the intersection of theology to social reality, Thiemann provides no clear reason why one should prefer any particular social arrangement or course of action to any other, including the one he purports to support – liberal democracy. Furthermore, he provides no *theological* rationale to explain why Christians should support or care about social pluralism in a democratic state.

That said, Thiemann does soldier on in attempting to engage liberal democracy, though it is striking that Thiemann's concrete proposals as to what public theological discourse in a pluralistic society might look like actually draws heavily from the work of John Rawls, and particularly reflects the ideas found in Rawls' *Political Liberalism*.

Like Rawls, Thiemann believes that public discourse in democracy ought to center around those policies best able to arise from an "overlapping consensus" of values.[47] Like Rawls, he believes that public discourse ought to be centered on non-coercive discourse designed to be persuasive.[48] Like Rawls, he believes that such discourse ought to reflect mutual respect for the various parties involved for one another,[49] and ought to reflect a public integrity and consistency.[50] Thus, despite his seemingly "post-liberal" perspective, when Thiemann attempts to lay out how the *practice* of public theology will look, his method begins to seem quite liberal.

---

44 Van Huyssteen, *The Shaping of Rationality* (Grand Rapids: Eerdmans, 1999), 75.
45 Van Huyssteen, *The Shaping of Rationality*, 75.
46 Van Huyssteen, *The Shaping of Rationality*, 75.
47 Thiemann, *Religion and Public Life* (Washington, DC: Georgetown University Press, 1996), 83 and passim.
48 Thiemann, *Religion and Public Life*, 121.
49 Thiemann, *Religion and Public Life*, 125–6.
50 Thiemann, *Religion and Public Life*, 137–41.

Indeed, one way to read Thiemann's *Religion and Public Life* is precisely as a theological counterpart to *Political Liberalism*. The principles contained in both books parallel one another quite nicely, and Thiemann provides a very persuasive account of the role of religion in American public life. What Thiemann lacks, however, is still a grounded *theological* justification of this parallel. Consider the following, very Rawlsian passage:

> The problem of contemporary pluralistic politics is this: We need to find some common ground on which to base policies designed to serve the public welfare, but given our cultural diversity, we are unlikely to discern universal principles on which we will all agree. If we are to forge some kind of overlapping consensus, we must identify those criteria which will allow us to seek a middle ground between universal norms agreed on by all and the conflicting and competing interests and preferences of grounds and individuals. In other words, conditions of publicity must designate a public space in which acceptable arguments are justified by criteria claiming less than universality but more than mere subjectivity.[51]

One can see very clearly the influence that *Political Liberalism* has had on Thiemann's analysis, but it is unclear how this analysis is rooted, as we saw Thiemann argue above, in the biblical narrative of promise. It seems as though, in practical terms, Thiemann leaves his post-liberal narrative presuppositions to the side in terms of the concrete questions of religion and political liberalism.

This, nevertheless, represents precisely what makes Thiemann a legitimately "public" theologian (in contrast to, say, Hauerwas, Milbank, or Rasmussen) despite his lack of consistency, namely his commitment to a free and open dialogue in a pluralistic society. Despite his methodological reserve in keeping the church theologically distinct from society, Thiemann is not content to fiddle while Rome metaphorically burns. For Thiemann, the good of society as a whole is a theological concern, one that can only be adequately addressed as theology acknowledges its need to participate in a discussion with the other institutions of society about what goods ought to be preferred. While the Christian conception of those goods is rightly defined by its experience of redemption in Jesus Christ, and the narrative in which that is the climactic event, it needs to be willing to discuss the social importance of those values in order to fulfill its particularly *public* task.

What Thiemann lacks, in addition to a firm grounding for his affirmation of liberal democratic structures, is a theory of society that would allow him to make the move from its internal theological presuppositions to an external understanding of the substantive good that Christians ought to will for the society as a whole. His narrativist approach to theology leaves him in a bind. On the one hand, he wants to argue that Christians have an obligation to engage with modern society. On the other hand, he relies on a theological method that provides no ability to do that. There needs to be some kind of mediating element in his theology that would allow him to say that the good promoted within the community of the church is translatable into a larger social good (though not necessarily *directly* translatable). However, as van Huyssteen notes, given Thiemann's presuppositions "all hope for finding a cross-

---

51 Thiemann, *Religion and Public Life*, 125.

disciplinary location for theological reflection as a plausible reasoning strategy is lost forever."⁵²

Next I want to turn to a theological outlook that does claim to have a strong theological vision of society, with the help of which we may begin to see a way to translate the good that the church proposes as its own into the larger social matrix.

James Skillen: The Spheres and Constraints of Public Life

James Skillen's approach to public theology represents a third aspect of the discussion of religion and public life. Whereas Tracy offers us a broad justification for the rationality of religious discourse in public life, and Thiemann demonstrates the need for an ecclesial perspective rooted within the commitments of the Christian faith, Skillen offers a comprehensive theory of society that can encompass social and political pluralism within a Christian understanding of society.

Key to Skillen's approach to religion and public life is his analysis of the highly differentiated nature of American society. Such differentiation requires a theological understanding of society capable of comprehending that differentiation in a way that avoids both collectivist and individualist options.⁵³ Like both Tracy and Thiemann, Skillen acknowledges and accepts the pluralist character of American society, and in the development of his approach seeks to find a way to justify Christian public participation in the midst of that pluralist setting.

Skillen sees the fact of social differentiation as the key component that enables one to analyze the variety of possible moral stands that can be taken by Christians vis-à-vis the modern world. In every analysis, if this differentiation is not given its due, the theory in question has a tendency to veer off into one of the dual temptations of individualism or collectivism. Alternatively, one may decide that theological analysis has no place in public life, and thus collapse moral analysis into either secularism or sectarianism. Skillen considers a number of exemplars of these unacceptable alternatives in the process of defining his own.⁵⁴

With regard to the importance of social differentiation, Skillen notes:

> Public-moral discourse today ... founders all too frequently on the error of ignoring the plural structure of society – an error arising from the fact that American citizens do not adequately recognize in their legal and political reasoning that human life is constituted by multiple obligations in a complex and differentiated society. In making this argument we

---

52 Van Huyssteen, *The Shaping of Rationality*, 76.

53 James Skillen and Rockne M. McCarthy, eds, *Political Order and the Plural Structure of Society* (Atlanta, GA: Scholars Press, 1991), 2

54 See in particular Skillen's analysis in *The Scattered Voice* (Edmonton: Canadian Institute for Law, Theology, and Public Policy, 1996). In this book, Skillen examines several perspectives from the right to the left end of the political spectrum in terms of their ability to appreciate the importance of differentiation in public life. In most cases, whether the subject of the critique is from the right or the left, Skillen articulates the strengths of their positions while demonstrating their failures to take social pluralism into account in their analyses. His critiques seem to be least pointed with regard to two categories he considers – the "sophisticated neo-conservatives" (chapter 4) and the "traditional and reflective liberals" (chapter 5).

are, of course, raising a fundamentally critical question about the adequacy of the liberal worldview, which is oriented by the religiously deep claim that individual freedom is the first principle of human existence and should be maximized. Thus, our questioning is not merely about contrasting legal and policy options that might arise from within the same basic view of social and political life. Rather, our questioning is about *both* those legal and policy options *and* the different root conceptions from which those policy options arise.[55]

Different segments of society, according to Skillen, are bound to have different moral conceptions and different responsibilities within the larger social body. To assume that any one moral or legal conception can fit all the circumstances of different institutions is to ignore the variable bases on which they exist. However, "there can be no legitimate omnicompetent community or institution in society, and therefore every question of moral responsibility must be framed in a way that allows for an answer to be directed to a specific, differentiated realm of competence and authority."[56]

Skillen's argument is rooted, as above, in the tension between the drive in American life toward excessive individualism and the drive toward overbearing government intrusion in the variety of civil institutions. However, the thrust of *Recharging the American Experiment* is rooted more toward providing a theological justification for a more limited role for government. Individualism gets less attention. His chief justification for his critique of government encroachment upon the different spheres of civil life is a moral one: "A law passed and enforced by government ought to exhibit the government's competence and jurisdiction. The simple fact that a majority wants a law, or that a law's aim is to advance individual freedom or some social good is not sufficient justification for it."[57] Rather the justification must be rooted in the specific legitimate role of government within a differentiated society. What this means, as he elaborates in a number of places, is that general appeals to ideas "such as justice, equality, freedom, fairness, love or mercy," are in themselves insufficient to justify government action.[58] In addition, the case needs to be made as to why it is *government* that should aid in achieving that end, rather than some other social institution. It is, in fact, *immoral* for government to exercise control over jurisdictions beyond its legitimate authority.[59]

The basis for Skillen's argument is found in the neo-Kuyperian doctrine of "spheres of sovereignty" in society. Abraham Kuyper summarized this idea of spheres of sovereignty in his *Lectures on Calvinism*:

> In a Calvinistic sense we understand hereby, that the family, the business, science, art and so forth are all social spheres, which do not owe their existences to the state, and which do not derive the law of their life from the superiority of the state, but obey a high authority within their own bosom; an authority which rules, by the grace of God, just as the sovereignty of the State does.

---

55 Skillen, *Recharging the American Experiment* (Grand Rapids: Baker Books, 1994).
56 Skillen, *Recharging the American Experiment*, 67.
57 Skillen, *Recharging the American Experiment*, 92.
58 Skillen, *Recharging the American Experiment*, 69.
59 Skillen, *Recharging the American Experiment*, 73.

This involves the antithesis between *State* and *Society*, but upon this condition that we do not conceive of this society as a conglomerate, but as analyzed in its organic parts, to honor, in each of these parts, the independent character, which appertains to them.

In this independent character a special *higher authority* is of necessity involved and this highest authority we intentionally call – *sovereignty in the individual social spheres*, in order that it may be sharply and decidedly expressed that these different developments in social life have *nothing above themselves but God*, and that the State cannot intrude here, and has nothing to command in their domain. As you feel at once, this is the deeply interesting question of our civil liberties.[60]

Each sovereign sphere in society, as directly accountable to God, is under no obligation vis-à-vis any other sphere, as no sphere has another above it.[61] Thus there is no theological basis upon which the state can claim authority over, for example, the sphere of the family, for the basis of family life is not found in any other social organ, but only in its status as a sphere created by God.

And it is precisely *in* the doctrine of creation that these various spheres of society are located. Skillen points out that the social differentiation for which he advocates is rooted in the social differentiation intended by God in the original act of creation. In discussing the social ontology of Herman Dooyeweerd, Skillen notes:

> The ontic identity of any particular institution or association, therefore, is to be found in the way that it expresses a particular type of social life in all the modal dimensions of the creation. That is to say, the ontic foundation of social life is neither substance in general nor "substantial" individual persons. Rather, it is the creation order which exists by design of the Creator and shows itself in the various creatures God has made. Human creatures exist in a variety of institutions and relationships each of which, with its own structural identity, is bound by all the norms of physical, rational, historical, linguistic, social, aesthetic, juridical, ethical, and other modes of life.[62]

Elsewhere he notes in a similar vein: "The differentiation of human responsibilities and institutions implies, from our point of view, that Christians should look for the underlying creational basis – the principled norms of God's creation order – by which to recognize the legitimate responsibilities of state, family, school, church, business enterprise, and countless professions and voluntary associations."[63]

But the rooting of institutional differentiation solely in the doctrine of creation creates its own problems. For one thing, it is not always clear just how firmly these institutions are intended to be rooted in creation. Does Skillen mean that God intended every institutional type in its contemporary form at the creation? Or rather,

---

60 Abraham Kuyper, *Lectures on Calvinism* (Grand Rapids: Eerdmans, 1931), 90–91.

61 This distinguishes the Kuyperian approach from the idea of subsidiarity as developed within the tradition of the Roman Catholic encyclicals. See Paul Sigmund, "Subsidiarity, Solidarity, and Liberation" in Lugo, ed., *Religion, Pluralism, and Public Life* (Grand Rapids: Eerdmans, 2000), 205–20. Skillen comments on this at length as well in *Political Order and the Plural Structure of Society*, particularly in chapter 20, which is an extended appreciation and critique of the social encyclical tradition.

62 Skillen, *Political Order and the Plural Structure of Society*, 405–406.

63 Skillen, *The Scattered Voice*, 208.

does he mean that God intended in a more general sense that human beings order their lives according to broad principles of social differentiation? If the former, then it seems as though Skillen does not pay adequate attention to the history of social differentiation that has taken place leading to the kind of social complexity that exists in liberal democracies. If the latter, it is unclear why the particular institutional forms that exist ought to be given any privileged position or direct and divinely mandated sovereignty.

But Skillen's seemingly affirmative evaluation of Dooyeweerd's social ontology suggests the former. If so, then Skillen runs the risk of reifying particular contemporary social orders in God's eternal will, thus not allowing for the possibility that social dynamics may necessitate change in social institutional formation. A stronger recognition of the contingency and historical boundedness of contemporary social forms would better enable Skillen to recognize the ambiguity of the way that institutional diversity, particularly in the United States, has evolved.[64]

Furthermore, it is not clear just why the diversity of social institutions that Skillen refers to have the kind of sovereignty that he assigns to them. A strong case could possibly be made that the family as a sphere of society has its own sovereignty and integrity apart from the state, but why educational institutions exactly? The same could be said of a variety of institutions to which he points. The fact that they *are* differentiated in modern society does not establish a case that they are created as such by the divine will. Skillen risks conflating "is" and "ought" in his attempt to justify the very particular roles that he assigns social institutions. A way ought to be made to understand social institutions as good, but as subject to historical contingency and open to new possibilities.

Furthermore, it is not clear what Skillen understands to be the role of other social institutions in the event that a given sovereign sphere fails to fulfill its societal mandate. What should happen if educational institutions fail in their own sphere to educate; or if medical institutions fail to heal? Skillen, with good reason, resists a doctrine of subsidiarity that would make these spheres subject within certain parameters to the state. But does the sovereign authority of these spheres mean that a popular mandate to, for example, place the state in charge of education, or social welfare, must *of necessity* be immoral if these other institutions are failing in their responsibilities? Skillen is unclear on this. Indeed, comments such as the following seem to imply that Skillen views *any* such thing as *prima facie* immoral: "Differentiated public-moral discourse requires the legal and political recognition of

---

[64] Skillen expresses a degree of skepticism toward analyses that are too historically rooted. He seems to regard the work of such figures as Moltmann and Miguez-Boniño as preferencing history *over* created order. He writes: "what is lacking in Miguez-Boniño's perspective ... is a developed philosophy of creation. While he looks ahead to the unfolding of a just and differentiated social order – an order which should come to expression in the 'corporality of history' he is no more able to provide an ontological basis for a differentiated society than was Burke Figgis or Groen. If history has brought us only injustice and oppression to date, why should we have confidence that the future will be different?" (Skillen, *Political Order and the Plural Structure of Society*, 371). One might point out in response that, in the face of an oppressive social regime, the rooting of common life in a social ontology, the result of which is the oppressive system itself, is no virtue.

both structural and confessional pluralism. Public law is morally legitimate not by virtue of majority vote and constitutionally legitimate procedures alone but only as it does justice to the confessional and institutional diversity of society."[65]

The ambiguities created by Skillen's rooting of his understanding of social differentiation in the doctrine of creation undermine what is otherwise a very solid point – a vibrant public theology needs a complex theory of society, and in particular a complex theory of civil society. Yet, for such a theory to be responsive to the new possibilities opened up in Jesus Christ, and the social demands made as a result, it cannot be rooted in the doctrine of creation but needs a more dynamic foundation.

Skillen does offer such an eschatological dimension to his analysis of social differentiation. The kingdom of God offers us a goal toward which social life may strive, although, he notes, "we must begin with the full and unhesitating acceptance of the fact that the kingdom of God – the City of God – cannot be identified with any state in this world."[66] Although "God *does* call governments to be ministers of his justice in the unfolding history of the creation."[67]

Skillen interprets the political implications of Christian hope as an aspect of the larger social reality of independent spheres within a differentiated society. "Politics, like every other sphere of earthly life, is a differentiated arena for service to God and neighbor."[68] The political sphere has no privileges that elevate it above the other spheres of human association. Nor is any particular historical moment able to be identified as either an instantiation of the coming kingdom or its vanguard. Christians may be legitimately called to participate in political life as in other social spheres. If Christians fulfill their vocations faithfully, Skillen argues, then the U.S. "can become more just, more balanced in its pluralism, less pragmatically reduced to isolated issues, less given to civil religious passion about its greatness and prosperity, more preoccupied with justice for its victims."[69] Such a politics "will seek to nurture a passion for a just and differentiated republic in which each individual and each legitimate non-governmental institution is given its due."[70]

Such an eschatologically oriented public life is still, however, rooted in the doctrine of creation, since "to function in the political arena, American Christians will have to act on the terms of God's will for his creation, not on the terms we wishfully create for ourselves."[71] The spheres of creation of which Skillen writes, as aspects of God's creation, are therefore taken up into the eschatological pattern of redemption, and remain inviolable in our anticipation of God's kingdom. If Christians allow their faith to flourish, and live that faith out in public life, signs of God's kingdom will be detected even in the midst of misery and fallenness.

We do, indeed, have every reason to hope confidently in the coming of God's kingdom, because the King of that kingdom has already been raised from the dead

---

65 Skillen, *Recharging the American Experiment*, 98–9.
66 Skillen, *The Scattered Voice*, 215.
67 Skillen, *The Scattered Voice*, 215.
68 Skillen, *The Scattered Voice*, 215.
69 Skillen, *The Scattered Voice*, 217.
70 Skillen, *The Scattered Voice*, 217.
71 Skillen, *The Scattered Voice*, 216.

and is seated at the right hand of the Father. His kingdom will have no end, and it will reach no limits. The multiple spheres of our earthly life, including the limited domains of political life where we should be working for the political common good, will one day find their complete, their ultimate realization in the communion of the saints of all time, face to face, with the One who rules all things.[72]

Eschatology then, becomes the ultimate confirmation of the Spheres of Sovereignty, and the kingdom of God becomes the *telos* of these differentiated social spheres. Nevertheless, this does allow for a progressive dynamism in Skillen's approach that, as we will see, makes for an interesting counterpoint to Moltmann's approach.

American Public Theology and Moltmann's Political Theology

The three approaches that we have examined make for an interesting set of comparisons and contrasts with Moltmann's evolving understanding of public theology. Moltmann's analysis of the intersections of religion and public life interweaves themes that can be discerned in Tracy, Thiemann, and Skillen's perspectives, while at the same time, Moltmann's own understanding of the cross and resurrection as touchstones for Christian public involvement color his approach and make it distinctive when compared to these other understandings.

Moltmann's most recent writing on the relationship between religion and public life is structurally similar to Tracy's approach in *The Analogical Imagination*. Moltmann, like Tracy, writes of the issues of theology as they are manifested in the church, in the university, and in the complex social setting of (post) modern life.[73] Moltmann understands, with Tracy, that theology is not simply one thing, but takes on different characteristics depending upon its setting and its audience. The "elective affinities" of various theological approaches, however, must remain, for Moltmann, rooted in the life of the church:

> These two theologies, the academic and the popular, must relate to each other, show consideration for each other, and learn from each other. If academic theology does not find its way to ordinary people, it loses its foundation. Without the church, Christian theology cannot exist as a university discipline. It will become diffused and lose itself in the science of religions. On the other hand, popular theology loses its reasonable character if it pays no attention to academic theology or if it despises theology's competence.[74]

As with Tracy, the church is a "generalized other" to which theology must respond. For Tracy the theologian may exist in a variety of relationships to the church, some critical, some supportive. For Moltmann, both church and academic theologian are

---

72 Skillen, *The Scattered Voice*, 223.

73 Moltmann, *Experiences in Theology*. Moltmann is particularly cautious of the abstraction of professional academic theology from the concrete congregational life, noting that "the more [academic theologians] adopt academic theology and make it their own, the greater their difficulty later in bridging the gulf between the 'educated' and the 'uneducated' in their congregations. Over against this academic theology, a 'congregational theology' has long since developed everywhere" (11).

74 Moltmann, *Experiences in Theology*, 11.

responsible to a third reality, the kingdom of God.⁷⁵ Yet, Moltmann also clearly sees the legitimacy of academic theology as residing in its reflection of the church's heritage: "Academic theology is nothing other than the scholarly penetration and illumination by mind and spirit of what Christians in the congregations think when they believe in God and live in fellowship with Christ."⁷⁶

As the church and the university together manifest dimensions of that reflection on the kingdom of God, they interact in a public way. The church is central to theological reflection, but it is only *"one form* of the kingdom of God in the history of this God-estranged world" and "its concern is always more than the church."⁷⁷ The public face of theology is the engagement of Christians within Tracy's spheres of, not only church, but university and society as well.⁷⁸

In terms of that social dimension, this has always been manifest in Moltmann's assertion of *political* theology. It remains in his recent reflections on public theology. What Tracy points to in terms of the instrumental qualities of the technoeconomic realm is echoed in Moltmann's critiques of the dominance of the market in cultural life.⁷⁹ Yet, unlike Tracy, Moltmann does not offer an analysis of social complexity that recognizes distinctions between that techno-economic realm and the realms of polity and culture. Moltmann does not seem to recognize a distinction between the economic and the political realms as he writes in terms of the need for a political theology in contrast to "global marketing." Tracy, conversely, roots his understanding of what precisely makes public theology "public" in an analysis of public life *per se*. This remains underdeveloped in Moltmann's approach, and affects both the analytic and interpretive dimensions of his public theological project.⁸⁰

This is also clear when we turn to a comparison of Moltmann and Skillen. Skillen's much more complex conception of social roles and relations gives him a distinct advantage over Moltmann in terms of the analytical role of public theology.

---

75 Moltmann, *God for a Secular Society*, 252.

76 Moltmann, *Experiences in Theology*, 13.

77 Moltmann, *God for a Secular Society*, 251. Italics in original.

78 Moltmann, like Tracy, makes the case that theology's importance in the university goes beyond its confessional components. He writes: "The more theology has turned into a training school for pastors and teachers, the more it has become a merely churchified study. The relationship of the theological faculties to their churches has become closer than their relationship to other faculties. So if the theological faculties are to go on existing in the universities, it is not just for themselves that it is important to look beyond the horizon of the churches and to be aware of social, overall-human and global affairs in the light of God's kingdom and his righteousness and justice. This is *also* important for the continued existence and function of the universities in our society, among human beings, and on this earth." *God for a Secular Society*, 255.

79 Jürgen Moltmann, "Ist der Markt das Ende aller Dinge?" in *Die Flügel nicht stuzen: Warum wir Utopien brauchen*, Teicher and von Wedel, eds (Dusseldorf, 1994), 85–108.

80 To be sure, Moltmann speaks frequently of "society." "Society" seems to be a generic term for Moltmann to designate the entirety of human public enterprise. It encompasses politics, the market, civil society, and more intimate communal bonds outside of family life. But what the dimensions of society are is not extensively dealt with by him, and he never puts an analysis of society at the heart of his explanation as to what the connection between his earlier "political" and current "public" approaches to society is.

Skillen's recognition of the complexity of public life as embodied in the pluralism of institutions within civil society allows him to offer a more nuanced picture of the way in which theology, social theory, and polity intersect in a liberal democracy. Moltmann offers his own theological justification for civil society in his conception of the exodus church, but without a sense of how that theological justification operates sociologically.

Moltmann and Skillen both consider how creation and eschatology inform conceptions of society. It is intriguing to note the distinction in their views. For Moltmann, all theology is understood in light of the history of promise confirmed in the resurrection of Jesus Christ. The reality of the cross and the anticipation of the kingdom of God form the basis for Christian social commitment. This perspective also informs the doctrine of creation. Moltmann does not view proper social forms, as Skillen does, as having their fullest forms in creation, but rather as moving in the anticipation of the coming kingdom of God. They are, as it were, "orders of redemption."

Yet there is an ambiguity in how Moltmann conceives of our destiny as rooted in our nature. On the one hand, he writes of the *imago Dei* as our "original destiny," rooted in human relationality as a reflection of the Trinity, and finding its fullest articulation in the relationship of husband and wife.[81] But our "messianic calling" is to be the *imago Christi*, which is found in the wider human community. Moltmann writes that "the true likeness of God is to be found, not at the beginning of God's history with mankind, but at its end; and as goal it is present in that beginning and during every moment of that history."[82] Additionally, he uses the terms "restoration" and "new creation" interchangeably at points, in a way that makes it unclear whether his eschatological vision is of a *restitutio ad integrim* or of a transformation of existing orders into something new.[83]

The answer seems to reside in his borrowing of the Blochian ideas of "tendencies and latencies." The future is never fully present in the now, but rather the seeds of new possibilities remain planted in our current circumstances, and need to be activated in order for their latencies to become real. Society may tend toward the articulation of new forms of social life that are more reflective of the coming kingdom of God.[84]

With Skillen, conversely, as we saw in the previous section, the eschatological fulfillment is precisely a confirmation of those properly ordered social relations given in creation. Skillen is also not seeking a *restitutio ad integrim*, but rather a completion of incomplete social forms that are in need of fulfillment.[85] In seeking to root social forms in creation, Skillen has a distinct advantage over Moltmann, in

---

81 Moltmann, *God in Creation*, 220.
82 Moltmann, *God in Creation*, 225.
83 See *God in Creation*, 226.
84 In *God in Creation* Moltmann disputes Bloch's attempt to reinterpret the importance of heaven as a utopian vision without the presence of God. Utopia, for Moltmann, in the sense of the transformation of present possibilities, is only possible if God moves us beyond that which is simply given in nature and history: "Without God's creative potentialities for the world, worldly potentialities remain determined by presently existing reality and are totally congruent with that" (180–81).
85 Skillen, *The Scattered Voice*, 215.

that he has a basis for articulating clear points of division between different social sectors, and therefore a stake in understanding the public place those sectors occupy. There is, for Skillen, a thread that connects properly differentiated contemporary social forms to their intended created shape and their future fulfillment. Each of these spheres is created sovereign by God and is intended to remain sovereign until it finds its final form in the kingdom of God. From the point of view of social analysis, this gives Skillen a solid starting point for interpretation and constructive public theology.

In some ways, it is Thiemann's approach to public theology that is most comparable to Moltmann's. Thiemann's insistence on the centrality of the church in the formulation of the public Christian character is very reminiscent of Moltmann's understanding of the church as the "contrast society" out of which Christian life is formed.

Thiemann articulates the importance of the church in light of the tradition and narrative that it embodies, whereas for Moltmann, the church is the community that is called to live in anticipation of the coming kingdom of God. The church for both defines Christian identity in the larger social context, and offers for Christians a basis for moral action.[86] Additionally, both recognize that the church as a gathered community of believers exists in and has responsibility toward the larger horizon of society.[87]

Both Moltmann and Thiemann are seeking to understand just how the church can be a community committed to a particular vision of the human good, rooted in particular revelatory events and traditions, and yet be responsive and relevant within a pluralistic society that does not always accept Christian grounds for moral commitments.[88] Both see in modernity both potential and risk to the Christian vision of a good society.[89]

Yet, as significant as their similarities are their differences, both in terms of general methodology and in terms of what they see to be the mission of the church. For Thiemann, the objective of Christian theology is to "'re-describe' the internal logic of the Christian faith"[90] Such re-description is not innately at odds with modern society (though it is also not innately compatible), but it does not have a direct correlational aspect, either.[91] The church is the community that inherits a tradition and narrative, which define how it exists in the world and how it responds to the issues raised in modern society. "Because public theology begins from the standpoint of faith, the theologian launches his or her inquiry with the conviction that those

---

86 See Thiemann, *Constructing a Public Theology*, 23ff. Moltmann, *The Church in the Power of the Spirit*, 66ff.

87 See Thiemann, *Constructing a Public Theology*, 19. Moltmann, *The Church in the Power of the Spirit*, 1.

88 Moltmann, *God for a Secular Society*, 5ff. Thiemann, *Religion and Public Life: A Dilemma for Democracy*, 121ff.

89 See particularly Moltmann, *God for a Secular Society*, 11ff. and Thiemann, *Constructing a Public Theology*, 35ff.

90 Ronald Thiemann, *Revelation and Theology: The Gospel as Narrated Promise* (Notre Dame: University of Notre Dame Press, 1985), 74.

91 Thiemann, *Constructing a Public Theology*, 23.

questions [of life's meaning and value] have been answered positively through the revelation of God in Jesus Christ."[92] In Thiemann's approach to public theology, "the goal is to identify the particular places where Christian convictions intersect with the practices that characterize contemporary public life."[93]

Moltmann begins from a very different methodological starting point. Public theology, for Moltmann, begins with the situation of Christians in the world, in their lives of suffering and celebration, grief, joy, sorrow, and triumph, all of which are reflected in the dialectic of Christ's crucifixion and resurrection: "As the theology of God's kingdom, theology has to be *public* theology: public, critical, and prophetic complaint to God – public critical, and prophetic hope in God."[94] As such, it is not bound to the church, but operates throughout society: "Public theology needs institutional liberty over against the church, and a place in the open house of scholarship and the sciences."[95]

For Moltmann, the church is the crucial embodiment of the community "on the way," living in anticipation of the kingdom in the midst of society.[96] The church is an open community of friendship through which the influence of God's reign extends out beyond its institutional boundaries.[97] The church exists in the service of the kingdom of God, and Christian life lived in anticipation of the kingdom overflows the boundaries of the church community in order to extend the *pro-missio* of Jesus Christ in *missio* to the world.[98] In tension with Thiemann's emphasis on the self-descriptive task of theology, for Moltmann, theology is responsive. And the church, rather than a community that embodies a narrative, is a community that exists in an open-ended relationship to a God who is active and present in history and social life. The task of public theology for Moltmann rests finally in a trusting response to the work of God in history, not in an application of a static tradition to changing circumstances.[99]

Conclusion

The diversity of American public theology, as well as the disputes as to what can properly be called the "public" dimension of theology, can make it difficult to discern what it is that ties these varied and sundry approaches together under one heading. What we have seen in considering the approaches of Tracy, Skillen, and

---

92 Thiemann, *Constructing a Public Theology*, 22.
93 Thiemann, *Constructing a Public Theology*, 22.
94 Moltmann, *God for a Secular Society*, 5.
95 Moltmann, *God for a Secular Society*, 5.
96 Moltmann, *The Way of Jesus Christ* (Minneapolis, MN: Fortress Press, 1993), xiv.
97 Moltmann, *The Church in the Power of the Spirit*, 316.
98 "Mission does not come from the church; it is from mission and in light of mission that the church is to be understood." Moltmann, *The Church in the Power of the Spirit*, 10.
99 This, indeed, is what can often make Moltmann frustrating to read. His theology is undergoing a constant revision, and as a result Moltmann's positions on some issues tend to be moving targets. Yet there does remain an underlying consistency rooted in that dialectical structure that I have already described in detail.

Thiemann, as well as their comparisons with Moltmann, is that each theological approach is constructively engaged with modernity, and attempts to discover in modern society those places of affinity that allow for the articulation of Christian values and principles in the midst of a contentious marketplace of ideas. Each of these approaches recognizes an enduring value in Christian faith and the way of life that it entails. Each approach also recognizes a value in the socially pluralistic context of liberal democratic society. Tracy, Thiemann, and Skillen each approach social pluralism differently, yet each recognizes that it is in some way both an unavoidable and salutary fact about modern society. The task of Christian theology is to operate with integrity within that framework.

Moltmann's own attempts to articulate a public theology share these features. Moltmann has recognized Christian public responsibility as central to a faithful life from his earliest work. Like Tracy, he sees it operating in society and the university as well as in the church. Like Thiemann, he recognizes a special place for the church in that formulation. And like Skillen, he recognizes that the kingdom of God is the goal that our socially differentiated society ought to be striving imperfectly to approximate. Yet, Moltmann's approach is also distinct from each of these approaches in the ways I have discussed.

A dimension remains missing from this discussion, however; a dimension without which Moltmann's public theology will be pure form without content, and thus incapable of providing ethical guidance for Christians on the concrete questions raised in the desire and struggle for a good society. This is the dimension of institutional pluralism as embodied in the sociological category of civil society. It is through a better understanding of civil society that we may be able to see how Moltmann's theological agenda may remain relevant in the midst of changing social circumstances.

PART III

RATIONALITY, CIVIL SOCIETY, AND THE ROLE OF THE CHURCH

Chapter 7

Theology, Reason, and Critical Theory

Introduction

In Part I, I described Moltmann's critique of modernity in the context of his use of both "political" and "public" as descriptive terms for the engagement of theology with social questions. Moltmann developed his point of view in dialogue with a number of different influences.[1] Key to understanding Moltmann's critical stance vis-à-vis modernity is his encounter with the critical theory of the Frankfurt School in the mid-1960s, particularly with Horkheimer and Adorno's *Dialectic of Enlightenment* and Adorno's *Negative Dialectics*. In the Frankfurt School, he found a philosophical and sociological critique of modern instrumental rationality that comported with his own emerging understanding of the cross as a critical principle for the evaluation of society. As his political theology took shape, it did so in constant conversation with the Frankfurt School.

Yet, the work of Adorno and Horkheimer is only capable of informing a Christian theology of the cross to a certain extent. Because their work was incapable of finding a route out of the contradictions inherent in modernity, its usefulness for Christian theology is finally limited by its own limitations. Even so, later thinkers continued to develop the Frankfurt School's themes, in an attempt to draw it out of the dead end of its pessimistic outlook. At the same time, Moltmann's political theology was experiencing its own limitations, as it sought a broader social lens through which to examine the public role of Christian faith.

In order to develop a fuller understanding of the critique of modernity, and in particular of instrumental rationality that Moltmann sees as being at the core of modernity's difficulties, in this chapter I want to consider the line of interpretation that runs from Max Weber's *Economy and Society*, through the Frankfurt School, to the Theory of Communicative Action developed by Jürgen Habermas and, to a lesser degree, Karl-Otto Apel.

Max Weber: The Rationality of Modernity

Turning first to Weber's theory, we must examine the connection that he makes between the rise of the modern bureaucratization of society and the increasing prevalence of what he terms "instrumental reason" (*zweckrationalität*). Instrumental reason in Weber's analysis is a particular mode of rationality that concerns itself specifically with the association of appropriate means to ends. Instrumental rationality

---

1 For an extensive treatment of those influences, see Douglas Meeks, *The Origins of the Theology of Hope* (Philadelphia: Fortress, 1974).

is "determined by expectations as to the behavior of objects in the environment and of other human beings; these expectations are used as 'conditions' or 'means' for the attainment of the actor's own rationally pursued and calculated ends."[2] The external world is, in this analysis, a tool for the purposes of achieving whatever ends the agent subjectively desires to pursue.

The counterpoint to instrumental rationality is termed by Weber "value-rationality" (*wertrationalität*). Value-rationality concerns itself with the ends for which instrumental rationality provides the means. Value rationality is non-consequentialist in its adherence to binding moral principles that motivate action. It is "determined by a conscious belief in the value for its own sake of some ethical, aesthetic, religious, or other form of behavior, independently of its prospects of success."[3] Value-rationality, as opposed to instrumental rationality, is thus deontologically oriented toward universal duties and obligations, which do not concern themselves with effects. "Value-rational action always involves 'commands' or 'demands' which, in the actor's opinion, are binding on him."[4] These demands are, furthermore, "unconditional."[5]

Both *zweck* and *wertrational* modes of reasoning are considered to be rational by Weber, and both stand in contradistinction to what Weber deems the fundamentally irrational modes of action represented by either traditional authority or affective feeling-states.[6] Weber notes that "value-rational action may thus have various different reactions to the instrumentally rational action. From the latter point of view, however, value-rationality is always irrational."[7] Weber continues:

> Indeed, the more the value to which action is oriented is elevated to the status of an absolute value, the more "irrational" in this sense the corresponding action is. For, the more unconditionally the actor devotes himself to this value for its own sake, to pure sentiment or beauty, to absolute goodness or devotion to duty, the less is he influenced by considerations of the consequences of his action. The orientation of action wholly to the rational achievement of ends without relation to fundamental values is, to be sure, essentially only a limiting case.[8]

Weber also takes into consideration questions of "formal" and "substantive" rationality. Formal rationality for Weber is simply the quantitative or calculative aspect of reason: "a system of economic activity will be called 'formally' rational according to the degree in which the provision of needs, which is essential to every rational economy, is capable of being expressed in numerical, calculable terms,

---

2 Weber, *Economy and Society* (Berkeley: University of California Press, 1978), 25.
3 Weber, *Economy and Society*, 24–5.
4 Weber, *Economy and Society*, 25.
5 Weber, *Economy and Society*, 26.
6 Weber, *Economy and Society*, 25.
7 Weber, *Economy and Society*, 26.
8 Weber, *Economy and Society*, 26. It is interesting that Weber does not see the corresponding situation: that of action oriented solely to value, as an equally limiting case, although he does admit that "it would be very unusual to find concrete cases of action, especially of social action, which were oriented *only* in one or another of these ways."

and is so expressed."⁹ Substantive rationality, by contrast, is defined simply as the category of considerations which are not so quantifiable.

> The concept of "substantive rationality," on the other hand, is full of ambiguities. It conveys only one element common to all "substantive" analyses: namely, that they do not restrict themselves to note the purely formal and (relatively) unambiguous fact that action is based on "goal-oriented" rational calculation with the technically most adequate available methods, but apply certain criteria of ultimate ends, whither they be ethical, political, utilitarian, hedonistic, feudal (*ständisch*), egalitarian, or whatever, and measure the results of the economic action, however formally "rational" in the sense of correct calculation they may be, against these scales of "value rationality" or "*substantive* goal rationality."[10]

Formal and instrumental rationality are associated for Weber, as are value and substantive rationality. Substantive questions are rooted in core values, while means are best considered with regard to formal and quantifiable measurements.

In the modern period, the rise of formal and instrumental rationality as the primary means by which economic activity was organized led, according to Weber, to a greater and greater economic efficiency and productivity. Communism and socialism, since they were based on more substantive considerations, were less rational.[11] On the other hand, the increasing dominance of these types of rationality led at the same time to an increase of bureaucratization in public life: "Bureaucracy ... is fully developed in political and ecclesiastical communities only in the modern state, and in the private economy only in the most advanced institutions of capitalism."[12]

How then do questions of value translate into the practical realm of public life? Weber argues powerfully in "Politics as a Vocation" that questions of substantive rationality cannot be the primary tool with which politicians act. Politics is about power and policy, and is thus not a realm in which questions of pure duty can be made the primary consideration. It is the realm of "isness" in which *wertrational* considerations cannot play a direct role.[13]

Weber contrasts the ethic proper to public life, an "ethic of responsibility," with an "ethic of absolute ends."[14] The ethic of absolute ends corresponds to a devotion to *wertrational* considerations in a realm where they are inappropriate, while an ethic of responsibility corresponds to a willingness to use the means appropriate to politics to achieve insofar as is possible the ends valued by the politician. The means in question is *violence*. Weber notes that "one can define the modern state

---

9   Weber, *Economy and Society*, 85.
10 Weber, *Economy and Society*, 85–6.
11 Weber, *Economy and Society*, 86. At the same time, Weber saw an increase in bureaucratization as an inevitable outcome of communist and socialist institutions. He therefore resisted the trends in *Verein für Sozialpolitik* to seek to bring greater "rationalization" to public institutional life. See John Patrick Diggins, *Max Weber: Politics and the Spirit of Tragedy* (New York: Basic Books, 1996).
12 Weber, *Economy and Society*, 956.
13 Weber, "Politics as a Vocation," 119ff.
14 Weber, "Politics as a Vocation," 116.

sociologically only in terms of the specific *means* peculiar to it, as to every political association, namely the use of physical force."[15]

But if violence is the means appropriate to politics, what ends is it appropriate for? Weber rejects the idea that power is useful for its own sake, but at the same time does not consider it appropriate for sociology to define ends proper to the state.[16] That does not mean, however, that Weber considers all ends to be created equal. He is strongly critical of the position of the mere "power politician," for whom politics is a tool to accumulate influence and personal sway, but he acknowledges that all politicians seek power: "He who is active in politics strives for power either as a means in serving other aims, ideal or egoistic, or as 'power for power's sake,' that is, in order to enjoy the prestige-feeling that power gives."[17] The ends which the politician pursues are subjective, but that does not mean, from Weber's perspective, that one cannot identify a meaningful political ethic.

For Weber, the contrast to the "ethic of ultimate ends," that is concerned only with principle and not consequences is an "ethic of responsibility," which seeks to use power for the achievement of ends beyond mere self-aggrandizement:

> [The politician] works with the striving for power as an unavoidable means. Therefore, the "power instinct," as is usually said, belongs indeed to his normal qualities. The sin against the lofty spirit of his vocation, however, begins where his striving for power ceases to be *objective* and becomes purely personal self-intoxication, instead of exclusively entering the service of "the cause." For ultimately there are only two kinds of deadly sins in the field of politics: lack of objectivity and – often but not always identical with it – irresponsibility .... The politician may serve national, humanitarian, social, ethical, cultural, worldly, or religious ends. The politician may be sustained by a strong belief in "progress" – no matter in which sense – or he may coolly reject this kind of belief. He may claim to stand in the service of an "idea" or, rejecting this in principle, he may want to serve external ends of everyday life. However, some kind of faith must always exist. Otherwise, it is absolutely true that the cure of the creature's worthlessness overshadows even the eternally strongest political successes.[18]

Some ethical foundation is, thus, necessary for the motivation of political life. But Weber attempts to steer a middle course between the belief that politics is about pure principle and the belief that it is about pure power. Politics is, rather, about the use of power to enact principle. It has to involve the calculation of means and ends, and it has to involve exposure to the temptations that are part and parcel of political life: "Everything that is striven for through political action operating with violent means and following an ethic of responsibility endangers the 'salvation of the soul.'"[19]

Politics for Weber is therefore a realm of instrumental rationality, but instrumental rationality is in the service of some ultimate end.[20] The fallacy behind the struggle for ethical purity in politics for Weber is the belief that the ultimate ends can themselves

---

15 Weber, "Politics as a Vocation," 77–8.
16 Weber, "Politics as a Vocation," 77.
17 Weber, "Politics as a Vocation," 78.
18 Weber, "Politics as a Vocation," 116–17.
19 Weber, "Politics as a Vocation," 126.
20 Weber, "Politics as a Vocation," 127.

become the means to their own achievement. On the contrary, Weber argues that once you have opted for politics as the avenue through which to achieve your ends, you need to rationally opt for the means appropriate to it – that is, violence.

Weber's ambivalence about the role of instrumental rationality in modernity is often apparent in his writing, although as a sociologist he saw his task as more descriptive than normative. Yet he continually pointed (as he does in "Politics as a Vocation") to the need for a larger meaning-system through which instrumental rationality could be morally utilized. The rise of instrumental rationality resulted in the "disenchantment" of the modern world, and resulted in the "iron cage" of modernity.[21] When his work was adapted by the Frankfurt School, the question of the normativity of instrumental rationality in modernity became a more pressing issue.

The Critical Theory of Max Horkheimer

Max Horkheimer endeavored to deal with the increasing prevalence of instrumental rationality in modern society through a series of attempts to analyze and critique the development of modern thought.[22] In opposition to the dominance of positivism in modern science and sociology, Horkheimer and his allies in the Frankfurt School sought to develop a "critical theory" of society.[23] This theory was intended to be rooted, not in a raw empiricism, but in a constructive approach to understanding social relationships.[24] Rather than being simply a descriptive system, it is understood to contain a normative element as well: "It is the task of the critical theoretician to reduce the tension between his own insight and oppressed humanity in whose service he thinks."[25] Critical theory is thus morally engaged in an attempt to overcome what was perceived to be the increasingly instrumental character of modern life.

Horkheimer attempts to bring together the Weberian insight into instrumental rationality and bureaucratization and a brand of Marxist historical materialism in order to lodge a critique, not only against bourgeois society in the West, but also (as his work developed) against communism.[26] Instrumental rationality, or as Horkheimer

---

21 Max Weber, *The Protestant Ethic and the Spirit of Capitalism* (New York: Charles Scribner's Sons, 1958), 181.

22 Max Horkheimer, *Critical Theory: Selected Essays*; *Eclipse of Reason* (New York: Continuum, 1974); *Critique of Instrumental Reason* (New York: Continuum, 1974); Horkheimer and Adorno, *Dialectic of Enlightenment* (New York: Continuum, 1972).

23 For commentary on the approach of the Frankfurt School in general and Horkheimer in particular, see Gary Simpson, *Critical Social Theory: Prophetic Reason, Civil Society, and Christian Imagination* (Philadelphia: Fortress, 2002); Rolf Wiggershaus, *The Frankfurt School: Its History, Theories, and Political Significance* (Cambridge: MIT Press, 1994); Stephen T. Leonard, *Critical Theory in Political Practice* (Princeton: Princeton University Press, 1990).

24 Max Horkheimer, *Critical Theory*, 221

25 Max Horkheimer, *Critical Theory*, 221.

26 See Max Horkheimer, *Eclipse of Reason*, 6. It is interesting to note, with Aronowitz, that "although Horkheimer worked openly with the Marxist theoretical tradition, he himself has never referred to his approach as 'Marxist.' This reticence is not an attempt to obscure his political position. It derives from the concept of critique employed by Marx himself to distinguish the dialectical method from the vulgar (positivistic) philosophy and political economy … . There

refers to it, "purposive reason," undermines the authenticity of human life and individuality and reduces human beings to pieces in a great social machine.[27] One can see here the continuity between Moltmann's critique of the "global marketing of everything," and the earlier critique of the Frankfurt School.

In the early period of his work, as represented in *Critical Theory*, Horkheimer believed that the purpose of critique was to develop an emancipatory consciousness for the sake of overcoming the instrumentalization of human life and the loss of individuality. Unlike Marx, Horkheimer did not view the exclusive agent of emancipation to be the proletariat. The proletariat was subject to false consciousness and reification as much as the bourgeoisie. Horkheimer writes:

> But it must be added that even the situation of the proletariat is, in this society, no guarantee of correct knowledge. The proletariat may indeed have experience of meaninglessness in the form of continuing and increasing wretchedness and injustice in its own life. Yet this awareness is prevented from becoming a social force by the differentiation of social structure which is still imposed on the proletariat from above and by the opposition between personal class interests which is transcended only at very special moments. Even to the proletariat, the world superficially seems quite different than it really is. Even an outlook which could grasp that no opposition really exists between the proletariat's own true interests and those of society as a whole, and would therefore derive its principles of action from the thoughts and feelings of the masses, would fall into slavish dependence on the status quo.[28]

The power of emancipatory consciousness would come, for Horkheimer, from the intelligentsia rather than the proletariat. This consciousness may even bring the intelligentsia into conflict with the proletariat, but this does not divest critical theory of its legitimacy:

> The theoretician whose business it is to hasten developments which will lead to a society without injustice can find himself in opposition to views prevailing even among the proletariat, as we said above. If such a conflict were not possible, there would be no need of a theory; those who need it would come upon it without help. The conflict does not necessarily have anything to do with the class to which the theoretician belongs; nor does it depend on the kind of income he has .... The possibility of a wider vision, not the kind possessed by industrial magnates who know the world market and direct whole states from behind the scenes, but the kind possessed by university professors, middle-level civil

---

may have been another motivation for Horkheimer's refusal to designate himself a Marxist. Marxism had undergone significant permutations in the hands of the Communist left after the Russian Revolution, and he may well have wanted to distinguish his approach." Introduction to *Critical Theory*, xiii. Simpson remarks: "Horkheimer eventually realized that he no longer was an ordinary Marxist, an orthodox Marxist. Still, in his self-understanding, he had not become non-Marxist. First, like Marx, he still was deeply troubled by the poverty and suffering of the working class. Second, like Marx, he still thought that the capitalist mode of production was the prime culprit for this suffering. Third, like Marx, he held to the conviction regarding immanent critique." Simpson, *Critical Social Theory*, 57.

27 See Horkheimer, *Eclipse of Reason*, 143.

28 Horkheimer, *Critical Theory*, 213–14. See also Georg Lukács, *History and Class Consciousness* (Cambridge: MIT Press, 1971) 52ff.

servants, doctors, lawyers, and so forth, is what constitutes the "intelligentsia," that is, a special social or even suprasocial stratum.²⁹

This stands in stark distinction to Marx's understanding of class-consciousness (although, it should be noted, in less contrast to Lenin's). Consciousness of the character and necessity of social freedom is neither guaranteed nor limited by one's social class, but rather is based upon a proper recognition of the constraints placed upon human freedom. "The New Prophetic agents appeared to be the critical theorists themselves! These aloof intellectuals ... possessed prophetic awareness of the contradictions of capitalism as well as philosophical insight into the rational potential inherent in Western ideals."³⁰

Yet, with the rise of fascism in Europe and the move of the Institute for Critical Studies to the United States, Horkheimer's perspective became more pessimistic. Gary Simpson identifies this pessimism as coming from two sources: First, his disillusionment with the potential for the proletariat to act as a revolutionary agent, and second, from his loss of conviction in the emancipatory potential of Western reason.³¹ This can be seen particularly in the final pages of *Dialectic of Enlightenment*, which he wrote with Theodor Adorno.³² Thus he writes: "It is not the portrayal of reality as hell on earth but the slick challenge to break out of it that is suspect. If there is anyone today to whom we can pass the responsibilities for the message, we bequeath it not to the 'masses,' and not to the individual (who is powerless), but to an imaginary witness – lest it perish with us."³³

For Horkheimer, then, the end of the enlightenment project does not yield a free society, or a free human identity, but yields only a collapse into objectification and bestiality.³⁴ Mass society has demonstrated itself to be subject to false consciousness and stultification, as instrumental rationality pacifies, and then objectifies it.³⁵ Far from leading to a liberating synthesis of Weberian and Marxist modes of critical thought, critical theory discovered instead through its analysis that instrumental

---

29 Max Horkheimer, *Critical Theory*, 221.

30 Simpson, *Critical Social Theory*, 57. It is interesting to note the similarities between what Horkheimer was arguing and what Antonio Gramsci speaks about in terms of the responsibilities of "organic intellectuals" in his *Prison Notebooks* (New York: International Publishers, 1971).

31 Simpson, *Critical Social Theory*, 58.

32 Adorno, in his own *Negative Dialectics*, reflects this disillusionment with the emancipatory power of rationality, although, unlike Horkheimer, he seeks to move beyond the dialectical structure of modernity in the terms laid out by Hegel and Marx, and seeks a solution in terms of *apophatic* mysticism: "at the approach of the mind, the absolute flees from the mind: its approach is a mirage. Probably, however, the successful elimination of any anthropomorphism, the elimination with which the delusive content seems removed, coincides in the end with that context, with absolute identity. Denying the mystery by identification, by ripping more and more scraps out of it, does not resolve it. Rather, as though in play, the mystery belies our control of nature by reminding us of the impotence of our power." 407. See also Wiggershaus, *The Frankfurt School*, 350.

33 Horkheimer and Adorno, *Dialectic of Enlightenment*, 256.

34 Horkheimer, *Eclipse of Reason*, 245ff.

35 See Horkheimer and Adorno, *Dialectic of Enlightenment*, 221.

rationality could not be overcome, and thus it can only be protested against in the name of the "imaginary witness" to whom it might be relevant.

Jürgen Habermas: The Recovery of Emancipation Through Communication

Against the pessimism and potential for despair represented in Horkheimer's disillusionment with the emancipatory character of reason, Jürgen Habermas represents an alternative rooted in recognition of the human capacity for communicative action.[36] Habermas sets his own theory against the Weberian assertion that substantive values are irrational in the public/political realm.

For Habermas, communicative rationality is the root of human agency, and stands over against Weber's instrumental rationality. Where Horkheimer took the Weberian distinction between *zweck* and *wertrationalität*, and despaired of finding an emancipatory link between the productive capacity of Western rationality and the liberative elements of Marxist class analysis, Habermas reconceives the nature of rationality itself. Social action is a communicative activity for Habermas, and so stands in opposition to pure instrumentality:

> Weber does not start from the social relationship. He regards as rationalizable only the means-ends relation of teleologically conceived, monlogical action. If one adopts this perspective, the only aspects of action open to objective appraisal are the *effectiveness* of a causal intervention into an existing situation and the *truth* of the empirical assumptions that underlie the maxim or the plan of action – that is, the subjective belief about a purposive-rational organization of means ... An actor behaves purposive-rationally when he chooses *ends* from a clearly articulated horizon of *values* and organizes suitable *means* in consideration of alternative *consequences*.[37]

This is not, for Habermas, an out-and-out rejection of Weber's sociology. Rather, Habermas sees within Weber important resources for the reconstruction of a theory of communicative rationality, under which Weber's theory of rationality may be subsumed. Habermas speaks of the "unofficial" version of Weber's project, in which "social actions are distinguished according to two action orientations – corresponding to the coordination of action through interest positions and through normative agreement."[38] Habermas endorses this "unofficial" version of Weber's project and develops his own on the basis of it.

Communicative rationality, for Habermas, is not a matter of a value-rationality such as Weber describes. It does not stand apart from natural human inclinations, but rather language is itself structured in such a way as to lead human beings into greater understanding of one another. The normative quality of communicative action is derived from the descriptive analysis of language:

---

36 Jürgen Habermas, *The Theory of Communicative Action*, 2 vols. (Boston: Beacon Press, 1984–87).

37 Habermas, *The Theory of Communicative Action*, I:281.

38 Habermas, *The Theory of Communicative Action*, I:284–5.

The concept of communicative action is presented in such a way that the acts of reaching understanding, which link the teleological structured plans of action of different participants and thereby first combine individual acts into an interaction complex, cannot themselves be reduced to teleological actions ... examples of the use of language with an orientation to consequences seems to decrease the value of speech acts as the model for action oriented to reaching understanding.

This will turn out to be the case only if it can be shown that the use of language with an orientation to reaching understanding is the *original mode* of language use, upon which indirect understanding, giving something to understand or letting something be understood, and the instrumental use of language in general, are parasitic.[39]

The original intent of language is not the coordination of means and ends, but rather the achievement of understanding. Language is originally oriented, not toward the creation of tools of domination, but rather of cooperation. The instrumental aspect of language descends from the corruption of its original function.

Contrary to Weber's argument in "Politics as a Vocation," then, the tool unique to political life is *not* violence. Coercion as the means by which the politician works to achieve his or her ends is not in any sense uniquely rational, and the exclusion of value-orientations from political calculation is not sustainable. If language exists to aid in achieving understanding within a social context, then communicative rationality is an integral part of public discourse, rather than that which is pushed to the realm of the "irrational." In communicative action "*all* participants harmonize their individual plans of action with one another and thus pursue their illocutionary aims *without reservation*."[40] It is through communicative action that other aims may be described or developed, but communicative action itself is prior to the construction of such aims.[41]

As a result, Habermas argues that the emancipatory character of rationality can be recovered through a relativization of this Weberian distinction to the theory of communicative action.[42] Yet Habermas does not think that all is well with modernity. The problem of the development of instrumental rationality in modern society may indeed produce the kind of objectification of human life that Weber and Horkheimer observed.[43] He discusses this under his distinction between the lifeworld and the system.

The lifeworld for Habermas is the background context of our concrete life-situations.[44] "Communicative actors are always moving *within* the horizon of their lifeworld; they cannot step outside of it."[45] In modern society, it comprises the realms

---

39 Habermas, *The Theory of Communicative Action*, I:288.
40 Habermas, *The Theory of Communicative Action*, I:293.
41 Habermas, *The Theory of Communicative Action*, I:294.
42 Habermas, *The Theory of Communicative Action*, I:7.
43 Habermas, *The Theory of Communicative Action*, I:366ff.
44 Habermas, *The Theory of Communicative Action*, II:122.
45 Habermas, *The Theory of Communicative Action*, II:126. Italics in original. He says elsewhere that "the lay concept of the lifeworld refers to the totality of sociocultural facts" (II:136).

of culture, society, and the development of personality.[46] Gary Simpson explicates Habermas's theory as follows:

> As background, the lifeworld provides resources informing the action, but doing so implicitly and tacitly, at least at first glance. Components of the "situation" might include *spatial* elements, like a group of construction workers at the site with a grocery market a block away; *temporal* elements, like an upcoming coffee break; a *theme*, like refreshments for the break; a *goal* like the purchase of drinks; a *plan* like having the new guy go to the store. The action that happens depends on how the actors define and interpret the situation. Definition and interpretations happen through the background resources provided by the lifeworld. The theme, goal, and plan already give evidence of considerable interpretations. Such situations are defined through the resources provided by a complex network that makes up the lifeworld, which is always present and thereby preexists the action. The lifeworld is the part of the iceberg floating beneath the surface of every situation.[47]

As the background context of all life-situations, the lifeworld operates in, with, and under every human context.[48] This is the case in both primitive and modern societies, although as society progresses toward modernity, the lifeworld moves toward greater rationalization, and begins to differentiate itself from the system through which human life is symbolically mediated.

Within modernity, the social system has become increasingly "detached" from the lifeworld. The system is the realm of material exchange and power allocation within society. "Whereas system differentiation in tribal societies only leads to the increasing complexity of pregiven kinship systems, at higher levels of integration new societal structures take shape, namely, the state and media-steered subsystems."[49] What this means in modern society is that "economic and bureaucratic spheres emerge in which social relations are regulated only via money and power. Norm-conformative attitudes and identity-forming social memberships are neither necessary nor possible in these spheres; they are made peripheral instead."[50] Whereas the lifeworld functions on the basis of the communicative-rational action of social agents, the system can operate independently, and as a result, lifeworld and system become "uncoupled" in modern society.[51] Thus, economic and state-administrative systems become dissociated from the larger lifeworld from which they develop, and operate according to instrumental as opposed to communicative standards.

The colonization of the lifeworld by these systems happens as a result of the process begun in the lifeworld. "The irresistible irony of the world-historical process of enlightenment becomes evident: the rationalization of the lifeworld makes possible a heightening of systemic complexity, which becomes so hypertrophied that it unleashes system imperatives that burst the capacity of the lifeworld they instrumentalize."[52] The result is that the lifeworld increasingly takes on the

---

46 Habermas, *The Theory of Communicative Action*, II:142.
47 Simpson, *Critical Social Theory*, 108. Italics in original.
48 See Habermas, *The Theory of Communicative Action*, II:134.
49 Habermas, *The Theory of Communicative Action*, II:154.
50 Habermas, *The Theory of Communicative Action*, II:154.
51 Habermas, *The Theory of Communicative Action*, II:154.
52 Habermas, *The Theory of Communicative Action*, II:155.

characteristics of the system, as it trades in power and wealth to the exclusion of communicative matters. The natural function of language to bring about situations of communicative action is thus subverted by the interchange relations of the system.[53] Habermas writes: "*From the perspective of the lifeworld*, various social roles crystallize around these interchange relations: the roles of the employee and the consumer, on the one hand, and those of the client and the citizen of the state, on the other."[54]

The possible result of this process is the complete domination of the lifeworld by the system. This would be maintained, according to Habermas, by a process of structural violence:

> The reproductive constraints that instrumentalized a life-world without weakening the illusion of its self-sufficiency have to hide, so to speak, in the pores of communicative action. This gives rise to a *structural violence* that, without becoming manifest as such, takes hold of the forms of intersubjectively possible understanding. Structural violence is exercised by way of systematic restrictions on communication; distortion is anchored in the formal conditions of communicative action in such a way that the interrelation of the objective, social, and subjective worlds gets prejudged for participations in a typical fashion.[55]

Habermas recognizes the possibility of avoiding this situation of structural violence through the reassertion and reconstruction of forms of communicative rationality within the public sphere through the apparatus of civil society. It is this apparatus of civil society that was lacking in the earlier analysis of Horkheimer, despite his occasional reflections on the nature of the family.

Conclusion

Civil society, for Habermas, provides an avenue through which morality may filter through the social system and the lifeworld in a way that communicative action may still be possible.[56] This is a subject that I intend to pursue at more length in subsequent chapters. However, at this point it provides a means of moving back from the sociological realm to the theological. It is interesting to note that Habermas, at least as of the writing of *The Theory of Communicative Action*, did not see religious modes of discourse as potentially communicative, but as authoritarian, and thus does not consider them as relevant for the reconstruction of communicative

---

53 Habermas, *The Theory of Communicative Action*, II:320. These interchange relations are enumerated by Habermas as, for example, labor power and income, in the interchange between the economic and private spheres, and taxes and mass loyalty in the interchange between the public and administrative spheres.

54 Habermas, *The Theory of Communicative Action*, II:319. Italics in original.

55 Habermas, *The Theory of Communicative Action*, II:187. Italics in original.

56 Habermas, *The Theory of Communicative Action*, II:173ff. See also Gary Simpson, *Critical Social Theory*, 113.

rationality within the colonized lifeworld.[57] Yet, for Habermas, as well as for Weber and Horkheimer, the secularization of modern society was tied in with the rise of instrumental rationality, reification, and the colonization of the lifeworld by the system. The religious question cannot be detached from the questions both of how meaning came to be potentially at risk in modern society and how its preservation and recovery may be accomplished.

In this regard, these three sociological thinkers share a common cause with Moltmann, for whom theology is precisely the key to the recovery of values within modern society. Like Weber, Horkheimer, and Habermas, Moltmann does not seek a reactionary return to a premodern stage of social formation, but rather seeks to move forward to a reconstruction of society that both carries forward the emancipatory promise of the enlightenment and seeks a critique of that social instrumentalization that he sees as dangerous to human (and indeed, global) life. He does not view the human situation as one in which we are condemned to dwell forever in the "iron cage" of modernity, but have the capacity thorough our worldly pilgrimage to induce the tendencies and latancies within modernity to develop in the direction of a liberative praxis within a new kind of community. The theory of communicative action provides a secular analogue to that theological agenda.

In order to better understand the possible pathways that Moltmann's approach to understanding the role of the church in society opens for us, however, it is necessary to consider more fully the form and structure of civil society as an element in the larger matrix of society, in which the church takes part. This will be the subject of the next two chapters.

---

57 Habermas, *The Theory of Communicative Action*, II:196. Although it must be said that Habermas has moderated his point of view on this matter to some degree. See "Transcendence from Within, Transcendence in this World" in Browning and Fiorenza, *Habermas, Modernity, and Public Theology* (New York: Crossroad, 1992), 226–50.

Chapter 8

The Evolution of the Theory of Civil Society

Introduction

In Part II, I examined the contours and content of public theology as it has been developed in the American context, and then brought it into conversation with Moltmann's own work on public theology. The key problems for Moltmann's approach emerged, as I have argued, from an inadequate consideration of the role of civil society in Christian public life. Without a theory of the basis and function of independent institutions in a society, public theology is easily co-opted by a theory of civil religion, or by a sectarian temptation to separatism. Given the problems absent such considerations, it is necessary to turn to consider the role of the church within civil society, as one among many institutions. In order to do this, we need to come to some understanding of what precisely civil society is, and what the term "institution" means in that context. By understanding the way the church's identity as a civil institution overlaps with but also differs from its theological identity, we can begin to identify more clearly some of the points of tension with which the church has to deal in order to develop a faithful and at the same time socially responsible public theology.

Without an understanding of the church's theological identity, public theology simply becomes civil religion. This fear lies at the heart of the analysis of those theologians who seek to create a hedge between the church and civil society.[1] They understand civil religion as lacking in any independent standpoint from which to criticize and transform its social context. Yet, without an understanding of the church's role within civil society, no public theology is possible. Rather, "public" theology is in such a context a misnomer. What exists is instead a more or less narrow brand of sectarianism, which can understand itself *solely* in opposition to society.[2] Such a theology also lacks any reformative or transformative potential in

---

1 For example, see Stanley Hauerwas and William Willimon, *Resident Aliens* (Nashville: Abingdon, 1989) and *Where Resident Aliens Live: Exercises for Christian Practice*. (Nashville: Abingdon Press, 1996); Milbank, *Theology and Social Theory* (Cambridge, MA: Blackwell, 1991); *The Word Made Strange: Theology, Language, Culture* (Cambridge, MA: Blackwell Publishers, 1997); Milbank, Ward and Pickstock, eds, *Radical Orthodoxy* (New York: Routledge, 1999).

2 It has been pointed out by some theologians, including Thiemann, Hauerwas, and Yoder, that the term "sectarian" as used in Ernst Troeltsch's sense of the word, can often be a less than helpful way of describing such groups. What often seems to be meant by the term is simply "bad," rather than any precise definition of the characteristics of the group. However,

society (although it does have the virtue of maintaining a critical stance to society, when it deals with its social context at all).

In order to clarify the concepts at issue, I will now turn to consider the development of the idea of civil society, examining its historical roots, as well as several aspects of it as it has developed and been refined through the last several centuries.

The Idea of Civil Society

In order to understand the church as a *part* of civil society, our first task needs to be the definition of civil society itself. This is no small task, and it is not my intention to provide a comprehensive analysis of the nature of civil society.³ What I do intend to offer is a brief overview of the history of the idea of civil society up to the 20th century, and then in the next chapter discuss some of the central elements of the theory that will be useful for the remainder of this book.

The concept of civil society can be traced back to Aristotle's discussion in his *Politics* of the *politike koinonia* (which could be translated as "civic community").⁴ According to Aristotle's conception, the *polis* is the natural end of human relationships, as humans are not capable of being without community. It is the outcome of the process of development in human community, the foundation of which is the

---

this accusation is incorrect. It may certainly be true that "sectarianism" can become a way of characterizing one's theological opponents without actually engaging them. But to say that this is possible does not imply that there is no real content to the term regardless. It seems that if we take the characteristics of Troeltsch's definition of a "sect" as voluntaristic, to some degree separatist, as resting on some internal idea of the "Christian order," and living "in preparation for and expectation of the coming Kingdom of God" then such a definition *can* be fruitfully used without necessarily arousing the suspicion of *ad hominim* attacks. Indeed, excepting the tendency to separatism, this term could well describe Moltmann's own theological approach. But separatism is the crux of the problem, as it prevents any meaningful influence on the larger social setting of life. See Ernst Troeltsch, *The Social Teaching of the Christian Churches*, 2 vols. (Louisville, KY: Westminster/John Knox Press, 1992), II:993. See also Heinrich H. Maurer, "Studies in the Sociology of Religion I: The Sociology of Protestantism," *American Journal of Sociology* 30 no. 3 (November 1924): 257–86; Benton Johnson, "On Church and Sect," *American Sociological Review* 28 no. 4 (August, 1963): 539–49; Peter L. Berger, "Sectarianism and Religious Sociation," *American Journal of Sociology*, 64 no. 1 (July, 1958): 41–4; Erich Goode, "Social Class and Church Participation," *American Journal of Sociology* 72 no. 1 (July, 1966): 102–11. For the critique of the term "sectarian," see particularly John Howard Yoder's critique of H. Richard Niebuhr in *Authentic Transformation*, Glen Stassen, ed. (Nashville: Abingdon, 1996). James Gustafson's response can be found in the introduction to the expanded edition of *Christ and Culture* (San Francisco: Harper & Row, 2001). Also of interest is Peter R. Gathje, "A Contested Classic," *The Christian Century* (June 19–26, 2002): 28–32.

3   This has already been quite ably done by Jean Cohen and Andrew Arato in *Civil Society and Political Theory* (Cambridge: MIT Press, 1992), among others.

4   Aristotle, *The Politics of Aristotle*, Ernest Barker, ed. (New York: Oxford University Press, 1958), Book 1, Chapter 1 {1252a15-1253a38}.

household.⁵ The *polis* is, in some sense, a "community of communities," made up of a variety of human associations, including familial, economic, judicial, and military arrangements. The *polis* may be organized in a number of different ways, but was at the same time (under a just system of rule) both a single entity and a collectivity of smaller groupings. "yet plurality and differentiation were dramatically integrated in a model that presupposed a single, homogeneous, organized solidary body of citizens capable of totally unified action – closer to our notion of community, a 'community of societies.'"⁶ The sense of pluralism that the term "civil society" has come to signify did not exist for Aristotle, although the roots of it are to be found there.

In Roman philosophy, Aristotle's terminology was translated into the Latin *societas civilis* and joined with the more cosmopolitan conception of society engendered by stoic philosophy.⁷ But there was not a great deal of development in the implications of the concept for social and institutional pluralism within society. The development of systems of guilds, hospitals, trading associations and other independent institutions in the late medieval period, supported by an emerging system of civil laws, was a decisive contribution to a greater sense of this pluralism, and added a layer of associational complexity to the earlier conceptions of civil society.⁸ The idea of humans as autonomous agents with the freedom to choose among the variety of contradictory ends within one society would be more fully developed during the enlightenment period.

During the enlightenment there was a renewed interest in the idea of civil society, precisely *because* it offered a way of conceiving of the social setting as open to a plurality of points of view. This element nevertheless took some time to develop. In Hobbes' *Leviathan*, the commonwealth was conceived of, not as a pluralistic society of participating members, but as an imposition of order on the natural state of chaos. As Hobbes says, the state of nature was "a war of each against all."⁹ As Daniel Elazar notes, this feeds into the covenantal framework he was developing as "in a state of nature the individual ... needs confederates to survive."¹⁰ While all human beings are created as equal, it is through their equality that warfare develops. The imposition

---

5   Cohen and Arato point to the ambiguity of Aristotle's conception at this point, noting that "the Aristotelian notion [of *politike koinonia*] did not allow for our distinction between state and society. The *polis–oikos* duality may seem to indicate the contrary, but the *oikos*, household, was understood primarily as a residual category, the natural background of the *polis*." *Civil Society and Political Theory*, 84.
6   Cohen and Arato, *Civil Society and Political Theory*, 85.
7   This can be seen particularly in Cicero's writings on the nature of the state, in which he clearly sees human society as broader than simply the *polis* and universalizes the moral demands upon society to include, not only the citizen, but all human beings as persons with innate dignity. See Marcus Tullius Cicero, *De Republica* (Cambridge: Harvard University Press, 1928). Ernst Troeltsch discusses some aspects of this in "Stoic Christian Natural Law and Modern Secular Natural Law," in *Religion in History* (Minneapolis: Fortress Press, 1991), 321–42.
8   See Cohen and Arato, *Civil Society and Political Theory*, 85.
9   Hobbes, *Leviathan* (Baltimore: Penguin, 1968), 185.
10 Elazar, *Covenant and Civil Society*, 33.

of order upon society is brought about precisely through the *elimination* of plurality and the vesting of absolute power in the hands of a sovereign. "In Hobbes's theory, the social contract creates a state, not society. The fusion of society is accomplished only by the power of the state ... . Thus the later construction in the *Leviathan* more or less left out the whole concept of civil society (i.e., the normative idea of free and equal citizens comprising the body politic)."[11]

A similar neglect of the concept of civil society as a sphere of association separate from the state can be seen in Rousseau's understanding of the social contract. In his understanding, the social transaction takes place between individuals and the state, with no intermediary institutions to act as buffers. Insofar as individuals are in society, they submit themselves to the "general will," and are thus subsumed under the authority of the state. They may, in Rousseau's words, be "forced to be free."[12] No subsidiary or parallel organs of authority exist. Rousseau envisions society as an organic whole, rather than as a contingent association or collection of associations, and so cannot imagine a diversity of authorities.[13]

Nevertheless, the concept took on increased importance in the work of Althusius,[14] Locke,[15] and Montesquieu,[16] each of whom recognized, in differing ways, a place for spheres of independent institutional sovereignty within the context of the larger society. Montesquieu's distinction between *l'etat politique* and *l'etat civile*[17] laid some of the theoretical groundwork for Tocqueville's later analysis of society in the United States, but it was in Locke's work that the recognition of institutional pluralism within a diverse society took firm hold.

One can see in Locke's *A Letter Concerning Toleration* that the importance of institutional pluralism for him was in no small measure tied to the question of

---

11 Cohen and Arato, *Civil Society and Political Theory*, 87. However, as Elazar points out, the structure of the state in *Leviathan* was covenantal and rooted in the confederation of individuals. Such confederations stood at the root of the social compact and allowed for the development of society. "At some point there must be the political equivalent of the Kierkegaardian 'leap of faith' to begin the covenanting process." Elazar, *Covenant and Civil Society*, 34.

12 Rousseau, "On the Social Contract," in *Basic Political Writings* (Indianapolis: Hackett, 1987) 150.

13 One may indeed suppose that Rousseau's understanding of society owes something to Paul's description of the church as a body (1 Cor. 12:27). Yet, while such an organic metaphor may be appropriate for a theological understanding of the church, which does indeed have a unitary identity when seen from the perspective of God's will for it and the world, such a metaphor becomes problematic and perhaps dangerous when applied to a diverse society *ante-Basilea*, since it presumes a unity which not only does not but cannot exist among diverse people, as well as a singular authority capable of enforcing a "general will" which, at least as Rousseau describes it, bears some resemblance to deity.

14 Johannes Althusius, *Politica* (Indianapolis: Liberty Fund, 1995).

15 John Locke, *Second Treatise of Government* (Indianapolis: Hackett, 1980); *A Letter Concerning Toleration* (Indianapolis: Hackett 1983).

16 Charles de Secondat Montesquieu, *The Spirit of the Laws* (New York: Hafner Publishing Company, 1949).

17 For a description of the distinction between these two realms, see Montesquieu, *The Spirit of the Laws*, 5.

religious freedom. The question of what church one belonged to was no matter over which government ought to have a say, since it was dictated solely by the conscience of the believer. No state could compel belief, and no church should finally be subject to any earthly authority. As he writes: "If anyone maintain that men ought to be compelled by Fire and Sword to profess certain Doctrines, and conform to this or that exteriour Worship, without any regard had unto Morals; if any endeavor convert them that are Erroneous unto the faith, by forcing them to profess things that they do not believe, and allowing them to practice things that the Gospel does not permit; it can not be doubted indeed but such a one is desirous to have a numerous Assembly joined in the same profession with himself; but that he principally intends by those men to compose a truly Christian Church, is altogether incredible."[18]

Locke's concern for religious tolerance was both a cause and an effect of his concern for limited government. Far from being able to endorse any idea similar to Rousseau's "general will," Locke understood the social contract to be of a very limited character. His interest included the effort to "distinguish exactly the Business of Civil government from that of Religion, and to settle the just Bounds that lie between the one and the other."[19]

Such boundaries were delimited by his understanding of the very short list of obligations that the state had to its citizens. As he notes, "the great and *chief end* … of men's uniting into commonwealths, and putting themselves under government, *is the preservation of property*."[20] Of course, this is not the sole reason for the existence of government as Locke understands it, but it is pretty close to the overriding reason. He does recognize other goods which the society can help engender, such as "Life, Liberty, Health, and Indolency of Body," but these things are always coupled with, and in some sense viewed as dependent upon "Money, Lands, Houses, Furniture, and the like."[21] It is for the preservation and the protection of the property rights of individuals that government is formed. Therefore, any government action which restricts freedom beyond that which is necessary for citizens to enjoy these goods is considered by Locke to be a violation of the social contract: "all Civil Power, Right and Dominion, is bounded and confined to the only care of promoting these things; and that it neither can nor ought in any manner to be extended to the Salvation of Souls."[22] Thus, the existence of churches and other institutions that serve to promote these human goods that are not directly under the supervision of the state are to be left to themselves.

Locke had, however, still not developed a particularly clear understanding of civil society as the sphere in which these institutions exist and mediate social life. It is not always clear what distinctions Locke means to make when he speaks of "civil society," "political society," "commonwealth," or "government." He often uses the terms as if they were interchangeable, yet at the same time recognizes that they have different connotations in that civil society makes political society and

---

18 Locke, *A Letter Concerning Toleration*, 25.
19 Locke, *A Letter Concerning Toleration*, 26.
20 Locke, *The Second Treatise of Government*, 66. Italics in original.
21 Locke, *Letter Concerning Toleration*, 26.
22 Locke, *Letter Concerning Toleration*, 26.

the commonwealth forms the government. Cohen and Arato see a clear attempt on Locke's part to make this separation, noting that "he distinguishes between surrendering power to society and to the government 'whom society has set up over itself' and even more emphatically (unlike Hobbes) between the 'dissolution of the society' and 'the dissolution of the government.'"[23] Nevertheless, they too recognize some of the ambiguities in Locke's formulation.

The Hegelian Theory of Civil Society

These early uses of the idea of civil society never sought to develop a strict definition of the term. That task was left to G.W.F. Hegel, who in *The Elements of the Philosophy of Right* developed a detailed classification of the strata of society, in which civil society was described as that collection of institutions which served to mediate between the family on the one hand and the state on the other.[24] As with all things Hegelian, this takes place in the dialectical process of universal development. In the case of his analysis of civil society in the *Philosophy of Right*, the development that is taking place is in the direction of a greater and greater realization of true freedom.[25] Freedom is embodied in a society that has a properly balanced relationship between family, civil society, and the state.[26]

Hegel makes the distinction in the *Philosophy of Right* among the three spheres of the development of freedom. The first moment in the dialectic is the abstract moment, the second the particular, and the third the universal.[27] The first is the realm of Abstract Right, in which is embodied those formal relationships of rights associated with contractual agreement and association.[28] This gets the least extensive treatment of the three moments in Hegel's system. More relevant is the realm of the Moral Life, when the individual recognizes him or herself not simply abstractly as a "person," but as a subject, who has the responsibility for discerning and acting on the basis of determinations of good and evil. It is in the realm of what he terms "social ethics" that questions of family, civil society, and the state become germane.

The realm of family life is rooted in nature. Human beings as social animals desire to be together for companionship, but also, more importantly, for reproduction. The family unit is the social embodiment of that natural relationship. As such, it is the least "rational" moment in the dialectic, in the sense that human beings are constrained to belong to a family unit. In civil society, there is a greater realization of freedom, as persons gather together in various associational groupings for achieving their own ends (which then become common ends). The state, according to Hegel, by virtue of being the embodiment of universal freedom, is the sublating moment of this dialectic, which transcends and incorporates the other two moments. "The

---

23 Cohen and Arato, *Civil Society and Political Theory*, 88.
24 Georg Wilhelm Freidrich Hegel, *Elements of the Philosophy of Right* (Cambridge: Cambridge University Press, 1991).
25 Hegel, *Philosophy of Right*, 35.
26 Hegel, *Philosophy of Right*, 62ff.
27 Hegel, *Philosophy of Right*, 62.
28 Hegel, *Philosophy of Right*, 67ff.

statist trend in Hegel's thought, anticipating Marx and especially Marxism, is clearly connected to the notion of civil society as *Gegensittlichkeit*, rooted in the analysis of the system of needs .... A state bureaucracy (the universal class, the class of civil servants) is called upon to deal with the dysfunctional consequences of the system of needs."[29]

As the associational moment in this dialectic, civil society has the advantage over the family of being voluntaristic and pluralistic (that is, one can belong to a variety of associations). Taylor points out that "civil society is the level of relations into which men enter not as members of a family, nor as members of some ethical community, as a state or a church, but just as men. It is a sphere in which men are related to each other as persons in Hegel's sense, i.e., as bearers of rights."[30] Hegel enumerates several elements in the nature of civil society. He begins by considering the three estates of society – the agricultural, the merchant, and the civil estates.[31] The agricultural estate is rooted in the ebb and flow of the natural world, as it depends on the vicissitude of nature to control its output. As such, it is not free to pursue more universal ends, but is to a large extent at the mercy of forces beyond its control.[32] The merchant estate (which includes not only merchants, but also crafts and tradespeople) is more universal in the sense that it makes use of and changes the goods of the agricultural estate for the purposes of engaging in the market.[33] It is, however, not entirely free. Because it needs to concern itself with the vicissitudes of the market, its concerns cannot be universal, but must be rooted in the particular. It is the class of civil servants (for example, the police, the courts, and so on), being free of the pressures of nature and the market, and having the means not to be beholden to outside interests, that has universal concern, in that it is concerned with the good of the whole society, not simply with one or a few elements within it.[34]

The economic system, as described by Hegel, which is embodied within these estates, is controlled by the "system of needs." The system of needs, as the name implies, is the embodiment of those things that human beings in society need in order to survive. Through the market economy, according to Hegel, individuals can meet those needs most efficiently, as long as there is a freedom of trade and the ability of individuals to follow their own ends in business.[35] The economy as an element of civil society thus has the virtue of being on the one hand the embodiment of particularistic and narrow interests of individuals, and at the same time lending itself to the realization of the common good.[36]

Finally, the three further organs of society developed by Hegel are the realms of the administration of justice, the police, and corporations.[37] The corporations feed

---

29 Cohen and Arato, *Civil Society and Political Theory*, 102.
30 Charles Taylor, *Hegel* (New York: Cambridge University Press, 1975), 432.
31 Hegel, *Philosophy of Right*, 234ff.
32 Hegel, *Philosophy of Right*, 236.
33 Hegel, *Philosophy of Right*, 236.
34 Hegel, *Philosophy of Right*, 237.
35 Hegel, *Philosophy of Right*, 230.
36 See Adam Smith, *The Wealth of Nations* (New York: The Modern Library, 1994), 15ff.
37 Hegel, *Philosophy of Right*, 240ff.

back once again into the system of needs by embodying those particularistic interests which are expressed universally through the corporation.[38] The administration of justice and the police (which for Hegel do not fall under the administration of the state, but of civil society) embody the concern of society as a whole that order be kept and contracts be honored. As such, they bring the realm of abstract right into the heart of civil society, by embodying through the civil and criminal law systems the particular settings in which that abstract right is applied. It is nevertheless through the state that the final unity of the elements of society is realized.

A few comments need to be made about the questions of pluralism and religious freedom in the context of Hegel's construction of civil society. Whereas for Locke, religion was expressly *outside* the state's responsibility, and existed as a question of free association within civil society, Hegel discussed the public import of religion under the doctrine of the state. Because of his metaphysical understanding of the state as a realization of the divine will in the social setting, Hegel could not take the view that questions of religion are a matter of indifference to the state. Rather, the state needs to decide the degree of tolerance it will have for religious diversity, depending on the degree of assent the religious community gives to the state's divine mandate:

> A relationship thus arises between the state and the religious community, and its determination is a simple one. It is in the nature of the case that the state fulfills a duty by giving the [religious] community every assistance and protection in the pursuit of its religious end. Indeed, since religion is that moment which integrates the state at the deepest level of the disposition [of its citizens], the state ought even to require all its citizens to belong to such a community – but to any community they please, for the state can have no say in the context [of religious belief] in so far as this relates to the internal dimension of representational thought. A state which is strong because its organization is fully developed can adopt a more liberal attitude in this respect, and may completely overlook individual matters which might affect it, or even tolerate communities whose religion does not recognize even their direct duties toward the state (although this naturally depends on the numbers concerned). It is able to do this by entrusting the members of such communities to civil society and its laws, and is content if they fulfill their direct duties toward it passively, for example by commutation or substitution [of an alternative service].[39]

Because the state has such a stake in questions of religious truth, it may compel acceptance of religion. But what is of particular note for our purposes is the placement of this discussion, not in Hegel's doctrine of civil society, but in his discussion of the state and its responsibilities. The church, as Hegel conceives it, is not a voluntary society but a fundamental organ of social cohesion, and thus to be administered by the state and not left to the vagaries of the system of needs.[40] One can still see this element reflected in the German *Kirchentuer* system.

---

38 Hegel, *Philosophy of Right*, 269ff.
39 Hegel, *Philosophy of Right*, 295. Editorial brackets in original.
40 This is because civil society, for Hegel, is a chaotic dimension of human life, rather than the seat of moral formation. As Kai Nielson notes: "Civil society referred to a social order, and most fundamentally, an economic order operating according to its own principles,

Hegel's conception of the nature of civil society has provided the theoretical foundation for much of the subsequent work on the subject, and his influence can be seen, not only in the continental reflection on the issue (both in Marxist and non-Marxist incarnations), but also in the Anglo-American world, insofar as it is in conversation with the German sociological tradition.

Tocqueville and the American Tradition of Civil Society

However, for a proper understanding of the American tradition, it is Alexis de Tocqueville who most clearly articulated the relationship between religious belief and civil society. Whereas in the European tradition Hegel was in some ways articulating and in other ways defining a singular dominant religious tradition that was deemed necessary for the proper functioning of society (although toleration for minority religions may be permitted), in the United States, the idea of religious pluralism was embodied in its founding document.

Tocqueville recognized the power and the risk of that religious diversity in his examination of American democracy, but also recognized the vitality of the American attempt to make it work. He argued that the freedom of association which allowed persons to choose from among several voluntary religious associations allowed for a tremendous degree of variation within American religion, at the same time democracy instilled a sense of unity which allowed citizens to sustain a common sense of purpose in spite of the lack of religious unity.[41]

The degree of individual involvement in religious life was also a question Tocqueville examined. Although it should have been the case that religious life languished without some official enforcement of religious observance, what he found was rather a vibrant and energetic religious life, in which participation in religious institutions was very high.[42]

From the point of view of social integration, then, the possibility of (relatively) free religious expression in the United States had a salutary effect from Tocqueville's perspective. The idea of religious institutions as voluntary associations opened up the possibility that the social function of religion need not be mandated by the state, but rather could develop organically through the freedom of individuals to choose among faiths in a free marketplace of ideas.[43]

---

independent of the ethical requirements of law and political association. It was, for both Hegel and the early Marx, part of social life where avariciousness and egoism, sometimes accompanied by economic rationality, were the order of the day. This part of social life lacked all qualities of warmth, solidarity, and moral cohesion at least supposedly characteristic of the *Gemeinschaften* of simpler societies." Kai Nielson, "Reconceptualizing Civil Society for Now: Some Somewhat Gramscian Turnings" in Walzer, *Toward a Global Civil Society* (Providence: Berghan Books, 1995), 42.

    41 Alexis de Tocqueville, *Democracy in America* (New York: Alfred Knopf, 1972), I:143.
    42 Tocqueville, *Democracy in America*, I:308.
    43 See Elazar, *Covenant and Civil Society*, 82.

Tocqueville also presented an alternative, more empirical view, to Hegel's schema by reasserting Montesquieu's distinction between civil and political societies.[44] Whereas Hegel only allowed for the realm of civil society in the context of specific social roles, Tocqueville recognized that the way in which mediating institutions interrelate, both with one another and with the state, affected their status within society:

> An association consists simply in the public assent which a number of individuals give to certain doctrines and in the engagement which they contract to promote in a certain manner the spread of these doctrines. The right of associating in this fashion almost merges with freedom of the press, but societies thus formed possess more authority than the press. When an opinion is represented by a society, it necessarily assumes a more exact and explicit form. It numbers its partisans and engages them in its cause; they, on the other hand, become acquainted with one another, and their zeal is increased by their number. An association unites into one channel the efforts of divergent minds and urges them vigorously towards the one end which it clearly points out.[45]

On the one hand are those agencies of civil society that relate to the realms of religion and civic morality and were somewhat removed from the direct involvement with political life.[46] On the other hand were political parties and associations dedicated to social change, which were members of political society and sought to influence the state's operation while not being part of the state proper.[47]

The Modern Synthesis of Civil Society

The 20th century attempts to formulate a view of civil society worked to bring together both the Hegelian systemization of civil society and the Anglo-American emphasis on the freedom of institutions within civil society. This is especially germane with regard to religion, which, as we saw, in the Hegelian system was subsumed by the state.

Within the context of the emergence of the modern state in Italy, pulled as it was between twin poles of democracy and fascism, Antonio Gramsci's analysis of civil society sought to avoid the problems inherent within both communist and fascist

---

44 Tocqueville, *Democracy in America*, I:191ff., II:106ff.; See also Cohen and Arato, *Civil Society and Political Theory*, 78.

45 Tocqueville, *Democracy in America*, I:192. While Tocqueville recognized the advantages of free association for public participation, it is interesting to recall that, for Madison, the chaotic possibilities embodied in such freedom were precisely what needed to be ordered into a federal system of government: "Liberty is to faction what air is to fire, an aliment without which it instantly expires," he wrote. "But it could not be less folly to abolish liberty, which is essential to political life, because it nourishes faction than it would be to wish the annihilation of air, which is essential to animal life, because it imparts to fire its destructive agency." James Madison, "Federalist 10," in *The Federalist Papers* (New York: New American Library, 1961), 78.

46 Tocqueville, *Democracy in America*, II:106ff.

47 Tocqueville, *Democracy in America*, I:192.

doctrines that all institutions of civil society would be subsumed by the state. In some ways, this is a problem that Marx inherited from Hegel, which was then passed down through the Marxist tradition. However, Gramsci recognized that in eliminating civil society as a separate integrative sphere of free determination, there existed in society no area of independent thought and will apart from the state.[48] In Gramsci's analysis, civil society was necessary as a realm of multiple associations, which may or may not be compatible with socialism, depending upon what ideology has hegemony in society. Under totalitarian systems, civil society disappears as the absolute state seeks to pull everything into its sphere of control. According to Gramsci:

> A totalitarian policy is aimed precisely: 1. at ensuring that the members of a particular party find in that party all the satisfactions that they formerly found in a multiplicity of organizations, i.e., at breaking all the threads that bind these members to extraneous cultural organisms; 2. at destroying all other organizations or at incorporating them into a system of which the party is the sole regulator. This occurs: 1. when the given party wishes to prevent another force, the bearer of a new culture, from becoming itself "totalitarian" – then one has an objectively regressive and reactionary phase, even if that reaction (as invariably happens) does not avow itself, and seeks itself to appear as the bearer of the new culture.[49]

As Cohen and Arato point out, in light of the identity of the characteristics of totalitarianism in both its "progressive" and "regressive" phases, "the defense of the Soviet Union by an antifascist must seem bizarre."[50] They attribute this inconsistency to Gramsci's "functionalist" approach to civil society and its role in preserving a capitalist system of domination. Nevertheless, Gramsci did perceive the need within all societies for the existence of a sphere of civil society, in which "alternative forms of association (worker's clubs, the new proletarian party form, or the 'modern prince'), intellectual and cultural life (the idea of the organic intellectual), and values that would help create a proletarian counter-hegemony that might eventually replace existing bourgeois forms."[51]

Talcott Parsons represents another major influence on the doctrine of civil society in the 20th century, which diverges from Hegel's normative path. Parsons saw civil society as embodying a societal community distinct from economic, political, and cultural spheres of life.[52] As Cohen and Arato point out, this "represents a synthesis

---

48 Within orthodox Marxism, following Marx's analysis in *Die Judenfrage*, civil society was seen as a realm of individualism and social fragmentation, in which personal interest governed over against the common interest and social cohesion could not be obtained. The goal, according to Marx, ought to be the abolition of both civil and political society and the reconstitution of the state along the lines of common interest. See Karl Marx, "On the Jewish Question," in *The Marx–Engels Reader* (New York: Norton, 1978).

49 Gramsci, *Prison Notebooks*, 265. Gramsci saw this developing most clearly in his encounter with Italian fascism, although the context arguably indicates that his understanding of "progressive" totalitarianism relates also to his opinion of the Soviet Union.

50 Cohen and Arato, *Civil Society and Political Theory*, 148.

51 Cohen and Arato, *Civil Society and Political Theory*, 151.

52 See Talcott Parsons, *The Social System* (London: The Free Press, 1951), 113ff. See also Parsons, *The System of Modern Societies* (Englewood Cliffs, NJ: Prentice-Hall, 1971).

of the liberal concept of civil society as differentiated from the state with the stress on social integration, solidarity, and community that typifies the sociological tradition initiated by Durkheim and Tönnies."[53] On the one hand is the individual autonomy and freedom to choose from among various associations, and on the other hand is the sense of belongingness to a larger community that serves the integrative role of civil society.

Civil society in Parsons' understanding is in some sense a keystone to modernity. The differentiation of the associational sphere from the economic, political, and cultural spheres allowed for the flexibility with regard to professional and personal decision as to the way and the degree to which public participation would take place, as well as the freedom to move within the economic and political spheres without necessarily being tied to preestablished kinship or caste identifications. Within civil society, cultural and social norms are inculcated within the person in such a way as to better enable one to cope within a larger society. Through the developments that took place within the industrial, democratic, and educational revolutions to which Parsons refers, the modern outlook was better developed and more successful in that it created an overlapping set of social "subsystems" that contributed to the stability of a diverse society.[54]

Conclusion

As the idea of civil society has developed through its various forms, it has emerged as a means of describing and explaining the reality and importance of institutional pluralism within society. As an intermediating sphere between the individual or family and the state, civil society provides a space for moral and spiritual development that both takes one beyond one's own personal preferences and inclinations, and yet also allows a realm of independence from the potentially overwhelming and depersonalizing spheres of the state and the market.

---

53 Cohen and Arato, *Civil Society and Political Theory*, 118.

54 Parsons, *The Social System*, 68ff. Cohen and Arato point out that Parsons finds himself in an inconsistent position vis-à-vis the relationship of these spheres to one another because he refuses to acknowledge the asymmetrical relationship between the differentiation of society from the state on the one hand and the economy on the other. They note Karl Polányi's analysis of the problems associated with the degree to which civil society is intertwined with the economy: "Instead of differentiation and complementary expansion, the industrial revolution produced an economic society (the market economy) that threatened to subsume and reduce autonomous social norms, relationships, and institutions. While one would hardly expect Parsons to be sensitive to the Marxian discussions of reification and commodification, it is indeed surprising that he does not examine Polányi's thesis that a self-regulating market produces an 'economization' of society, against which a program of the self-defense of society emerged in the nineteenth century." *Civil Society and Political Theory*, 122. See also Karl Polányi, *The Great Transformation: The Political and Economic Origins of Our Time* (Boston: Beacon Press, 1957). Polányi saw an unfettered and unregulated market mechanism as a threat to the existence of society in all of its dimensions, human and environmental, but also economic: "Even capitalist business itself had to be sheltered from the unrestricted working of the market mechanism" (*The Great Transformation*, 192).

As we have seen, in the early development of the concept, it was unclear just what place the church held in the larger social setting. Was it an aspect of the state as Hegel would have it? Or was it instead a member of civil society, a voluntary association in which individuals participated of their own volition, rather than out of compulsion? As the idea of religious freedom and the fact of religious pluralism began to more fully pervade modern society, Tocqueville's understanding of the role of religion came to predominate, and the voluntaristic understanding of religion's place in society became more widely accepted. Religious organizations, including the church, are now understood in most modern settings to exist in the civic realm.

And yet, what is the theological importance of this placement of the church within civil society? As I will examine in the next chapter, and explore in more depth in the final part of this project, the church exists as both an institution within civil society, with particular social roles that it shares with other religious institutions, and as a theological entity – the body of Christ – which has a mission which can be both compatible with and stand in tension with its social role. That dual identity is an important aspect of how I want to describe the church's public role. But in order to do so, I want to turn next to a consideration of the way that the church engages in moral and spiritual formation within civil society.

Chapter 9

Civil Society and the Church's Public Role

Introduction

In the previous chapter, I traced some of the key moments in the development of the idea of civil society. From its roots in the Greek conception of the *polis*, through the development of modern political theory, the idea of civil society has served to describe important elements of human civic life, although its proponents by no means always agreed on what those elements were. For our purposes however, it is important to consider what role the church plays within the complex of social institutions of which it is a part. Furthermore, what is the theological significance of the church's place within the institutional realm of civil society?

In this chapter, I will examine more closely some of the key factors that contribute to an understanding of the role of institutions within civil society. I will then look at two major ways of understanding social pluralism within society in the Christian tradition. The subsidiarity model, a keystone of Catholic social teaching, offers a way of seeing social differentiation as an important element of a just society. The covenantal model, more associated with Protestantism, both converges with and diverges from the subsidiarity model in important ways. After considering these two models, I will turn in the final section to consider how the church exists within society both as a civil institution, functioning as other institutions within civil society, and as a theological entity, existing in the service of the Christian missionary project. Both of these identities will become important for understanding the church's public role in modern society.

The Central Elements of Civil Society

What then are some of the essential elements of civil society in light of this discussion? Certainly there is no one formulation of the structure of civil society that meets with universal assent. However, a number of generalizations can be made.

First, civil society is in some sense a mediating sphere between the individual or family unit and the state.[1] In standing between these two other spheres, it serves the

---

1 As I noted earlier, for Hegel, the family was the realm of the private sphere of life, set apart from civil society. This can also be seen in Tönnies description of the family as a *gemeinschaft*, a private sphere set apart from the public *gesellschaft*. See Ferdinand Tönnies, *Community and Society* (New York: Harper & Row, 1957), 34. Conversely, the more recent reflection on the concept of civil society locates the family within it as an institution among

cause of social cohesion by, on the one hand, not allowing society to be composed of isolated and merely autonomous atoms with no real relationship with one another, and on the other hand not being subsumed by the larger undifferentiated social whole.² The former is a problem that exists within political philosophies that rely too much on the idea of "individual free choice" without an understanding of the checks that are necessary to allow individuals to cohere within a society. This is a classic problem for political theory, visible in both the right and the left, for example, in Rousseau and the French tradition. In seeing society as an imposition on the individual spirit and a chaining of the conscience, Rousseau had romanticized the ability of individuals to come together for the purposes of mutual aid without some mediating structure to refine and organize their actions.

The latter, however, is a problem that can be seen, for example, in Hobbes' anti-revolutionary political philosophy, in which all power derived from and returned to the state as sovereign. There was no mediating space between the individual and the social whole. It is also the flip side of Rousseau's individualism, insofar as he also relies so strongly on the "general will" as the expression of social solidarity, which is willing to coerce participation if members refuse to recognize its sovereignty.³

Second, the sphere of civil society is the realm of association and participation. It exists to create a space within which individuals can form relationships and develop alliances for the purpose of pursuing mutual benefit and development.⁴ Depending

---

other institutions. This is rooted initially in Gramsci's analysis, but has been taken up by the primary theoreticians on the issues. Thus, for example, Jean Cohen writes: "I understand civil society as a sphere of social interaction distinct from economy and state, comprised above all of associations (including the family) and publics." ("Interpreting the Notion of Civil Society," in Walzer, *Toward a Global Civil Society*, 37). The earlier version to which Hegel refers can also be found in Althusius, and can probably be related back to Aristotle's conception of the *oikos* as the foundation of the *polis*. See Elazar, *Covenant and Civil Society*, 21.

2   Both of these dangers are recognized in Emile Durkheim's description of social relationships, as he describes them in *The Division of Labor in Society*. These "abnormal forms" of association result in either an "anomic" or a "forced" relationship among the parts of the social whole, necessitating, in Durkheim's analysis, a renewed attention to mediating forms of association, which contribute to moral formation. He locates these within what he calls "professional groups." He notes: "For a professional morality and code of law to become established within the various professions in the economy, instead of the corporation remaining a conglomerate body lacking unity, it must become, or rather become once more, a well-defined, organized group – in short a public institution." *The Division of Labor in Society* (New York: Free Press, 1984), xxxvi.

3   This should not be read to mitigate Rousseau's influence on Durkheim. As Lewis Coser notes: "In the *Division*, the collective consciousness, a conception that Durkheim largely developed in derivation from Rousseau's 'general will' and Comte's 'consensus,' is conceived as the major cement that binds people in their mechanical solidarity" (Introduction to *The Division of Labor in Society*, xix).

4   This is a key element of the importance of civil society for Bellah and friends. In this realm is the possibility for "civic friendship" recognized and developed and the various institutions of civil society "do manage to communicate a form of life, a *paideia*, in the sense of growing up in a morally and intellectually intelligible world": Robert Bellah, *et al.*, *Habits of the Heart* (Berkeley: University of California Press, 1996), 282. Robert Putnam also points to

on the theory of civil society under consideration, this element within it may include such institutions as political parties and labor unions, but need not. Cohen and Arato envision a model of civil society that utilizes the features of political society developed within the French tradition, and expand and apply it in light of the Gramscian distinction of the economy from civil society. Thus, they view such organizations as existing in a kind of middle position, connecting civil society indirectly to both the state and the economy, without at the same time belonging specifically to either.[5]

Insofar as civil society exists to allow a space for participation in public life, it is important to understand it as enabling social change to take place. But social change need not only take place within the realm of politics. Indeed, the role of the church in civil society is often conceived of not as necessarily involving the direct involvement in politics, but as engaging in a process of moral formation within its own community in such a way that individuals will then participate in the political life of the larger society in a way that is reflective of the church's teaching. Nevertheless, it is at the same time true that most churches within the United States invest some of their resources in direct political activities, either through lobbying agencies, or through contributions to other non-governmental agencies that work to change public opinion on the governmental level. At the same time, these denominations invest even more in social service agencies and charities, which participate through direct action to ameliorate social problems.[6]

Third, civil society has an integrative role insofar as it creates a place within society where individuals can feel affiliated within a larger meaning system, while at the same time not being overwhelmed by or coerced by the size and scope of state power.[7] While as the sphere of mediating institutions civil society provides such a space, as the sphere of social integration it gives that space its meaning and content. What makes the existence of spheres of free association and participation important in a society is precisely that it allows individuals a sense of social cohesion and meaning that is manageable and in which they can perform meaningful work, without being constrained by either political or economic necessity.[8]

Additionally, institutions within civil society often provide meaning-making systems of symbolization and ideology. They offer a *raison d'être* within society that does not exist for the individual as isolated self, the market as realm of exchange, or the state as the realm of social power and coercion, and in fact transcends all

---

this aspect of association in *Bowling Alone* (New York: Simon & Schuster, 2000), and elaborates on the possibilities of this idea (with Lewis Feldstein) in *Better Together* (New York: Simon & Schuster, 2003).

5   See Cohen and Arato, *Civil Society and Political Theory*, 18–20.

6   For discussion of some of these issues, see Ram A. Cnaan, *et al.*, "Bowling Alone But Serving Together: The Congregational Norm of Community Involvement," Mark A. Warrant, "Faith and Leadership in the Inner City: How Social Capital Contributes to Democratic Renewal," and David E. Campbell and Steven J. Yonish, "Religion and Volunteering in America," all in Smidt, ed., *Religion as Social Capital* (Waco, TX: Baylor University Press, 2003). See also Putnam and Feldstein, *Better Together*, particularly Chapter 1 and Chapter 6.

7   See Durkheim, *Division of Labor in Society*, 296–8; Parsons, *The Social System*, 54ff.

8   See Cohen and Arato, *Civil Society and Political Theory*, 22–3.

three.⁹ Individuals cannot make such meaning for themselves (or at least cannot sustain it), and the state has no need for it, since it relies on coercive force. It is within civic institutions that forms of identity (and often critique) are developed and examined.¹⁰ The very existence of "civics" classes in high schools, or the degree of social indoctrination that takes place in a civic institution such as the Boy Scouts or a church youth group points to this integrative role. At the same time, civic institutions can also develop critical and even prophetic perspectives on society, allowing as they do for the articulation of minority perspectives in a friendly atmosphere.¹¹ Thus, for example, black churches in the civil rights era provided a safe space from which to offer critical assessments of the status quo, while at the same time offering a means of being integrated within a smaller society, which accepted African Americans for who they were, rather than on the basis of a racist ideology.¹²

Fourth, civil society is of necessity *pluralistic*, that is, as the sphere of institutions and free association, it necessarily becomes a realm that is resistant to attempts to unify it under a single ideological or political point of view.¹³ If there is only one institution, then there is no civil society, since by definition, civil society is the social sector where a multitude of institutions can compete and cooperate in the marketplace of ideas for the sake of promoting their own ends and agendas.¹⁴ This has both intellectual and activist components. Individuals may join associations

---

9   Durkheim alludes to this in the preface to the 2nd edition of *Division of Labor in Society*, in which he discusses the importance of professional groups in creating spheres of solidarity in modern society. "If anomie is an evil it is above all because society suffers through it, since it cannot exist without cohesion and regulation. Thus, moral or legal rules essentially express social needs which society alone can identify. They rest upon a climate of opinion, and all opinion is a collective matter, the result of being worked out collectively. To be shot of anomie a group must thus exist or be formed within which can be drawn up the system of rules that is now lacking" (xxxv).

10   See Robert Bellah, *The Broken Covenant: American Civil Religion in Time of Trouble* (Chicago: University of Chicago Press, 1992), particularly 164ff.

11   Bellah, echoing the Troeltchian church/sect/mystic typology, notes that the virtues of both the church type's public openness and the sect type's dimension of social critique are necessary in understanding the potential power of public religion: "If there is to be an effective public church in the United States today, bringing the concerns of biblical religion into the common discussion about the nature and future of our society, it will probably have to be one in which the dimensions church, sect, and mysticism all play a significant part, the strengths of each offsetting the deficiencies of the others." *Habits of the Heart*, 246. See Tocqueville, *Democracy in America*, I:915.

12   This points to the ugly underside of civil society as well, in that at the same time it may support organizations that offer salutary moral formation, it also supports institutions that inculcate diabolical ideologies. Thus, the "white citizens councils" during the same era were also institutions of civil society that engaged in an integrative task, but one which may be justly criticized as a perversion of the aim of civil society.

13   See Cohen and Arato, *Civil Society and Political Theory*, 18ff.

14   This is rooted in the Anglo-American conceptualization in the freedom of association, as represented in Locke's *Letter Concerning Toleration* and in Tocqueville's description of the variety of associations in American life. In the German conceptualization of civil society, it is described in Hegel's *Philosophy of Right* as a component of the system of needs, which sets up a

either because they agree with the intellectual basis for its existence, or because it includes activities that are attractive. Most of the time, both elements are present to a greater or lesser degree.

Fifth, civil society is *voluntaristic*. In providing a realm of free association within the larger society in which individual conscience can prevail in the choice of institutional commitment, civil society is necessarily voluntaristic.[15] Persons cannot be compelled to join particular associations or commit themselves to institutions that do not reflect their own point of view. This principle flows from the integrative dimension of civil society, in that in order for individuals within society to be able to socially adjust to the reality of social life, they must be free to choose the institutions to which they are themselves inclined to gravitate, rather than be forced into institutions to which they are not drawn. While many an athletic parent may wish their son were the star quarterback rather than a philatelist, it is essential to the moral and psychological development of the child that he be allowed to associate himself where he wishes.[16]

The institutions of civil society come in myriad forms. They include not only institutions specifically dedicated to civic integration and participation, but voluntary associations committed to providing social services, philosophical or artistic or naturalistic interests, as well as religious interests. The complexity of institutions within civil society makes it difficult to pin down the ways in which civil society can be spoken of as a singular *thing* rather than simply as a mash of different things grouped together under a single heading. However, this discussion ought to serve to demonstrate the ways in which civil society is a particular mode of social being in the larger whole of society. By mediating between the individual and the state, civil society provides a means of social cohesion that, as Gramsci noted (not necessarily positively), serves to stabilize modern society and enable it to sustain itself in the midst of changing circumstances. Societies based either on kinship systems or state mandate cannot be so flexible and thus are less able to respond to altered conditions.[17]

Additionally, civil society has the potential to break down and transcend the fetters of its relationship to particular nation-states and move into an international and potentially global arena. Recent reflection on the emergence of a *global* civil society demonstrates that the various tasks of civil society are not limited to its effectiveness for a particular country, but can create associations among members

---

variety of mediating institutions in the public sphere of society. See Robert Putnam's discussion of the issue in *Bowling Alone*, 337ff.

15 In the United States, this point is particularly important with regard to ecclesial membership. With a constitutional separation of church and state, there is no external compulsion for individuals to join churches or religious organizations. The free-choice element of religious involvement is a distinctive characteristic of the American understanding of civil society, as compared, for example, to Germany. Tocqueville noted this as well. See *Democracy in America*, I:305ff.

16 See Parsons, *The Social System*, 36ff.

17 See Durkheim, *The Division of Labor in Society*, 334.

around the world.[18] In writing of the nature of governance on a global stage, David Held and Anthony McGrew write:

> With the global communications revolution, citizens' groups and NGOs have acquired new and more effective ways to organize across national frontiers and to participate in the governance of global affairs. Whereas for much of the twentieth century international diplomacy was essentially an activity conducted between consenting states, the existence of suprastate organizations, such as the UN and the WTO, has created new arenas in which the voice of peoples – as opposed to simply governments – is increasingly heard. Some view this as a global associational revolution in which citizens, communities and private interests organize to influence the conduct and content of global governance. Across the entire global agenda, on issues from the ecological to the ecumenical, NGOs and transnational movements give expression to the concerns and interests of an emerging transnational civil society.[19]

The mediating function of civil society thus can no longer be said to be limited to the translation of interest and identity between individuals and states, *per se*. It rises above the state as a locus of concern and takes in the entire world. The nature of the church as an institution is itself exhibit number one on this point. The church, in the broad ecumenical sense, is not limited by national boundaries (although in the case of some national churches, it may lean in that direction). The World Council of Churches and the World Alliance of Reformed Churches, as well as the Roman Catholic and Anglican Communions, are evidence of the international reach and scope of the church as an institution.[20]

I will now turn to look at the way in which the church's role in a larger social context has been understood in two of its most influential theoretical incarnations: the idea of subsidiarity in Roman Catholicism, and the covenantal theories that emerged from the Reformed tradition.

Subsidiarity and Covenantal Association in Catholic and Protestant Analysis

A key distinction in the question of civil society, as it relates to Christian discourse, is the model of society with which one works. There are two central models that are

---

18 See Albert Paolini, *Between Sovereignty and Global Governance: The United Nations, The State, and Civil Society* (London: Macmillan, 1998); Riva Krut, *Globalization and Civil Society: NGO Influence in International Decision-Making* (UN Research Institute for Social Development, 1997); Benjamin Barber, *Jihad vs. McWorld*, rev. edn (New York: Ballantine Books, 2001); William F. Schultz, *In Our Own Best Interest: How Defending Human Rights Benefits Us All* (Boston: Beacon Press, 2001).

19 David Held and Anthony McGrew, *Globalization/Anti-Globalization* (Oxford: Blackwell, 2002), 68.

20 And particularly as the institutional identity of the church shifts more to the southern hemisphere, the global concerns of the church may shift as well. Concerns which were pressing when the impetus for action in the church came primarily from Europe and North America may come to seem less important, while issues related to the concerns of Africa and Latin America move to the fore. See Philip Jenkins, *The Next Christendom: The Coming of Global Christianity* (London: Oxford University Press, 2002).

preeminent in this discussion. The first is the subsidiarity model most fully explored and developed within the Roman Catholic tradition. The second is the covenantal model, developed within the Protestant, and particularly the Reformed tradition. In this section, I will consider both models, each of which fruitfully contributes to a fuller understanding of a Christian interpretation of civil society.

The subsidiarity model was first articulated as a theory of social and religious organization in a comprehensive sense by Leo XIII in the encyclical *Rerum Novarum*.[21] Paul Sigmund refers to this as "the founding document of modern Catholic social thought."[22] It was more fully developed by Pius XI in *Quadragesimo Anno*[23] and by John Paul II in *Centismus Annus*.[24] During this period, it underwent development, as I will discuss. Its elements can also be seen in the development of the U.S. Catholic bishops' letter *Economic Justice for All*,[25] which I will also discuss.

Rerum Novarum is primarily a dual critique of both the socialist movements of the late 19th century and the abuses of capitalism during the same period. Its first target is socialism, which, according to the encyclical "is highly unjust, because it violates the rights of lawful owners, perverts the functions of the State, and throws governments into utter confusion."[26] Private property and the institutions of civil society are given by God for the purpose of the preservation of the social order. The complex differentiation of creation is the intention of God. Socialism, according to the interpretation of this encyclical, breaks down the naturally differentiated order to overcome social inequalities, but in so doing, it "injures the very ones whom it seeks to help, contravenes the natural rights of individual persons, and throws the functions of the State and public peace into confusion."[27]

Nevertheless, this is not to say that *Rerum Novarum* offers an unqualified support of a kind of *laissez-faire* capitalism. At the same time it supports the existence of traditional economic and familial structures, it also supports the right of workers to organize for the preservation of their own rights in the workplace. Employers are exhorted to give their workers their due: "Assuredly, to establish a rule of play in accord with justice, many factors must be taken into account. But, in general, the rich and employers should remember that no laws, either human or divine, permit them for their own profit to oppress the needy and the wretched or to seek gain from another's want."[28]

---

21 Leo XIII, *Rerum Novarum* (Boston: St. Paul Editions). Originally promulgated, 1891.

22 Paul Sigmund, "Subsidiarity, Solidarity, and Liberation," in Lugo, ed,, *Religion, Pluralism, and Public Life*, 208. One must note that "subsidiarity" as a descriptive term for social organization does not appear in the encyclical, although the idea that the term embodies does.

23 Pius XI, "Quadragesimo Anno," in Skillen and McCarthy, eds, *Political Order and the Plural Structure of Society*. Originally promulgated, 1931.

24 John Paul II, *Centismus Annus* (Boston: St. Paul Editions). Originally promulgated, 1991.

25 National Conference of Catholic Bishops, *Economic Justice for All* (Washington, D.C.: United States Catholic Conference, 1986) (hereafter USCCB).

26 Leo XIII, *Rerum Novarum*, 7.

27 Leo XIII, *Rerum Novarum*, 15.

28 Leo XIII, *Rerum Novarum*, 19.

A few points ought to be noted about the lines of argument laid out in this encyclical. First, although subsidiarity itself does not make an appearance in this document, its argument is rooted in the diversity of civil society. This diversity itself is rooted in God's design for social order. In this social order, there is a hierarchical structure, in which various institutions are organized relative to one another – thus, individual, familial, social and political life are intertwined in an organic system of relations.[29]

Second, rights and responsibilities of these various institutions are emphasized. With regard to both workers and employers it is pointed out that they are accountable to God as well as their social setting for their various activities. The state has a responsibility to hold the various members of society to their tasks. "Therefore, those governing the State ought primarily to devote themselves to the service of individual groups and of the whole commonwealth, and through the entire scheme of laws and institutions to cause both public and individual well-being to develop spontaneously out of the very structure and administration of the State. For this is the duty of wise statesmanship and the essential office of those in charge of the State."[30]

Finally, the key to the theological understanding of the structure of society is the idea of the "common good" – that all institutions of society have a responsibility to promote, not simply their own individual goods and aims, but the good of the whole.[31]

These themes are developed and expanded in *Quadragesimo Anno*, and the term "subsidiarity" is introduced to describe the division of labor that is to be sought among institutions within society. Once again, the primary targets are socialism and liberalism, but the context also raises questions about how the church is to respond to fascism. Although mistaken by some as an endorsement of fascist corporatism, the encyclical is in fact a sharp criticism of it.[32]

In the encyclical, subsidiarity is elaborated as a process by which "the supreme authority of the State" allows "subordinate groups" authority over subsidiary areas of institutional life.[33] It is not for the state to have sole control over every aspect of human endeavor, but rather "those in command should be sure that the more perfectly a graduated order is preserved among the various associations, in observance of the

---

29 See Paul Sigmund, "Subsidiarity, Solidarity, and Liberation," 209.

30 Leo XIII, *Rerum Novarum*, 29.

31 Leo XIII, *Rerum Novarum*, 43. The encyclical makes the distinction between "public" and "private" societies. It notes that "Although private societies exist within the State and are, as it were, so many parts of it, still it is not within the authority of the State universally and *per se* to forbid them to exist as such" (44). It is noteworthy that the state is seen in this document as the encompassing institution to which others are subordinate. This is an element that, as Sigmund notes *contra* Skillen and McCarthy, has faded from recent Catholic social thought. (See, Sigmund, "Subsidiarity, Solidarity, and Liberation," 219). See David Hollenbach, *The Common Good and Christian Ethics* (New York: Cambridge University Press, 2002).

32 See Skillen and McCarthy, eds, *Political Order and the Plural Structure of Society*, 173 n.13.

33 Pius XI, "Quadragesimo Anno," 167.

principle of 'subsidiary function,' the stronger social authority and effectiveness will be, and the happier and more prosperous the condition of the State."[34]

Once again, the justification for this arrangement is the health of the social whole.[35] Individuals ought to be free to engage in any number of associations voluntarily and without state compulsion, for whatever purposes they desire. Once again, Pius XI specifies the need for the allowance of workers to organize, but he notes that labor organizations are not the only institutions that are good and necessary for a vibrant social life:

> Moreover, just as inhabitants of a town are wont to found associations with the widest diversity of purposes, which each is quite free to join or not, so those engaged in the same industry or profession will combine with one another into associations equally free for purposes connected in some manner with the pursuit of the calling itself. Since these associations are clearly and lucidly explained by Our predecessor of illustrious memory, We consider it enough to emphasize this one point: People are quite free not only to found such associations, which are a matter of private order and private right, but also in respect to them "freely to adopt the organization and the rules which they judge most appropriate to achieve their purpose." The same freedom must be asserted for founding associations that go beyond the boundaries of individual callings. And may these free organizations, now flourishing and rejoicing in their salutary fruits, be set before themselves the task of preparing the way, in conformity with the mind of Christian social teaching, for those larger and more important Guilds, Industries, and Professions, which We mentioned before, and make every possible effort to bring them to realization.[36]

All legitimate forms of associational life are essential for the health of the social organism. And furthermore, as Pius notes, it is not simply imprudent, but actually *immoral* for higher institutions to take over the tasks of properly functioning subsidiary organizations: "Just as it is gravely wrong to take from individuals what they can accomplish by their own initiative and industry and give it to the community, so also it is an injustice and at the same time a grave evil and disturbance of right order to assign to a greater and higher association what lesser and subordinate organizations can do."[37] As all members of society exist as parts of a cohesive social whole, however, they all share a common lot. This element has been discussed recently under the category of "solidarity," especially in the context of the debates around liberation theology, where this term has become particularly prominent.

The critiques of both encyclicals of liberalism also encompass a critique of democratic forms of governance, as Paul Sigmund notes: "Despite the fact that incipient or functioning Christian Democratic parties were emerging in many countries in Europe, the Vatican still harbored a suspicion of democracy as inherently anticlerical."[38] However, Sigmund also notes that the hierarchical view of subsidiarity has developed in the century of discussion around it to more and more acceptance of

---

34 Pius XI, "Quadragesimo Anno," 167.
35 Pius XI, "Quadragesimo Anno," 170.
36 Pius XI, "Quadragesimo Anno," 168–9.
37 Pius XI, "Quadragesimo Anno," 166–7.
38 Paul Sigmund, "Subsidiarity, Solidarity, and Liberation," 210.

democratic principles of governance.[39] Nevertheless, if the ideas of the common good and social solidarity imply that there must be a comprehending institution that, as it were, has "veto power" over the plurality of forms of institutional life, then there is a risk to democratic governance in the principle of subsidiarity. However, the recent uses of the principle, particularly in the U.S. Catholic bishops' document *Economic Justice for All*, affirm a strong view of pluralistic democracy. In their affirmation of the need for a participatory, or "contributive" form of justice in society,[40] as well as in their rejection of "statist and totalitarian" solutions to problems of economic life,[41] the bishops affirm the need for a democratic form of common life in which all members of society have a right to participation. Of particular interest is the red thread that runs through the entire discourse on subsidiarity – namely, that it is rooted, from *Rerum Novarum* onwards, in terms of the principles of human rights.[42] This is made a central tenet of the bishops' letter, as they note that "Catholic social teaching spells out the basic demands of justice in greater detail in the human rights of every person. These fundamental rights are prerequisites for a dignified life in community."[43] They note that "These rights are bestowed on human beings by God and grounded in the nature and dignity of human persons. They are not created by society. Indeed, society has a duty to secure and protect them"[44] Those things that are enumerated as basic human rights, such as not only political and civil rights, but also rights to "life, food, clothing, shelter, rest, medical care, and basic education" are considered as minimal, rather than an exhaustive, list of what is required for human provision.[45] They are, as the bishops note: "the minimum conditions for life in community"[46]

Skillen and McCarthy, in their criticism of the principle of subsidiarity, note that it "does not ... seem to safeguard society from moving in either a collectivist or an individualist direction. It does not appear strong enough to resist purely pragmatic tendencies whether coming from above or below."[47] This may be a debatable presumption, but it may serve as a transition to the other major theory, which Skillen and McCarthy prefer, namely, the covenantal view of social pluralism.

The covenantal view of social pluralism developed out of the Reformed approach to Christian theology in the 16th century and following.[48] First articulated by Heinrich Bullinger, it derived the plural character of society from the affirmation

---

39 See Paul Sigmund, "Subsidiarity, Solidarity, and Liberation," 210.
40 USCCB, *Economic Justice for All*, 36.
41 USCCB, *Economic Justice for All*, 60.
42 See Leo XIII, *Rerum Novarum*, 10.
43 USCCB, *Economic Justice for All*, 40.
44 USCCB, *Economic Justice for All*, 41.
45 USCCB, *Economic Justice for All*, 41.
46 USCCB, *Economic Justice for All*, 40.
47 Skillen and McCarthy, eds, *Political Order and the Plural Structure of Society*, 388–9.
48 Of course, as Daniel Elazar described so thoroughly in his four-volume series, *The Covenantal Tradition in Politics*, the roots of this tradition extend as far back as biblical Israel and the covenantal structure of God's relationship to his chosen people. Its development in the Reformation period drew upon these biblical themes for its elaboration, and justified its own perspective on the basis of this view of God as the One who covenants with his people.

that God's covenant with humankind encompassed both spiritual and social life: "The covenant was, therefore, the centerpiece of the Christian religion and the cornerstone of the Christian state. It was the moral foundation of society and of religion."[49] Bullinger discussed the concept of covenant or *foedus* at length, arguing that the covenant of God that was given by God to Adam and Eve, and Abraham and his descendents, continues through the history of Christianity (and furthermore, that the origin of Christianity is in fact found in the covenant of God with Adam and Eve).[50] This covenant ought to dictate for Christians the entirety of the way they should live their lives, and thus extends to the administration of law and authority of the magistrates.[51] As McCoy notes, Bullinger's approach to covenant did not deal with social complexity in the way that subsequent federal thinkers would, although it does have some traces of that element.

It is Johannes Althusius who developed the covenantal tradition into a kind of pluralistic political federalism, in which various offices were distinguished by the agreements and associations of the various members. Daniel Elazar notes that "the foundations of Althusius' political philosophy are covenantal through and through. *Pactum* (covenant) is the only basis for legitimate political organization."[52]

Althusius's political theory is rooted in a doctrine of "consociation" (*consociendai*) or association.[53] Members of society exist "symbiotically" with one another.[54] He writes that the citizens or "symbiotes" "pledge themselves each to the other, by explicit or tacit agreement, to mutual communication of whatever is useful and necessary for the harmonious exercise of social life."[55] Rather than a unitary social unit, however, the symbiotic relations among persons in society are organized into various compartments of life, some private, some public.[56] But the aim of all human associations is to contribute to the happiness of the social whole. Thus, Althusius notes that "a commonwealth is best and happiest when magistrates and citizens bring everything together for its welfare and advantage, and neither neglect nor despise anyone who can be helpful to the commonwealth."[57]

See Elazar, *Covenant & Polity in Biblical Israel*, *Covenant and Commonwealth*, *Covenant & Constitutionalism*, and *Covenant and Civil Society*.

49 Charles McCoy and J. Baker, "Heinrich Bullinger and the Origins of the Federal Tradition," in *Fountainhead of Federalism: Heinrich Bullinger and the Covenantal Tradition* (Louisville: Westminster/John Knox Press, 1991), 26–7.

50 See Heinrich Bullinger, "The One and Eternal Testament or Covenant of God," in *Fountainhead of Federalism*, 134.

51 See Bullinger, "The One and Eternal Testament or Covenant of God," 114.

52 Daniel Elazar, "Althusius' Grand Design for a Federal Commonwealth," in Johannes Althusius, *Politica* (Indianapolis: Liberty Fund, 1995), xli.

53 Althusius, *Politica*, 17.

54 Althusius, *Politica*, 17.

55 Althusius, *Politica*, 17.

56 Althusius, *Politica*, 27.

57 Althusius, *Politica*, 22.

Althusius's understanding of social pluralism is such that he recognizes the internal integrity of various social institutions, including foundationally the family.[58] God has called together the various persons into society for mutual aid and benefit. Althusius writes:

> From what has been said, we further conclude that the efficient cause of political association is consent and agreement among the communicating citizens. The formal cause is indeed the association brought about by contributing and communicating one with the other, in which political men institute, cultivate, maintain, and conserve the fellowship of human life through decisions about those things useful and necessary to this social life. The final cause of politics is the enjoyment of a comfortable, useful, and happy life, and of the common welfare – that we may live with piety and honor a peaceful and quiet life, that while true piety toward God and justice among the citizens may prevail at home, defense against the enemy from abroad may be maintained, and that concord and peace may always and everywhere thrive. The final cause is also a conservation of a human society that aims at a life in which you can worship God quietly and without error. The material of politics is the aggregate of precepts for communicating those things, services, and right that we bring together, each fairly and properly according to this ability, for symbiosis and the common advantage of the social life.[59]

In the interests of this social concord and flourishing, individuals may associate in a variety of ways, including not only the family and the commonwealth, but other associations as well: "Voluntary associations may establish their own statutes in the framework of public law and in harmony with their *jus commune*, which is customarily written in the association's records."[60] Indeed, the existence of a diversity of modes of associational life was essential to the good of society:

> Althusius emphasized that the greatest safeguards for liberty were to be found in the structuring of the body politic into five permanent associations: two private – the family and the collegium – and three public – the city, the province, and the commonwealth. It was through those permanent structures that individuals were able to function, to be represented, and to preserve their liberties. The private sphere was real and was protected not by abstract principle alone but by the constitutional authority and political power of the family and the collegium as private institutions. The individual for Althusius (as for the Bible) was a reality because every individual was created in God's image with his or her own soul. But individuals did not stand naked in the face of powerful public institutions, rather they were protected by being located within families and collegia.[61]

---

58 I say "foundationally" because Althusius begins with a discussion of the family as the root of those private associations of persons out of which other social institutions emerge. Theologically, this can be seen as rooted in the primal relationship of Adam and Eve. Althusius also seems to be following the Aristotelian approach, in which the commonwealth develops from familial relations.

59 Althusius, *Politica*, 24.

60 Elazar, *Covenant and Commonwealth*, 321.

61 Elazar, *Covenant and Commonwealth*, 316. The collegia were the various independent associations in society into which individuals freely entered for mutual support and enrichment. Thus, for example, universities, guilds, and churches all represented collegia within society. "Secular collegia are those composed of magistrates and judges or people engaged in common

This rooting of social life in the belief in God's covenantal will for humanity had striking implications for the political development of Europe and the United States. Particularly in those lands where Reformed Christianity predominated, the idea that society was held together by covenantal bonds among diverse people in multiple consociations in society was raised to the level of religious obligation, and public responsibility was made a question of faith. The Puritans were particularly innovative in this regard. They "wove together covenantal theories of citizenship, political structure, and history to lay the foundation for modern federalism. Moreover, this theory was not detached speculation but a reflection of their activity in establishing covenanted churches and public associations to secure the common good."[62]

The stream of covenantal thought developed by Abraham Kuyper provides another dimension of its relationship to the idea of social pluralism. Kuyper's development of the idea of "spheres of sovereignty" emerged out of his own Calvinist presuppositions about the covenantal nature of society, and the appropriate social organization that this entailed.

As with the subsidiarity view, Kuyper approached covenantal life as an organic whole.[63] Calvinism, as a "life-system," for Kuyper establishes, as for Bullinger, a comprehensive way of looking at the world, rooted in covenant with God. Kuyper excoriates those social contract theories of governance that are rooted in both popular sovereignty and the sovereignty of the State, arguing that they ignore the central role of God in the vitality of social life.[64] Rather God has ordained the various spheres of society to have their own sovereign role, which cannot be abrogated by others. Kuyper notes:

---

agricultural, industrial, or commercial pursuits. An ecclesiastical collegium is composed of clergymen, philosophers and teachers" (316). Note that both economic and ecclesiastical institutions are represented as collegia, in a way that is distinct from Hegel's division of institutions within civil society.

62 William Johnson Everett, *God's Federal Republic: Reconstructing Our Governing Symbol* (New York: Paulist Press, 1988), 112.

63 See Abraham Kuyper, *The Problem of Poverty* (Grand Rapids: Baker, 1991), 52. Skillen and McCarthy seem critical of the specific way in which the subsidiarity tradition goes about establishing the organic unity of society, preferring the covenantal view of Kuyper, but they do not seem to criticize an organic view of society *per se* (as long as it is properly construed as clearly differentiated and pluralistic). The key distinction is between the view of organism as representing a unity in the subsidiarity tradition, and representing a harmony of the whole in Kuyper's approach. See Skillen and McCarthy, eds, *Political Order and the Plural Structure of Society*, 382–9. Kuyper makes an important distinction between the state and society in this regard, as the state is deemed to be a mechanical structure, whereas society is organic (See Kuyper, *Lectures on Calvinism*, 91). Heslam writes: "In stressing the organic nature of society, Kuyper was reacting not only to individualism but also to the mechanicism and scientism prevalent in the intellectual world at the end of the nineteenth century. In opposition to these theories, which taught that society was governed by neutral forces that operated in terms of cause and effect, he argued that society should instead be understood as a moral (*zedelijk*) organism, in the sense that it was held together by groups sharing common philosophical positions." Peter S. Heslam, *Creating a Christian Worldview* (Grand Rapids: Eerdmans, 1998), 155.

64 See Kuyper, *Lectures on Calvinism*, 85–8.

In many different directions we see therefore that sovereignty in one's own sphere asserts itself – 1. In the social sphere, by personal superiority. 2. In the corporative sphere of the universities, guilds, associations, etc. 3. In the domestic sphere of the family and of married life, and 4. In communal autonomy.

In all these four spheres the state-government cannot impose its laws, but must reverence the innate law of life. God rules in these spheres, just as supremely and sovereignly through his chosen *virtuosi*, as He exercises dominion in the sphere of the State itself, through his chosen *magistrates*.[65]

The sovereignty of God and the divine will establish incontrovertibly the independence of the various spheres of society, so that it cannot be said that either state fiat or popular will has any right to overtake the duties of these spheres.

Max Stackhouse selectively draws on these traditions to accent similar themes in his own consideration of the intersection of public theology and civil society. As with Kuyper, he roots his approach in a covenantal understanding of social pluralism, arguing that preserving a well-ordered social pluralism is central to a healthy civic life. "It simply is not the case that civil society can remain healthy if family life dies, if schools decay, the arts degenerate, and businesses close."[66] With Kuyper, Stackhouse recognizes the various social spheres as having a sovereignty with regard to one another, which should not be violated lightly. Civil society is, Stackhouse argues, "a wider arena, where church members participate in forming the potentially covenanted groups of the common life, each one having a vocation into which the others ought not unduly intrude, but all subject to influence by a religiously informed social ethics able to carry beyond the church gathered in worship."[67]

In this view, covenant is closely affiliated with the idea of vocation in Christian life, and both together illuminate the plural character of human social life: "The concept of vocation not only relates to our personal lives but has direct meanings for a multiplicity of public institutions as well."[68] Vocation is not simply a matter of individual callings, and it is certainly not to be confused with the identification of a career. Vocation is rather the calling that each individual and institution has to follow God in a particular way. Stackhouse continues:

> Putting the matter this way, to be sure, means that this concept of vocation bears within it a theological conviction about pluralism in society, one in which creation and history require multiple "spheres," "arenas," or "orders" of life. Each one must ask, "why do we exist as a community?" Schools and colleges, courts of law and hospitals, art museums and research institutes, manufacturing corporations and labor unions, churches and legislatures – all have distinctive vocations. They are called to fulfill certain functions of and for humanity, and they must do so with excellence and clarity of purpose, or they are subject to either critique and transformation or destruction. If a university becomes a political party or a psychiatric center, if a corporation becomes a military camp or a charity organization, if a church becomes a museum or a court of law, it has betrayed its central vocation. Each

---

65 Kuyper, *Lectures on Calvinism*, 96. Italics in original.
66 Max Stackhouse, *et al.*, *Christian Social Ethics in a Global Era* (Nashville: Abingdon Press, 1995), 27.
67 Stackhouse, *Christian Social Ethics in a Global Era*, 27.
68 Stackhouse, *Public Theology and Political Economy*, 25.

sector of the common life is called by God to define, obey and enhance the specific values and purposes that are proper to it.[69]

Covenant ties into this as the ordering principle from which the proper relations among persons and institutions are derived and understood. It serves as the bond of obligation that ties social actors together in communal responsibility.[70]

Within institutional life, this communal responsibility entails the preservation of certain basic institutional forms that are necessary for the survival of any society. Stackhouse lists five such institutions: The family, political institutions, economic institutions, a cultural-linguistic system, and religion.[71] He argues, along similar lines to Kuyper, that in order to preserve a well-ordered social life, these institutional spheres need to remain distinct from one another: "Something is lost to civilization if any one of these systems is collapsed into one or several of the others. If, for example, family life becomes only a means of economic gain, political power, or adaptation to cultural stereotypes, something of the innate dynamic of human sexuality is destroyed and is likely to appear in distorted forms elsewhere in the society."[72]

Of additional interest for Stackhouse is the question of how the various professions, as expressions of individual vocations in the midst of a pluralistic society, should be understood. The various forms of professional life in modern society, such as teaching, law, medicine, or art, have been shaped by Christian theological reflection and/or missionary activity in arriving at their modern form. In the case of teaching, for example, Stackhouse writes that, although institutions for instruction are common in all societies, the development of Western education through Christian ministry has a distinctive form:

> What was important about these schools is that they were distinct in principle and in social organization from the core institutions of life and thus provided an area of critical learning that took the student outside of the direct control of these institutions. Schools abstract people from their primary involvements and allow them to develop analytical tools with which to critically evaluate the structures and dynamics of the core institutions.[73]

---

69 Stackhouse, *Public Theology and Political Economy*, 25–6.

70 Stackhouse, *Public Theology and Political Economy*, 26. Stackhouse notes elsewhere in a similar vein: "According to the biblical view, humans are free in the sense that we can and must make choices, but we are not free to do whatever we wish. We have the most profound aspects of human identity *conferred* upon us in love by a reality beyond us. To that we *must* be faithful – not in the sense that we are, as puppets, manipulated to, but that we ought to, if we are to be truly human." Stackhouse, *Creeds, Society, and Human Rights* (Grand Rapids: Eerdmans, 1984), 34. Here we see the close tie of vocation and covenant once again. In vocation, we have the most important elements of our identity given to us, and this leads us into relationships of responsibility, with the source of that identity, but also with other human beings.

71 Stackhouse, *Public Theology and Political Economy*, 163–4. See also *God and Globalization*, where these ideas are more fully explored.

72 Stackhouse, *Public Theology and Political Economy*, 164.

73 Stackhouse, *Public Theology and Political Economy*, 168.

In other words, such institutions, emerging from the Christian vocation to seek God in covenantal responsibility, offer an arena of differentiation through which individuals can come to a clearer awareness of who they are within their various social roles.

These various professions are linked with particular institutions of civil society, and thus civil society is affected by the Christian understanding of vocational responsibility in covenant. Covenant as an idea thus extends beyond the intra-Christian understanding of the relationship between God and the Church as a theological institution. Rather, the idea of covenant also encompasses the sociological effects of the church's role as a civic institution. The theological dimension cannot be isolated only in the church's self-understanding, for it has repercussions for what the church does sociologically and in the persons created through its action.

Similar things could be said with regard to the Catholic doctrine of subsidiarity. In providing a framework through which institutional life can be theologically conceived, and by virtue of which institutional pluralism can be understood to be not only possible but also necessary for the proper organization of social life, the doctrine of subsidiarity contributes to the theological reflection on civil society, aiding in understanding the public implication of theological issues.

These two theoretical constructions for the plurality of public life in society have been the dominant modes of theological reflection in the 20th century on the nature of the differentiation within society and on the Christian attitude toward such diversity. They have allowed both Catholics and Protestants, in their respective ways, to engage in the complexity of social life and to militate for or against particular policies or organizations that are deemed to reflect or stand contrary to their own aims or the public good. This has been fruitful for democratic development and has offered the church a way of maintaining its integrity in the face of competing social claims. Let us turn now to consider the way that the church exercises that integrity in the midst of a complex social matrix.

The Church's Public Responsibility

It has certainly not been universally recognized that the church is an institution of civil society. Hegel, in particular, was notable for putting the church within the realm of the state, as I noted above, due to the way religion was made territorial and a matter of the prince's preference at Westphalia. But in the United States, the question of the status of religious life and the church's role evolved according to the outlines described by the covenantal tradition that influenced Locke, rather than the statist approach of Hegel. The question of the public relevance of religion thus becomes a question of the degree to which churches are entities independent of state control, and can thus wield an independent influence on the consciences of their members while at the same time fulfilling the roles mandated for institutions within civil society.

But the question then becomes what the status of the church actually is among the various institutions that constitute civil society. As discussed above, civil society contains not only the so-called "civic" organizations, such as the Kiwanis Club or Chamber of Commerce, but also associations dedicated to a wide variety of interests, including religious interests. Whether it be the Roman Catholic Church, or the Theosophical Society, groups who come together for the purpose of exploring the nature of religious truth constitute precisely the kind of interest group that fits within civil society precisely *because* they take the individual outside of him or herself and family into a larger compass of human association, and yet preserve the individual from being swallowed into a unitary social organism.

The church as a social institution provides a sphere of conscience into which an individual may enter for the purposes of meaning-making and solidarity with others, and yet which is neither compulsory nor transitory. Religious institutions in general fulfill their social function by providing a stability and cohesion which allows individuals to decide their own level of involvement and participation, and which at the same time encourages a greater degree of participation than the minimum.[74] It is within the context of such a safe space that the church (as well as other religious institutions), can fulfill the various roles that are required of an institution in civil society.

The church fulfills its integrative role within society in part through its person-forming activity. Through the inculcation of values in its members, and an understanding of the necessity for Christian faith to work itself out in the world through good work, the church develops in its members an appreciation for the social responsibility incumbent upon them. Thus, through work in missions, charity, face-to-face work with those in need, or participation in the various social events sponsored by the church, members come to understand themselves as related to a social context that is both larger than themselves, and yet itself associated with an even greater social context.

This integrative role within the church may be connected with the idea of evangelism, or the bringing of the good news to others.[75] Often it will involve becoming associated with people whom the members would never have met individually, and taking part in events that as individuals the members would never have considered, or which would not have been accessible to them.[76]

Additionally, the church does indeed, as Peter Berger points out, create a meaning-making structure for human life, and give resources to allow individuals to resist a sense of *anomie* and dislocation.[77] The "human world" which the church

---

74 Thus, while the individual may become associated within a religious organization simply by attending worship regularly, the complex web of relationships, which develops through that association, only manifests itself when the individual interacts with and participates in other activities with the members of that community. While worship is indeed the central function of most religious communities, part of their function within civil society is to allow individuals to forge those relationships that can be pursued outside of the worship experience. See Cnaan, *et al.*, "Bowling Alone But Serving Together" in Smidt, ed., *Religion as Social Capital*.

75 See Steven S. Maughan, "Civic Culture, Women's Foreign Missions, and the British Imperial Imagination, 1860–1914," in Trentman, ed., *Paradoxes of Civil Society* (New York: Berghan Books, 2000), 199–222.

76 See Robert Putnam, *Bowling Alone*, 66.

77 Thus, as a process of "world construction," Berger argues, religion serves the purpose of aiding in the ordering of social life. He writes: "Religion is the human enterprise by which a sacred cosmos is established. Put differently, religion is cosmization in a sacred mode. By sacred

represents provides a narrative in which the individual, as a member of the "body of Christ" can have significance as an individual as well as a sense of belonging as part of a group. The sociological significance of Paul's metaphor of the body (1 Cor. 12:12–31) cannot be underestimated, as he recognized within this image that individuals need both of those aspects – individual significance and belonging – to be integrated within the social system. The absence of a sense of the person as an individual leads to a loss of identity and an inability to take initiative or make independent judgments, while at the same time the lack of a sense of belonging deprives the person of important elements in socialization. The results in either deficiency can be dire.[78]

At the same time, there is a danger of too much emphasis on the integrative role of the church to the exclusion of other roles. The church may do a very good job of integrating the individual into its own worldview and outlook, but if it is not at the same time connected to a recognition of the larger social space in which both the individual and the church operate, then the result is not a properly functioning institution within civil society, but rather a failure of the institution actually to be civil. The resultant sectarianism separates the church from the society in an inauthentic and self-deceptive way.[79] Thus, it is important to keep this aspect of the church's social role in tension with the others.

The second role of the church within civil society is connected with its task of *participation*. As William Everett points out, the public church is a "theaterola" in which individuals can develop and practice a public persona through which they may relate to society, both as a whole and in its various parts.[80] By providing a space for social participation, the church develops persons as actors in the larger social play, in which they may regard themselves and be regarded by others as necessary for the proper functioning of the institution. Thus, persons learn what it means to be responsible, not only for themselves, but also for others and for a community as a whole. Within the church, persons begin to learn the value of *publicity* through which they may interact with and engage the world.[81]

This does, however, imply a particular kind of church. It implies that the church as an institution is in some sense democratic and participatory. The more hierarchically a church defines itself, and the less important the role of the laity is within the overall

---

is meant here a quality of mysterious and awesome power, other than man and yet related to him, which is believed to reside in certain objects of experience." Peter Berger, *The Sacred Canopy* (Garden City, NY: Anchor Books, 1969), 25.

78 See Emile Durkheim, *Suicide: A Study in Sociology* (Glencoe, IL: Free Press, 1951). Berger notes: "To be in society is to be 'sane' precisely in the sense of being shielded from the ultimate 'insanity' of such anomic terror. Anomy is unbearable to the point where the individual may seek death in preference to it. Conversely, existence within a nomic world may be sought at the cost of all sorts of sacrifice and suffering – and even at the cost of life itself, if the individual believes that the ultimate sacrifice has nomic significance." *The Sacred Canopy*, 22.

79 Inauthentic, because the church in these circumstances denies an essential element of its being in the world; self-deceptive, because it does so by assuming that it can be something that it cannot be – a socially isolated being.

80 William Johnson Everett, *God's Federal Republic*, 157.

81 Everett, *God's Federal Republic*, 135–44.

decision-making and water-carrying aspects of the church, the less effectively it is going to carry out this task. The more that the church encourages individual initiative vis-à-vis the institution and allows space for persons to take on leadership roles within the ecclesial body, the more likely it will be that the members will develop this sense of participation and publicity with regard to it.[82]

This is not, however, to imply that members of churches with more hierarchical structures are incapable of developing this sense of participation and publicity. Rather, it is simply that they may not learn it from the church, or may learn it only in the way other church traditions have shaped the culture. One of the advantages of civil society is precisely in its ability to answer social needs in a variety of ways within one society. While the church may in some cases not be capable of developing certain characteristics of the person, other institutions may.[83]

Again, another role that the church can fulfill vis-à-vis its function within civil society is precisely in its character as a voluntary association. This is an element that is key to understanding how the church functions in the United States. James Luther Adams and H.R. Niebuhr were both impressed by this flexibility implied in the kind of social movement that occurs around churches.[84] Whatever the possible objections to his analysis, Niebuhr did point out that where one begins religiously need not be where one ends. Rather, within the United States in particular we see religion largely as a matter of choice.[85] Being born into a particular religious community does not necessarily mean that one is destined to remain there. Indeed, persons may often switch religious affiliations a number of times over the course of a lifetime.

This is not necessarily a good thing from an ecclesial perspective, for it can tend to lend an element of consumerism to what is, after all, supposed to be a matter of rightly expressing the relationship between individuals and God. If church membership is contingent on that which proves most attractive to a large number of people, then the question of whether or not the gospel is being truly preached within

---

82 See Miroslav Volf, *After Our Likeness*; David S. Cunningham, *These Three Are One*. Both of these authors root their understanding of human freedom relationally within the church in their understanding of the human implications of the doctrine of the Trinity. In this regard, they are following after the work that had been done by Moltmann, particularly in *The Trinity and the Kingdom* and *History and the Triune God* (New York: Crossroads Publishing Co., 1992).

83 It is interesting to note the work on public theology that has been done within the Roman Catholic Church in the United States over the past 40 years or so, emerging from the subsidiarity understanding of social differentiation. Certainly one can point to figures such as John Courtney Murray to find examples of earlier trends toward publicity and openness within Roman Catholic theology, but the flourishing of these ideas really only began to emerge after Vatican II. The theory of subsidiarity gave the church a basis for a greater embrace of social pluralism that helped in the formulation of Vatican II principles, and has remained an important theoretical factor since then.

84 See H.R. Niebuhr, *The Social Sources of Denominationalism* and J.L. Adams, *Voluntary Associations* (Chicago: Exploration Press, 1986). At the same time, Niebuhr was negatively disposed toward the differentiation among ecclesial bodies, seeing it as a sign of weakness within Christianity. Adams, on the other hand, was positively disposed toward it.

85 See Bellah, *Habits of the Heart*, 219ff.; Putnam, *Bowling Alone*, 65ff.; Wuthnow, *Christianity and Civil Society* (Valley Forge: Trinity Press International, 1996), 16ff.

it may fall by the wayside. Nevertheless, the voluntarist strain within American religious life has the social advantage of adding to religious diversity. It enriches civil society precisely *because* it puts pressure on the churches as institutions to make a public account of themselves, and explain why they are relevant, necessary, and desirable within society.[86]

This brings us to another element of the reality of the church within civil society, namely the encounter with religious and philosophical pluralism. The cold hard fact of Christian existence in the United States is that it no longer holds pride of place as *the* normative religious tradition. Rather it is one among many religious traditions, most of which function as institutions within civil society alongside the church.[87] When looked at alongside the voluntaristic aspect of civil society, it appears that such religious diversity contributes to the robustness of social life. Pluralism here is more than simply a question of religious toleration by a majority of a minority religious tradition or traditions. The pluralism that is alive in the United States adds to the robustness of civic life precisely because of the element of choice mentioned above.

With such a diversity of religious tradition within the United States, individual religious communities, and the various Christian churches in particular, are required to articulate their worldview in a way that is not only attractive to those who are outside of their religious traditions, but also persuasive to those within those traditions. The penalty for complacency in the midst of such a situation of pluralism is often a declining membership and a failure of spirit in the members of those religious communities.

Additionally, such pluralism calls on religious communities to become more civic-minded as well as more civil toward religious and perspectival difference. The requirements of being participants in civil society from which they all benefit puts the onus on religious communities to act more responsibly with regard to questions of interfaith dialogue and communication than they might otherwise. To the degree

---

86 One must be very cautious here. While the "marketplace of ideas" may indeed be a venue for arriving at truth, it may just as often be a venue for intellectual hucksters and con artists. The relative success of a particular mode of worship or type of theology in the end does not say a whole lot about its truth-value or actual relationship to God. Rising membership does not necessarily imply divine favor any more than falling membership means divine displeasure. The most that can be said in either case is that one has caught the *zeitgeist* and the other hasn't. Nevertheless, it ought to give pause to any religious institution when it sees declining rolls within its own ranks while the numbers rise in other institutions. While emulating other institutions may not necessarily be called for, such churches ought at the very least be exploring why their own numbers are falling.

87 On this subject, see Diana Eck, *A New Religious America* (San Francisco: Harper & Row, 2001). Eck points out that, while the Christian tradition was, through most of the history of the U.S., the normative tradition, within the last 30 years since the rise of non-Christian and even non-Western religious traditions in the United States has resulted in a considerable change of context of which the United States as a whole needs to take account. Pluralism has always been a fact of U.S. life from its inception. However, despite the existence of other, marginalized religious traditions, the pluralism was largely a matter of negotiating among segments of the Christian world, rather than between Christians and non-Christians.

that a religious community recognizes itself as an institution within civil society, it will be open to the participation of other religious communities within the same society.

The converse of this, namely, the exclusion from dialogue of the "unacceptable" religious communities, suggests that a faith group sees itself as somehow uniquely privileged within the culture or society and as, in a way, "more equal" with regard to civic life. Thus, it emphasizes its own participation and influence within society as a whole without regard for the degree to which it does not in fact represent the whole of society, but only a portion of its members. To recognize that the pluralism within civil society puts upon a religious institution the responsibility to hold its own truth claims in reserve to some degree requires a great deal of epistemological modesty, but in a certain regard such responsibility is imposed upon any religious group by the reality of its own position within the civic order. Within a liberal democratic society in which religious pluralism is a reality, any attempt by one or a few religious groups to claim any real practical advantage over the others will be met by the countervailing forces of all of those others against it.[88] Thus, it is in the interest of all religious groups to protect some form of equilibrium among diverse religious groups in society.

At the same time that the church has these responsibilities along with all other religious groups within civil society, in enacting those responsibilities the church also takes a risk – it risks the possibility that its message will be co-opted for the purposes of the larger society in ways that are at odds with the actual content of that message. If, as Moltmann's theology suggests, the purpose of the church is its witness to the kingdom of God and the status of Christ as the messiah, then such cooptation is a danger that strikes right at the heart of the church's being. Because this message relates not only to the spiritual but also to the social reality (that is, the *basilea* as the reign of God on earth as it is in heaven), the possibility of cooptation is always a reality for the church in a way that it might not be for a less socially oriented religious group. The theological reality of the church implies a public reality, a set of standards for morality and behavior that are relevant, not only to the church but also to the world as a whole. The kingdom of God, as a *kingdom*, implies actual social conditions through which the principles that rule are made manifest in the world. The theological reality of the church thus leads to very real practical

---

88 This does not imply that Christians should not bring their own conceptions of substantive good to the public conversation. On the contrary, as David Hollenbach notes, "equal citizens can start from different understandings of the good but go on to participate actively in defining and pursuing the good that they share in common" (*The Common Good and Christian Ethics*, 12). Earlier, Hollenbach relates his own approach to Aristotle's understanding of public life in the *polis*: "Aristotle understood that the free males of Athens could be treated as equal citizens even when they held different understandings of the good life. The public domain of equal citizenship was the place where different understandings of the good life were to be debated and argued about. The public sphere was the forum where a working idea of the common good was to be forged" (11). Within modern society, the multiplicity of conceptions of the good makes such a forging a challenge, but this should not imply that substantive conceptions of the good need to be left aside. But there must be genuine discussion of their validity.

consequences in the way in which Christians ought to live their lives and strive to structure their society.

But, as H.R. Niebuhr pointed out in *The Kingdom of God in America*, it is precisely because of such a social dimension to its theological purpose that the church's message can be turned against itself and made to correspond to ideals that run counter to it. Whether it is in the chain of ideas that leads from the Bible to the Puritan desire to become a "city on a hill" to Ronald Reagan's invocation of that phrase to support an aggressive Cold War Americanism, or the link from Christ's teaching on poverty through the apocalyptic theology of Joachim of Fiore to Thomas Münzer's peasant rebellion, the walk from the idea of the kingdom of God to the identification of the kingdom with particular human movements and ideologies is easily made and always stalking Christianity's public life.

Thus, Robert Bellah's (later abandoned) endorsement of the idea of civil religion as that which provides an impetus for public morality and virtue contains within it the risk that the cooptation of the sociological calling of the church will be put to uses that run directly contrary to its theological calling.[89] While Bellah rightly notes that "such moral and religious understandings produce both a basic cultural legitimation for a society which is viewed as at least approximately in accord with them and a standard of judgment for the criticism of a society that is seen as deviating from them,"[90] he fails to see that the intermingling of certain social values within the church can result in a loss of that critical judgment in the name of an identification of the society with God's will of divine providence. In such situations, there needs to be a rediscovery of the theological meaning of the church's task.

Conclusion

The concept of civil society is the product of both historical and conceptual development that has gone through a number of distinct phases. The analysis of civil society has on the one hand (to steal a phrase from Hegel), like Minerva's owl, risen only at dusk to arrive at an understanding of the way that social forms have developed and interacted with one another. On the other hand, having arrived at an analytical understanding of civil society, the recognition of its importance to the cohesion of society has led to a normative appreciation of the need to encourage and develop distinct and independent spheres of human association and interaction. Thus, the pluralism of institutional life in modern society is seen as being a prerequisite for the maintenance of a free and stable public life.

To the degree that social fragmentation has contributed to the decline of civil society as a realm of free association, public life is impoverished and placed at risk. Thus, the analyses of Bellah, Putnam and others have served to call attention to the way that individualism as a cultural condition undermines social cohesion. The question is whether and to what extent it is necessary to take some action to restore it.

---

89 See Bellah, *The Broken Covenant*, 164ff.
90 Bellah, *The Broken Covenant*, xvi.

It is here that the theological dimension of civil society needs to be recognized as a crucial dimension of the discussion. Both the Roman Catholic subsidiarity approach and the Reformed covenantal approach to conceiving of social differentiation have contributions to make to the understanding of what stake theological concepts have in public life. Both recognize the complex and sometimes conflicting interactions of diverse institutions within society. Each also recognizes social pluralism as a gift and intention of God, part of God's positive will for a properly functioning human society. Without such a theological viewpoint, civil society may well be seen to be simply a convenient set of social arrangements, as optional and disposable in the face of political or economic pressures. Civil society is thus always in danger of that "colonization" of which Habermas speaks insofar as it is not recognized as an innately human social arrangement. Sociological and philosophical conceptions of civil society can thus only take us so far. What is needed is an understanding of civil society that can provide a theological basis for its preservation and expansion.

Public theologies such as those that we explored in Chapters 5 and 6 begin from a presumption of social differentiation in modern society, and seek to address the theological issues that attend that differentiation. In various ways, American public theologians such as Tracy, Skillen and Thiemann have sought to understand the church within society as offering a contribution to the understanding of the social good.

In his theology, Moltmann, influenced more by the continental and Hegelian conception of civil society than by the Toquevillian understanding, has offered a less nuanced understanding of social differentiation, and as a result has not been able to offer as compelling an affirmation of the pluralistic aspects of modern life as his American counterparts. Nevertheless, as we observed in Chapter 2 his understanding of the idea of the Exodus Church offers a resource for understanding the role of Christians within civil society that is in need of further development and application.

It is a delicate balance that needs to be maintained between the theological and sociological tasks of the church. The risk taken by too strong an emphasis on the theological task of the church is the collapse of its social responsibility and a retreat to sectarian separation from the social context. For Moltmann, the image of the kingdom of God, the theme of covenant as promise, and the doctrine of vocation (also seen in Stackhouse's own understanding of the theological significance of civil society) give him the resources to put forward a vision of society that is in accord with God's will for all human beings, rather than for a select set. Yet, at the same time, the risk taken by too strong an emphasis on the sociological task of the church is a transformation into a co-opted civil religion.[91] The balance can only be maintained by recognizing it as a part of the mission of the church to engage in *both* critique and support of the social setting. The critique emerges from the church's norm as based, as Moltmann would have it, on the anticipation of the kingdom of God and the call of

---

91 Both Bellah and Moltmann comment on the advantages and risks of civil religion in Rouner, ed., *Civil Religion and Political Theology* (Notre Dame: Notre Dame University Press, 1986).

society to make that norm its own ideal. The support emerges, as we have discussed in this chapter, from the church's role as a mediating institution.

In Part IV I will attempt to integrate the various themes that I have been exploring throughout this project – the nature of public theology, the particular importance of Moltmann's theology, and the philosophical and sociological dimensions raised in the theory of civil society.

PART IV
SOCIAL ETHICS AND THE EXODUS CHURCH

Chapter 10

Public Theology, Critical Modernism, and the Kingdom of God

Introduction

If the theory of civil society provides us with a sociological clue to what the church's role in public life may include (and vice versa, if theology can tell us something of the importance of civil society), then we need to understand the way in which the themes of our previous chapters interact with the questions raised earlier in this book particularly with the questions of modern public life raised in the several approaches to public theology, and the theological themes raised by Jürgen Moltmann's work. In the final three chapters, I would like to provide some synthesizing comments that may allow these three elements to combine creatively and constructively in the Christian moral life in society.

I would like to begin with a brief summary of where we have been so far in this book. We began with a consideration of Jürgen Moltmann's theological project, in light of the persistent problems raised within modernity, particularly his concern with what he terms the "global marketing of everything." We then explored the development of Moltmann's theological project, with an emphasis on its social dimensions, which operate within what I have termed a "dialectic of transformation and critique." We then explored how several important theological themes interplayed within Moltmann's work in the development of his understanding of the character of the church as an "exodus community." This concept forms the core of how I want to understand the relationship of Moltmann's work to the theory of civil society.

In Part Two, I brought Moltmann's thought into dialogue with the tradition of American public theology by comparing Moltmann's thought to several key figures in the movement. Of particular importance were the intersections between their thought and his on the nature of Christian public action. Points of intersection were found between Moltmann's thought and different dimensions of David Tracy, Ron Thiemann, and James Skillen's different approaches to public theology. What was missing in Moltmann's approach, I argued, was a robust conception of social pluralism, without which his thought would lose its practical trajectory.

In Part Three, I attempted to reconstruct that missing dimension of Moltmann's thought through an analysis of the idea of civil society, tracing the idea through several historical permutations, and then articulating some of the key characteristics that render the theory of civil society important for the idea of the church.

In this final part, I will be returning to these themes in order to tie them together and offer an explanation of how they may be understood as a set of mutually affirming and critical companions in the continuing development of an understanding of public theology in a pluralistic society. I will first turn to a discussion of the relationship of public theology to modernity, arguing that theology best serves its role in society, not in rejecting it and setting itself apart, but in understanding itself as a brand of "critical modernism," which both participates in and seeks the transformation of its social setting. I will then turn to the idea of the kingdom of God as a normative regulative principle for gauging Christian public participation. In the next chapter I will consider more closely the ethical task of the church in modern society in light of our earlier discussion of public theology and civil society.

Public Theology and Critical Modernism

Public theology relies for its viability on a concern with the broad public space of society. Within this public space, there are lesser and greater degrees of association and agreement. In order to respond creatively to the various intersecting spheres of social life, public theology needs a way of understanding itself in relation to society that is not at the same time a complete mirror of that society.

Liberal democracy, which has been formed in no small measure by theological themes that have become identified with public theology, is also deeply penetrated by the themes of philosophical modernism. Public theology cannot choose not to acknowledge that element of its own history in liberal democracy if it is to have a voice within society; otherwise, the result will be a privatization of religious understanding that leaves the public square "naked."[1] Yet the concerns of thinkers, such as Stanley Hauerwas, for whom an identification with modernity and liberalism are a threat to theological integrity, cannot be ignored.[2] A critical modernism, such as Moltmann's, which can both affirm those elements in modernity that are creatively open to the realization of theological ends and at the same time critique those elements that are fundamentally flawed, may provide resources for a reconstructed engagement of theology with liberal democracy, and provide a foundation for Christian social ethics.

Critical Modernism

In arguing that public theology functions best as a brand of critical modernism, I am aware that modernism itself is often seen as passé. Yet critical modernism could itself be viewed as a brand of postmodernism, such as Paul Lakeland has described.[3] Moltmann has also described his own Christology as "postmodern."[4] In using the

---

1 See Neuhaus, *The Naked Public Square* (Grand Rapids: Eerdmans, 1984). Also of interest on this point is Carter, *God's Name in Vain* (New York: Basic Books, 2000)..

2 This is, of course, a recurrent theme for Hauerwas. See particularly his *The Peaceable Kingdom*. Also of interest are Hauerwas and Willimon, *Resident Aliens* (Nashville: Abingdon, 1989) and *Where Resident Aliens Live* (Nashville: Abingdon, 1996).

3 Paul Lakeland, *Postmodernity: Christian Identity in a Fragmented Age* (Philadelphia: Fortress Press, 1997).

4 Moltmann, *The Way of Jesus Christ* (Minneapolis, MN: Fortress Press, 1993), xvi.

term "critical modernism" here, I am not attempting to pick a fight with those who prefer the term "postmodernism." However, in describing the process of affirmation and critique that I see taking place between theology and modernity, it is necessary for me to stress *both* the critical aspect *and* the modernity. Whatever may come in the future, for the present public theology has not moved beyond nor abandoned modernity. Even if it has gained some critical distance from modernity because of its theological focus, they remain in dialogue. Thus, "critical modernism" represents my intent more accurately than "postmodernism."[5]

Earlier, I examined the dominance of instrumental rationality in modern public life. The prevalence of game theory and cost-benefit analysis in the determination of public policy and foreign affairs has created a very limited moral discourse in public life. Additionally, the liberal emphasis on individualism has made it increasingly difficult to argue for communally formed and sanctioned value-systems in modern society. These elements combined have served to privatize religious experience and remove questions of value from public relevance.[6]

If this were all there was to modernity, then it would be justifiable for Christians to reject it as a basis upon which to build a theological project. Yet, the counter-current in modernity, represented by Jürgen Habermas and others, offers a way of reconceiving modernity's compatibly with a Christian social ethic. Communicative rationality maintains the value and substantive rational elements of moral and religious discourse at the same time it recognizes the importance of instrumental reason. It provides a place for the discussion of moral principles in the midst of a disputed social system, and simultaneously insists on the equal worth of actors in the midst of a communicative discourse. Habermas, along with Rawls, Schrag, Benhabib and others, provides a complementary philosophical touchstone to the instrumental reason of modernity that remains relevant for theological discourse.[7]

---

5   A carefully qualified use of the term "postmodern" would be a perfectly acceptable substitute for what I am arguing here. It is certainly true that the perspective I am promoting is not based upon a wholesale affirmation of modernity, but recognizes its limitations and potential destructiveness. Yet any postmodernism that is engaged in public theology would of necessity be a "constructive postmodernism" of the kind advocated by van Huyssteen in *The Shaping of Rationality*.

6   At the same time, it must be noted that such marginalizing of religious expression in public life has not necessarily ended the public discussion of religion. On the one hand, Stephen Carter has argued that it has rather made the public expression of religious perspectives into something along the line of a "hobby." Interesting perhaps. Personally motivating, but not finally relevant. See Carter, *The Culture of Disbelief* (New York: Basic Books, 1993). On the other hand, the rise of public religious expression in Evangelical Christian circles, as well as in fundamentalist corners of the Islamic, Hindu, and Buddhist world have created a great deal of public relevance for religious expression, although not necessarily in a positive or constructive way.

7   This theme is extensively explored throughout Habermas's work, particularly in *The Theory of Communicative Action*. See also Rawls, *Political Liberalism* (New York: Columbia University Press, 1996); Calvin Schrag, *The Resources of Rationality*; Seyla Benhabib, *Situating the Self: Gender Community and Postmodernism in Contemporary Ethics* (New York: Routledge, 1992). Also of interest for his work in recovering the Aristotelian tradition in a modern context

But critical modernism has to deal with the other side of this as well. If modernity remains relevant for theological discourse, how may theological discourse remain relevant to modernity? Under what conditions is it possible for the substantive ethical questions raised in religious discourse to become meaningful within an instrumentalized marketplace of ideas?

To be sure, as long as instrumentality and quantification remain the only guideposts by which rationality is judged, these substantive questions cannot be raised. Religion will continue to be pushed to the margins as private at best, and probably increasingly to the irrational. In order to break through this set of assumptions, public theology needs to engage the premises of instrumental rationality, and argue for a complementary understanding of rationality based upon a "wide reflective equilibrium" within philosophical discourse.[8] Such an approach would allow for the openness of discourse in the public sphere without placing the stringent limitations on acceptable types of discourse that are imposed in much public discussion. This leads to a recognition that public theology functions best when it places itself, not above other fields, nor outside of the realm of criticism, but within a communicative setting as a discursive practice.

Public Theology as a Discursive Practice

The wide reflective equilibrium of which I am writing relates to what Rawls refers to as the distinction between "thin" and "thick" conceptions of the good.[9] Within a pluralistic social setting, Rawls argues, "thick" conceptions of the good cannot reach consensus. A "thin" conception is necessary for social consensus, one that embodies only the general principles of formal justice within the social system. Fiorenza points out that there is a dialectical relation that exists between these two categories:

> The dialectical relation is that in any society there will be a mutual reciprocity between the "thin" and "thick" conceptions. If the "thin" conception is what is essential to justice and premises of primary goods, then fuller conceptions of the good should be consistent or should cohere with these essentials and premises. Likewise, the fuller conceptions will necessarily influence what is considered essential to the "thin" conception of the good. The distinction is important insofar as societies do, in fact, have an integrating and an overlapping consensus on significant moral issues. Nevertheless, concretely and

---

is Charles Taylor, *Sources of the Self* and *Philosophical Arguments* (Cambridge, MA: Harvard University Press, 1995).

8 See Rawls, *Political Liberalism*, 8, and passim; Fiorenza, "The Church as a Community of Interpretation," in Browning and Fiorenza, eds, *Habermas, Modernity, and Public Theology*, 81; Schrag, *The Resources of Rationality*, 178. Schrag actually goes farther and suggests the need for a "wider" reflective equilibrium in the definition of rationality. "This," he argues, "would refigure and expand the range of reason, making its alignment with the social sources of thought and the practices of everyday life more explicit, and provide a corrective to recurring tendencies of privileging a belief-centered approach to rationality" (178–9). See also Michael Stenmark, *Rationality in Science, Religion, and Everyday Life* (Notre Dame: University of Notre Dame Press, 1995).

9 See Rawls, *A Theory of Justice* (Cambridge, MA: Harvard University Press, 1971), 395ff., and *Political Liberalism*, 178ff.

historically, one has to explore the dialectical relation between the "thin" and the "thick." This relation raises the issue between the reconstructive interpretation of normative traditions within society and their relation to "thin" conceptions. It also raises the question: Where does public discourse take place about this interrelation between fuller and more substantial conceptions of the good and the "thin" conceptions about which there is overlapping consensus?[10]

Public theology, as a representative discourse within liberal democratic society, brings to the discursive process a particular "thick" conception of the good, rooted in the church's particular identity as the anticipatory community. Through its own sense of tradition and obligation, it engages in a hermeneutical assessment of its social situation, as what Fiorenza calls an "interpretive community."[11] As such, it has an obligation to engage openly with these other conceptions of the good within liberal democracy for the purposes of making its own conceptions of the good relevant within its social context. Fiorenza points out how Christians have contributed to such a discourse: "the churches as communities of interpretation of normative traditions have contributed to public policy in recent years. They have issued public statements on such controversial issues as nuclear warfare, the economy, and the death penalty ... they have dealt with issues concerning the nature and priority of diverse social goods."[12]

Such a process of interpretation does not take place in a vacuum, but precisely in the process of argumentation and discourse by which broader (and perhaps also "thinner") social conceptions of the good are to be determined.[13] Society is based upon the presupposition of the possibility of at least some minimal discursive consensus, that may allow individuals within divergent interpretative communities to function in a viable relation to one another.[14] The church as an interpretive community is not isolated within its interpretive perspective, but brings that perspective to the table in dialogue, for the purposes of hammering out something akin to its own substantive moral conceptions in public life.

Although Moltmann never provides an extensive discussion of precisely *how* the church *per se* remains in dialogue with is social setting, he does presume such a

---

10 Fiorenza, "The Church as a Community of Interpretation," 83.

11 Fiorenza, "The Church as a Community of Interpretation," 83.

12 Fiorenza, "The Church as a Community of Interpretation," 83. One may also note that the church's contribution to public discourse is certainly not limited to policy discussions, but operates on every level of civil society to present its normative interpretation to the larger social body, whether through nongovernmental organizations, local churches, educational institutions, and so on. Policy is only one realm where such interpretation is necessary and possible.

13 See Rawls, *Political Liberalism*, 10ff.

14 Nicholas Rescher argues that a broader conception of overlapping consensus rooted in communicative discourse is finally a utopian pipe-dream. Yet his own proposal for the maintenance of social cohesion in the midst of pluralism is not substantially different from Habermas's conception, despite Rescher's claims to the contrary. See Nicholas Rescher, *Pluralism: Against the Demand for Consensus* (New York: Oxford University Press, 1993), 127ff.

dialogue in his discussion of the church's role.[15] Although as an "exodus community" the church maintains an identity that cannot be reduced to its surrounding culture, that identity remains "open" with regard to culture.[16] The identity of the Christian community is not circumscribed by its narrative. Rather, it is particularly through that narrative that the Christian community may become open to the world, reflecting as it does the story of God's openness to the world. In the story that the Christian tradition tells itself about God's interaction with humankind and creation, we can find a model on the basis of which to promote the kind of discursive practices that are necessary to critically engage and work toward the transformation of modernity.[17]

A model of public theology that presumes such a set of discursive practices, and self-consciously seeks to engage, with an attitude of openness, with the cultural world of which it is a part, possesses the possibility of offering both a substantive moral framework for Christian action in society, and also a contribution to the kind of "thin" conception of justice that may be more reflective of precisely those same substantive principles.[18] There is certainly no basis for a criticism of a liberal conception of justice in the absence of an attempt to bring the particularities of Christian tradition into discourse with the other contenders in the marketplace of ideas in civil society. If Christian ethics is to be *social* ethics, then there must be a

---

15 Consider, for example, the extended discussion in *Experiences in Theology*, in which he explores the various "mirror images" of liberation theology. Again, in *God for a Secular Society*, his entire project is premised on a continuation of such dialogue. Despite the absence of an articulated theological basis for such discursive praxis, he actually engages in it reflexively throughout his theological project.

16 As we have seen at a number of points, the idea of "openness" remains a key concept for Moltmann. The church is to be open to society, as Christian relationships are to be based on a doctrine of "open friendship," and the intratrinitarian dynamics of God are based upon an "openness" to one another. The continual recurrence of the motif of "openness" suggests a strong inclination on Moltmann's part toward precisely the kinds of trends that Habermas and others have talked about under the heading of "discourse ethics." In order to judge how fully Moltmann's approach is compatible with a Habermasian understanding of dialogue, it would be necessary for Moltmann to engage more directly with Habermasian philosophy, which he has not yet done in any explicit way. However, it is worthwhile to note the recent works that have considered these connections. Most particularly, Hyun-Sook Kim's *Christian Education for Postconventionality: Modernization, Trinitarian Ethics, and Christian Identity* (Seoul: Kangnam Publishers, 2002) attempts to approach questions of Christian education and practical theology through a juxtaposition of Moltmannian and Habermasian categories. Gary Simpson in "*Theologia Crucis* and the Forensically Fraught World: Engaging Helmut Peukert and Jürgen Habermas" (in Browning and Fiorenza, eds, *Habermas, Modernity, and Public Theology*, 173ff.) brings Moltmann's theology into direct dialogue with Habermas. Both of these attempts recognize some affinities in the programs of Habermas and Moltmann, while also recognizing that each brings resources to the discussion of public theology that the other lacks.

17 This is a point that Tracy makes in his description of the hermeneutical task of public theology. He writes: "The heart of any hermeneutical position is the recognition that all interpretation is a mediation of past and present, a translation carried on with the effective history of a tradition to retrieve its sometimes strange, sometimes familiar meanings" (*The Analogical Imagination*, 99).

18 See Fiorenza, "The Church as a Community of Interpretation," 85.

groundwork from which social critique can take place. And this must be done in the context of an open public space.

Public Theology as Christian Social Ethics

Public theology acts responsibly with regard to questions of substantive moral claims to the degree that it is able to formulate an ethical approach that is relevant within the context of larger social claims. "It refers to the *engagement* of a living religious tradition with its public environment – the economic, political, and cultural spheres of our common life."[19] How this engagement is to take place depends in large measure on the commitment that Christians have to the kind of dialogical practices detailed above. It is certainly possible to formulate a coherent Christian ethic without reference to the cultural surroundings in which Christians live, but such an ethic would be impoverished by its narrow focus. In effect, such an ethic would be so immersed in its own presuppositions that it would be incapable of responsible reflection outside of a predetermined set of symbols and issues. It would be a fossilized and sterile ethical viewpoint.

By contrast, a public theology that is self-consciously committed to a Christian *social* ethic remains cognizant of its own tradition and narrative as the "thick" vantage point from which it surveys the ethical landscape. It is committed to look beyond its own interior perspective and respond to that which lies before its eyes. But if it is to see clearly then it has to make constant reference to those interpretive lenses through which it views the world. There are three dangers associated with this: First, a theology that attempts to be public without such a reference will forget its own grounding and risk collapsing into a merely civil religion, with only a thin veneer of Christian theology to overlay it; second, it may become so self-conscious of its narrative presuppositions that it fails to see beyond them, myopically looking *at* the very lenses that it is intended to see *through*; third, it may constantly reinterpret and selectively critique its theological framework, re-grinding, as it were, the lenses to such a degree that they cease to be effective tools for clarity of sight.

A Christian social ethic rooted in a public theology must then be engaged in a process of translation. That is: the act of interpreting the meaning of its normative framework in relation to a particular set of social circumstances requires that public theology be "multi-lingual" in the public realm. It could speak to many specific situations and spheres of life. I stress that this does not imply an abandonment of precisely those "thick" dimensions that make up its substantive moral claims. On the contrary, the act of translation is precisely that which takes place in dialogue in seeking to make the elements of that thick description comprehensible across the boundaries of divergent language-games.

Translation in this sense is rooted, not according to a predetermination of the kind of outcome desired by the translator, but by the process of interactive discourse with the various parties and special vocabularies of different spheres themselves.

---

19 Robert Benne, *The Paradoxical Vision* (Philadelphia: Fortress Press, 1995), 4. Stackhouse's approach in *God and Globalization* challenges Benne's division of social categories as overly simplified.

The principles of a discourse ethic rooted in both a respect for all participants in the discussion and an intent to allow for all voices to be heard sets the agenda through which translation may take place.[20] Additionally, it is necessary that the translator be engaged in an honest explication of his or her position within the public space of discussion. Habermas speaks of this in terms of the general presentation of a discourse ethic, writing:

> It belongs to the communicative intent of the speaker (a) that he perform a speech act that is *right* in respect to the given normative context, so that between him and the hearer an inter-subjective relation will come about which is recognized as legitimate; (b) that he make a *true* statement (or *correct* existential presuppositions), so that the hearer will accept and share the knowledge of the speaker; and (c) that he express *truthfully* his beliefs, intentions, feelings, desires, and the like, so that the hearer will give credence to what is said.[21]

Translation under these circumstances becomes a process of *disclosure* and *articulation* of one's interpretive framework in relation to a critical public space. The goal of such disclosure may certainly include the intent to learn and/or convince. But more primarily, the goal is to achieve a condition of understanding between the translator and the audience.[22]

Christian social ethics has a responsibility to engage in such a process of disclosure and articulation relative to its own "thick" description of the world. This means undertaking the task of making its theological foundations comprehensible across a large disciplinary spectrum. Again, the goal is primarily understanding, as well as persuasion and normative guidance. In this regard, the ethical task of public theology can be seen, to use Tracy's approach, to address the "generalized others" of academy and society through the process of discourse that emerges out of its explicit (yet also often critical) commitment to the description of reality articulated by the church in the act of interpreting its own key texts and traditions.[23]

Not all theological concepts may be equally relevant to all public fields. In terms of social ethics, I want to bring this discussion back around to Moltmann's theological project, and consider those concepts that he develops that are particularly fruitful for this kind of discussion.

The Kingdom of God, Society, and Ethical Norms

In Chapter 2, I explored the various dimensions of Moltmann's theology through an articulation of its dialectical structure. Moltmann's thought reflects the critical modernism about which I have been writing, in that his perspective remains rooted in and affirmative of many of the concerns developing out of the enlightenment – in particular questions of human freedom and dignity, democracy, and the establishment of social justice. His critique of "the global marketing of everything"

---

20 Benhabib, *Situating the Self*, 30–1.
21 Habermas, *The Theory of Communicative Action*, I:307–8.
22 Habermas, *The Theory of Communicative Action*, I:308.
23 See Tracy, *The Analogical Imagination*, 21–2.

parallels Habermas's critique of the colonization of the lifeworld by the system.[24] Moltmann's emphasis on the centrality of the church as the messianic community is an attempt to rearticulate a theology rooted within the Christian lifeworld that has the capacity to resist systemization. But this is done less through an accent on mutual humanistic understanding than through an emphasis on the identification of God with the world in Christ, an articulation of utopian Christian hope, and an insistence on a moral way of life rooted in a consideration of the person and work of Jesus Christ. He subordinates, but does not repudiate, the Kantian, deontological accent present in Habermas (and Rawls) to an eschatological transformational teleology. There are three elements of Moltmann's theology that I want to consider in this section: the ethical implications of his understanding of anticipation, his appropriation of Ernst Bloch's idea of "tendencies and latencies" as they relate to the reconstructive potential of modern society, and the question of how the particular elements of Christian claims may be understood as having universal value.

Anticipation and Ethical Norms

As Moltmann conceives of it, the kingdom, as the norm by which the ethical standards of the Christian lifestyle are established, creates certain expectations, both as to the way in which Christians will interact with one another, and how they will act with regard to the world. The "messianic ethic" that Moltmann endorses consists of several principles.[25]

The messianic ethic is established on the basis of the life and teaching of Jesus Christ. Such an ethic, while rooted in these teachings, is not epistemologically limited to the believing community however, because, as Moltmann notes: "the messiah is a public person."[26] As a public person, his teaching establishes a particular Christian approach to ethics that cannot be gainsaid or ignored. To be a Christian in public life is precisely to bring the specificity of Christ to the public problem:

> If there is no specifically Christian ethic, then the acknowledgment of Christ is itself called into question; for then Jesus' message cannot have been ethically meant, in the sense of making a public ethical claim. It was then either purely religious, and hence non-political; or wholly apocalyptic, and hence without relevance for changes in the world

---

24 See Moltmann, *God for a Secular Society*, 153 and passim; Habermas, *The Theory of Communicative Action*, vol. 2.

25 As I have already noted, Moltmann has nothing that could be considered an "ethics" in the sense of an extended volume on questions of moral norms or responsibilities and their bases. *On Human Dignity*, though it advertises itself as being about "political theology and ethics," has many ethical implications but is not really an ethical treatise. Similarly, *Politische Theologie – Politische Ethik* represents another attempt at ethical engagement, but again, in an unsystematic and uncomprehenisve manner. The most extended treatment of the basis of ethics in Moltmann's work is found in *The Way of Jesus Christ* where he writes in some detail about the principles of a "messianic ethic." I will concentrate on this material in this section. However, it should be noted that Moltmann's theology is thoroughgoingly ethical in both its intent and in its execution. What is lacking is an attempt to summarize its ethical approach in one place.

26 Moltmann, *The Way of Jesus Christ*, 117.

itself; or confined to personal life, and hence without any relation to the public conditions in which personal life is lived. But can Jesus then still be called the messiah in a sense that is in any way relevant? ... If it is taken seriously, then the confession of Jesus as the Christ also involves a practical discipleship that follows the messianic path his own life took; and this means an ethic which has to be made identifiably Christian.[27]

The nature of such a messianic ethic needs to find a way to speak within an often ambiguous social context while remaining connected to the kingdom that Christ preached. This entails following the way of Christ along several paths: In his proclamation of the messianic Sabbath, in his preaching of the messianic Torah, and the messianic Peace that he proclaimed.

Moltmann links his concern with the importance of the Sabbath with an ecological ethic and an ethic of ecological justice. The messianic Sabbath is connected for Moltmann with the idea of the year of Jubilee, or the year of the Lord's favor.[28] In his proclamation that God "has sent me to proclaim the release of captives, the recovery of sight to the blind, to let the oppressed go free, to proclaim the year of the Lord's favor" (Lk. 4:18–19), Christ proclaims, not simply a temporary amelioration of the suffering of the miserable, but a complete reconstitution of society.[29] For Moltmann, the declaration of this requires a "contrast society" to stand in the midst of the unredeemed world on its behalf.[30] This is for Moltmann a genuine public alternative, and not a "retreat to commitment" on the part of the church. He writes:

> Not least, the messianic interpretations of God's year of liberation through Christ, and the alternative programme of the community of Christ, acquire increasing general plausibility the more our present day political, social and economic systems destroy people and devastate the nature of the earth. Where the acts of men and women have in this way brought "the end" so close for so many people and so many living things, it is reasonable and wise to look round for alternatives.[31]

The same approach can be seen in Moltmann's understanding of the importance of the messianic Torah as an ethical category. In opposition to a potentially antinomian understanding of Christian freedom (that is, that "faith in the gospel frees people from the requirements of the law"),[32] Moltmann argues instead for an interpretation of the gospel as the "fulfillment" and extension of the Law to all the nations. "Through love, the community of Christ fulfils the Torah in the dawn of the kingdom of God."[33]

---

27 Moltmann, *The Way of Jesus Christ*, 117–18.
28 Moltmann, *The Way of Jesus Christ*. See *God in Creation*, 276ff.
29 Moltmann, *The Way of Jesus Christ*, 122. See Moltmann's extended discussion of the church's solidarity with the poor and dispossessed in *The Church in the Power of the Spirit*, 76ff.
30 Moltmann, *The Way of Jesus Christ*, 122.
31 Moltmann, *The Way of Jesus Christ*, 122.
32 Moltmann, *The Way of Jesus Christ*, 122.
33 Moltmann, *The Way of Jesus Christ*, 123. This element of obedience to the law ties in to some of the deontological elements of Habermas's project. In particular, see Habermas's

Key to Moltmann's analysis of the ethical significance of the Law is his reconceptualization of the gospel, not as release from the Law, but as a *"messianic interpretation of the Torah* for the Gentile nations."[34] In this interpretation, according to Moltmann, "we hear the voice of the end-time Wisdom of God, which from the beginning gives life to all created beings, and does not desire their death."[35]

Moltmann interprets the Beatitudes of Matthew according to this understanding, arguing that "its intention is certainly the revival and gathering of the whole people of God, Israel – but the Israel of the messianic era."[36] He continues:

> Jesus' Sermon on the Mount is addressed to the people. In so far it is open to the world, and is universal in its trend and thrust. But men and women are called to follow Jesus, and to keep the messianic Torah. This is represented by the throng of men and women disciples. By way of *antitheses*, "the law of Christ" is related to Israel and the law of Moses. By way of *the beatitudes* it is related to all human beings who hear it. The Sermon on the Mount therefore offers the ethic of a particular community, the messianic community of Christ. But this ethic is directed to the redemption of the whole people (*ochlos*) and claims universality.[37]

The law of Christ is the constitutive ethical mandate of the community of those who follow Christ. It is therefore "bound to contrast with the ethics of existing society, since the ethics of society as it exists are in contradiction to the liberation of the messianic Sabbath, and the justice of the approaching kingdom of God."[38] The messianic lifestyle of which Moltmann writes at a number of points entails living a life that takes seriously the innate connection between *believing* in Christ and *following* Christ. "Hope for God's kingdom and the experience of poverty among the people; the community of brothers and sisters, and the discipleship of Christ – these things are a unity."[39]

What this means, particularly with regard to the Sermon on the Mount, is expounded by Moltmann under the category of the "messianic peace." Moltmann argues that the ethic manifested by the Christian community is an ethic founded upon nonviolence. "The presupposition here is that humanity's real sin is the violence that leads to death; and that consequently humanity's salvation is to be found in the peace that serves our common life."[40] This implies that the Christian community, standing as a contrast society and obedient to the messianic Torah of Jesus Christ, is morally obligated to live as a community free from violence and coercion. The goal is to break the cycle of violence that is based upon the *lex talionis*:

---

discussion of the link between Kantian and discourse ethics in *Moral Consciousness and Communicative Action*, 196ff.

34 Moltmann, *The Way of Jesus Christ*, 124. Italics in original.
35 Moltmann, *The Way of Jesus Christ*, 124.
36 Moltmann, *The Way of Jesus Christ*, 124.
37 Moltmann, *The Way of Jesus Christ*, 125. Italics in original.
38 Moltmann, *The Way of Jesus Christ*, 125.
39 Moltmann, *The Way of Jesus Christ*, 126.
40 Moltmann, *The Way of Jesus Christ*, 127.

The vicious circle of violence and counter-violence is broken. Non-resistance to evil shows up the absurdity of evil. Evil's strength is violence. Evil's weakness is its wrongness. Counter-violence supplies evil with its supposed justification, and often enough stabilizes it. It is only the non-violent reaction which robs evil of every legitimation and puts the perpetrator of violence in the wrong, "heaping burning coals on his head" (Rom. 12:20). The rule of violence is built upon anxiety and terror. Where the rulers are unable to rouse either anxiety or terror, their violence loses its effect. This is the weakness of violence, and this is where the non-violent conquest of an act of violence starts. Gandhi understood the Sermon on the Mount correctly: talking about non-violent resistance, he said that counter-violence was better than resignation, but that non-violent action was better than counter-violence.[41]

The public implication of this for Moltmann is not, it seems, a divestiture of political power or public responsibility, but rather it "does oblige everyone to engage in a continuous struggle to make every exercise of power subject to law; for to subject the exercise of power to law is the first stage in the conquest of violence."[42] This is an important qualification for Moltmann, and one that is often ignored by his critics. The abolition of the cycle of retribution is a matter of *process*, not *principle*. The messianic hope that underlies Moltmann's ethical thought does not seek to establish the kingdom, but to anticipate it. As such, it always says both a yes and a no to the world in which it lives.

Thus, the subjection of violence to the rule of law is neither a presumption of the kingdom nor a recognition of its impossibility. Rather, it is a practical step toward the realization of the norms of the kingdom in social life. It is, he notes, a "first stage." He continues: "The second stage in conquering the rule of violence is the solidarity of the people in rejecting that rule, and their refusal to co-operate with it in any form."[43] This implies a love for enemies and a desire to see the messianic rule of Christ actualized in social life. "In loving one's enemies one no longer asks: how can I protect myself, and deter my enemies from attacking me? The question is then: how can I deprive my enemy of his hostility?"[44] Moltmann clearly views this

---

41 Moltmann, *The Way of Jesus Christ*, 129. It is worth asking how the word "better" is used in this passage. Presumably Moltmann means "morally better." Yet Moltmann's conception of questions of moral good does not leave adequate room for a tragic dimension that could be forced to acknowledge that violence, while never a good (so in that sense, not "better" than anything), may nevertheless be the only available option for those who will not allow themselves to be resigned. While acknowledging Moltmann's point that "anyone who considers the Sermon on the Mount to be in principle impossible of fulfillment, mocks God; for God is the creator and lover of life, and he gives no commandments that cannot be fulfilled" (127), I would wish Moltmann to respond more fully to the question of whether a commandment that is not in principle impossible is nevertheless not at the same time universally *possible*. In other words, nonviolence may be, and perhaps most often is, the best possible moral approach, but are there never circumstances under which it is not a viable possibility, even if it is in principle feasible? It is this lack of recognition of a tragic dimension to Christian ethics that is the most serious flaw in Moltmann's understanding of the messianic dimensions of Christian lifestyle.

42 Moltmann, *The Way of Jesus Christ*, 130.

43 Moltmann, *The Way of Jesus Christ*, 130.

44 Moltmann, *The Way of Jesus Christ*, 131.

as an attainable stage within history, although he does not offer any details as to how this stage may be achieved or what it might look like. He seems to advocate it as a principle of international law and as a means by which nation states may strive to utilize power in the search for human rights, but he does not go into great detail on the issue.[45]

This brings us back to the dialectical characteristic of Moltmann's theology. On the one hand, we see his conception of the church as a "contrast society" living according to principles of the messianic Torah and the nonviolent ethic of the kingdom. Yet on the other hand, we see Moltmann's conviction that Christians may live out the implications of the gospel in a public and socially viable way. The dialectical structure of Moltmann's project enables him to hold these two principles in tension with one another through a movement between an ethical optimism and an ethical realism that allows him to see society as being on the move toward the realization of these goals, but not yet there.[46]

The ethical optimism of Moltmann's position emerges from his understanding of the church as the "first fruits" of the messianic community.[47] As the exodus community, the church has a responsibility to witness to the norms of the kingdom, and to stand on the side of those norms against the "realism" of an unredeemed social system. Speaking of nuclear arms, he writes: "The modern systems of deterrence and retaliation are logical enough in themselves, but their logic is the logic of universal death."[48] The challenge of the exodus church is to present the logic of the kingdom and its associated ethic as an alternative to this "logic of universal death." Moltmann sees this as a concrete possibility in a social situation in which the lines of demarcation between "friend," "stranger," and "enemy" are broken down by the prospect of nuclear annihilation. But this is only possible insofar as the Christian community recognizes itself as embodying a concrete alternative to the given social system. The community's public witness is rooted in its missionary consciousness, and its recognition of God's redemption as meaningful for the world, and not only for Christians.

However, Moltmann also recognizes that such victories, when then occur, are likely to be partial and perhaps transitory. There is a real possibility of martyrdom for those who seek to embody the principles of the kingdom in public life.[49] The symbol of the cross continues to stand within the community as a call to the recognition that the triumph of the kingdom over the institution of evil is an *eschatological* reality. All victories are indeed only partial and perhaps temporary, and there is no inevitable

---

45 Moltmann, *The Way of Jesus Christ*, 130.

46 Yet, it must be said, in the main Moltmann's ethical optimism predominates over his ethical realism. It is clearly the focus of his attention, with his realism operating as a subtext that must be teased out of the details of his argument. As a result, the public aspect of Moltmann's theology can often appear to be utopian in a negative sense, in that it is not apparent just how the ideals which Moltmann espouses can be given concrete historical and social form. It is this aspect that a close reading of his work and an attention to the idea of the "exodus community" can reveal.

47 Moltmann, *The Way of Jesus Christ*, 135.

48 Moltmann, *The Way of Jesus Christ*, 132.

49 Moltmann, *The Way of Jesus Christ*, 130.

progress toward the kingdom, but only the slow and incessant struggle to draw out from history those trends that may be turned to an articulation of the meaning of the kingdom in history and society. One cannot presume in advance the character that such trends may take, or where they will call the church.

Tendencies and Latencies in Modern Society

Despite Moltmann's critical stand toward the abuses of modernity, and his critique of its instrumentality, Moltmann does acknowledge a Blochian conception of tendencies and latencies within society that create a realm within which Christians may engage in both critique and affirmation of society. Recall that for Bloch, the central motivating category of human action is the longing for the *noch nicht*, the not yet. This manifests itself in our cultural life through expression in fantasy, dream, myth, and fairy tale, as well as through social action on behalf of utopian possibilities. For Bloch, the realization of the desire for our true "home" is always before us, an unrealizable state of futurity toward which we perpetually strive.[50] Moltmann's affinity with Bloch is strong at this point, as he also sees this utopian longing as an expression of genuine Christian passion for the coming kingdom of God.[51]

The struggle to realize the utopian possibility within the context of the world in which we live was spoken about in the categories of "tendencies and latencies," by which Bloch means those possibilities within the existing world that bring us toward a closer approximation of utopian hope.[52] The anticipatory consciousness of the utopian imagination recognizes grounds in the world that exists for an optimistic engagement in the struggle for social transformation.[53] This is not a blind optimism, but an optimism based upon both a "cold" analysis of "the limited possible,"[54] which unmasks illusions and ideological presumption, and a "warm" analysis of "the prospect-exploration of What-Is-In-Possibility goes towards the horizon, in the sense of *unobstructed, unmeasured expanse*, in the sense of the Possible which is still unexhausted and unrealized."[55] The first is a limit-principle set on what may conceivably be achieved in the world, while the second looks at the horizon with which reality may converge.[56]

For Moltmann, these tendencies and latencies describe the aspects of modern society that Christians may affirm and seek to develop. The Christian stance toward modern society is not one of pure negativity, but rather a recognition, a "pre-apprehension" (*vorshein*) of the world as it is coming to be. The church as exodus community understands the world in its futurity, and lives that reality within the

---

50 Bloch, *The Principle of Hope*, 16, and passim.
51 Moltmann, *Theology of Hope*, 203.
52 Bloch, *The Principle of Hope*, 18, and passim.
53 See Bloch, *The Principle of Hope*, 4, and passim; Moltmann, *Theology of Hope*, 32, and passim.
54 Bloch, *The Principle of Hope*, 208.
55 Bloch, *The Principle of Hope*, 209.
56 Bloch meditates for some time on the various ways in which "possibility" may be understood, distinguishing, for example, between that which is "formally possible," "factually-objectively possible" and "objectively-real possible." See *The Principle of Hope*, 223ff.

world as it is. This is what Moltmann means when he says of the kingdom: "it is not 'the not-world'; it is the world which is now already turning anew to the future of God because it follows the call to freedom."[57] With regard to Christian action in society, this implies that "Christianity is not in the church but rather the church in the world."[58]

To recall Moltmann's classic formulation in *The Crucified God*, this pre-apprehension of the kingdom in society is found in those movements which stand against the world as it exists, which is to say, the instrumentalized world of technological rationality. It is "in the slums and peace movements"[59] and in "student communities"[60] that the anticipations of the not-yet-conscious reality of the kingdom may be found in modern society.[61] This continues to be reflected throughout Moltmann's work, and he reiterates the same thing by insisting in *Experiences in Theology* that "inasmuch as the gospel heralds Christ's coming parousia, we can see it as Christ's parousia in the world that heralds it."[62] The task of the Christian community is precisely to reflect that coming in every aspect of social life.[63] It is a matter of *action in the world* and not institutional identity that defines Christian life, and that action takes place on every social level in the activity of "looking for the city that is to come" (Heb. 13:14).[64] Moltmann writes:

> This "searching for" means ... breaking out from what is given towards the future which is promised, but is not yet visible (in fact, on the contrary, it is concealed) and is contrasted to "having." ... Hebrews 13:13 connects this searching with confidence in what has been announced but has not yet appeared, with "let us go forth outside the camp" and in this way parallels it to the *exodus* of Abraham and Israel. The openness towards the future of the promise, the leaving-oneself and the emigration from the "lasting city" implies that Christianity does not have its center in itself but rather in the future. It is the community of hope.[65]

What are the tendencies of modern society that Moltmann sees as "pre-apprehensions" of the coming kingdom? Clearly they are connected to those ethical principles discussed above: The messianic Sabbath, Torah, and Peace that are embodied in the teaching of Christ and the lifestyle of the Christian community. At those points of

---

57 Moltmann, *The Church in the Power of the Spirit*, 83.
58 Moltmann, *Hope and Planning* (New York: Harper & Row, 1971), 143.
59 Moltmann, *The Crucified God*, 18.
60 Moltmann, *The Crucified God*, 22.
61 It bears noting that, though these societies are identified by their opposition to the technological rationality of modern society, which Moltmann refers to as the "global marketing of everything," the movements are not "anti-modern" *per se*, but are rather for Moltmann a reflection of the possibilities for moving forward through modernity in anticipation of the kingdom. What Moltmann is speaking of here is neither "counter-modern" nor deconstructive, to use Paul Lakeland's terminology, but rather a late-modern critique of a particular mode of modernist rationality.
62 Moltmann, *Experiences in Theology*, 102.
63 See Moltmann, *Theology of Hope*, 304ff.; and *Hope and Planning*, 143.
64 See Moltmann, *Hope and Planning*, 146.
65 Moltmann, *Hope and Planning*, 146. Italics in original.

intersection with a more "secularized" modern world, we may find these tendencies beginning to develop.[66] Thus, in movements for peace, for economic justice, and for ecology, we can find these pre-apprehensions and tendencies beginning to appear.[67] Similarly, in movements for political liberation from oppression, for the restoration of human rights, and the protection of the innocent we can see these tendencies developing as well.[68] In broad terms, the principles of freedom, democracy, and human rights that we discussed earlier embody forward historical motion that Moltmann sees as an essential part of the anticipation of the kingdom of God.

Once again, it should be noted that Moltmann's own tendency to speak in broad terms often undermines the sociological or ethical application of his ideas. He provides a very large canvas on which to paint the picture of the coming kingdom, but so often it is in the details that the painting takes on life. *Which* peace movements, and *which* strategies for economic justice represent genuine pre-apprehensions of the coming kingdom needs elaboration if we are to affirm that any particular movement is going in the right direction. On the one hand, Moltmann's reference to the messianic Sabbath, Torah, and Peace provide a means by which we could possibly critically assess various movements, but again, the question of the tragic option is not addressed. The same can be said of economic strategy. If the goal is providing economic justice, it is not clear *a priori* which types of movements can establish that. This can only be discerned through an examination and evaluation of the results of various strategies on the basis of the ethics of the kingdom. The lack of such an evaluative stance limits Moltmann's ethical effectiveness, and makes him most useful in terms of his broad principles, but not in terms of an evaluation of institutional structures or policies, nor in terms of concrete proposals for reform.

Yet the community of hope and expectation does not anticipate the possibility of the kingdom in society without a cost. As Moltmann's theological approach is identified with this dialectic of affirmation and critique, so the hope in anticipation is to be met by a suffering in the present in that anticipation.

In this regard, again, the church is a contrast society, in that it undertakes its anticipatory mission in critical opposition to the world as it is constituted. It envisions a society that is the fulfillment of what existing society is called to be, and seeks to actualize that vision proleptically in the present. "Christian hope ... is not empty promises of another world; rather, it places those concerned here and now in the front line of the apostolic event, in the midst of the pain of love."[69]

---

66 Rasmussen rightly points critically to the fact that Moltmann's detection of streams of tendency and latency in modernity tends to fall almost exclusively on the left end of the political spectrum. Moltmann's affirmative stance toward modernity is largely an affirmative stance toward movements that embody modernist principles of freedom and equality, and then seek to find a foundation for those principles in Christianity. See Arne Rasmussen, *The Church as Polis*, 164ff. Whether or not Rasmussen is finally correct about the derivation of these affinities for Moltmann, the impression that one could legitimately draw from Moltmann's corpus is of a theology in support of one very specific corner of modernity.

67 Moltmann, *God for a Secular Society*, 51ff.
68 Moltmann, *Experiences in Theology*, 183ff.
69 Moltmann, *Hope and Planning*, 147.

A hint of what this may mean ethically is found in Moltmann's statement about "the place of sanctification" which is "so to speak, pregnant with the future."[70] This sanctification is found especially on the margins of society "where ... dishonour and disgrace are found."[71] The love that leads Christians to seek the hints of the coming kingdom within the existing world, also leads toward those who are forgotten by the existing world, and leads to a solidarity with those who are outcast and godforsaken.[72] Moltmann writes:

> Suffering springs from the passion of love and it is this love which directs the interest of Christianity outwards away from itself. The Christian does not shape love and the world out of the utopia of faith, but rather out of the fantasy of love. For this reason, the suffering of Christians becomes the form of Christ in the world. To live under the lordship of Christ means to take on oneself that suffering which the "Yes" of real love brings into the world.[73]

In the final analysis, the exodus community realizes the possibility of anticipation through that love that is willing to suffer on behalf of the future toward which it strives, and is willing to make common cause with those social movements with whom they share an ethical and anticipatory affinity for the future. It is in this type of social action that the process of critical assessment of modernity takes place for Moltmann, and in the context of which the various streams of modernism appear affirmatively in his work.

Christian Norms and Practices as Embodiments of Universal Moral Claims

How universal are the principles that derive from a specifically Christian conception of the nature and future of society? If the norms that Christians embrace as defining their ethical universe are in fact not graspable as a universally rational set of moral principles, how can they be understood to be valid moral claims? The church, although Moltmann acknowledges its role as a contrast society, nevertheless realizes its mission precisely in referring to the universal horizon of the principles to which it adheres.[74] The way in which Moltmann roots his whole theological project in

---

70 Moltmann, *Hope and Planning*, 148.
71 Moltmann, *Hope and Planning*, 148.
72 Moltmann, *Hope and Planning*, 148.
73 Moltmann, *Hope and Planning*, 148. Note that the phrase "fantasy of love" is probably not an ideal translation of the German. The German word "*phantasie*" can be rendered in English as either its cognate "fantasy" or "imagination." Imagination seems to embody more accurately what Moltmann is arguing here: Namely that love sparks a new way of construing the world, in which new possibilities of social relation can arise.
74 This is key to understanding the distinction between Moltmann's approach and the approach of a narrative theology that grounds its theological epistemology on the particularity of the church's story. For Moltmann, the church's existence is only provisional, and does not define a unique way of knowing. Rather, the church *responds* to a knowledge that is universally given in the resurrection of Jesus Christ. Whatever contrast the church may have in the surrounding social context, it recognizes itself as responding to a universal truth that represents *society*'s true nature and highest good.

the understanding of God's historical action and futurity enables him to say that Christian theology recognizes in its particular witness that which is universally true, but unrecognized in a secularized and instrumentalized society.[75]

Universality for Moltmann manifests itself in several ways. First, it manifests itself pneumatologically, in the action of the Holy Spirit in the world. Second, it manifests itself eschatologically, in the action of God in history in the bringing about of the kingdom. And third, it manifests itself cosmologically, in the birth of the new creation out of the old.

In the action of the Holy Spirit in the process of redemption, we see the action of God taking place on both a personal and a social level in the dynamics of conversion and sanctification. For Moltmann, conversion defines the means by which the kingdom becomes manifest in history, and transformative in terms of social values and aspirations. It functions, though, not only on an individual level, but on all levels of human life:

> The conversion to which the gospel about the nearness of God's kingdom calls, cannot be limited to either private or religious life. It is as all-embracing and holistic as the salvation of the new creation itself. Conversion takes hold of people, *and* the conditions in which people live and suffer. That is to say, it takes place in personal life, life in community, and the systems which provide an order for these ways of living. In its trend and thrust, conversion is as all-embracing as the coming kingdom of God, whose proclaimed closeness makes conversion possible and necessary.[76]

The Holy Spirit is the Spirit of redemption and reconciliation in history. It is also the Spirit of liberation and rebirth to new life.[77] The Holy Spirit justifies and sanctifies as well, and it does all of these in every dimension of human life.[78] In the personal experience of conversion to Christianity, and in the repentance and regeneration that this entails, the Spirit also signals the possibility of a new way of life: a way of life rooted in healing and fellowship.[79]

Even more radically, the conversion made possible in the Holy Spirit makes possible new modes of social organization, including what Moltmann calls the "culture of sharing" that stands in contrast to the global marketing of everything.[80] These new possibilities are marked by an ethic of acceptance of the unacceptable, and the welcoming of the outcasts.[81] Moltmann writes: "the kingdom of God which Jesus proclaims and which he demonstrates through his dealings with the poor, the sick, sinners and tax collectors does not merely bring the lordship of God over his own creation; it also brings the great and joyful banquet of the nations."[82]

---

75 Moltmann, *Theology of Hope*, 216ff., *The Crucified God*, 65ff., *Experiences in Theology* 163ff. See also the essay "The Revelation of God and the Question of Truth in *Hope and Planning*, 3–30.
76 Moltmann, *The Way of Jesus Christ*, 103.
77 Moltmann, *The Spirit of Life* (Minneapolis: Fortress Press, 1992), 99ff., 144ff.
78 Moltmann, *The Spirit of Life*, 123ff., 161ff.
79 Moltmann, *The Spirit of Life*, 180ff., 217ff.
80 Moltmann, *The Way of Jesus Christ*, 101.
81 Moltmann, *The Way of Jesus Christ*, 112ff.
82 Moltmann, *The Way of Jesus Christ*, 115.

At its heart, the work of the Holy Spirit is embodied in new fellowship that reconstitutes social life in Christ. This fellowship transcends questions of class and culture, or time and gender. It is also not limited to the church as an institution. Rather, it is found in the free action of Christ's Spirit. Moltmann recognizes the broader social context and universal intention of the Spirit when he seeks to understand it in "Christian experiences of the natural communities in home and family, work and civic life" as well as "the voluntary groups of concerned people who are brought together by world problems and developments – peace, environmental, and third-world groups" as well as other modes of human interaction."[83]

Turning to the eschatological dimension of universality, we again must confront the ideas developed in Chapter 2 on the subject of promise and fulfillment. The resurrection of Christ is, for Moltmann, the assurance of a promise that is to be fulfilled for the entire world. Although sin, evil, and death are still realities to be dealt with in the world, Christianity recognizes them as already overcome in Jesus Christ, not only for or in the church, but with regard to reality *per se*. The future defines the reality that we are living, it is not defined by it. And the future is the realm of the fulfillment of the promises of God.[84] History, in the sense of the tragic march of human suffering and retribution, is overcome in the realization of the promises of God. The world is redeemed from history in the presence of God.

The implications of this are, for Moltmann, messianic in the sense that they are representative of the spread of the messianic impulse out of Judaism and Christianity and into the world at large, and apocalyptic in the sense that they involve the radical overturning of the instrumental character of modern society, and the cracking open of the fixity of historical opportunities and the flourishing of new social options.

The eschatological dimension of universality is morally normative particularly with regard to the principles of the kingdom of God discussed above. The world as it is currently constituted cannot abide the ethics of the kingdom, and so therefore the church operates as a contrast society and seeks to anticipate the kingdom in the plurality of institutional milieus in which Christians move in civil society. Yet that which the world does not see in its own tendencies and latencies is eschatologically available as a new way of life for the world as a whole. What is done piecemeal by the exodus community is simply the foretaste of that which is done in the kingdom for the world.

Cosmologically, this theme is extended and developed into an understanding of the new creation of all things. For Moltmann, the final destiny of the world is not simply the completion of a process begun in history, and it is not a return to the garden. Rather, the cosmological implication of the redemptive and salvific work of God is found in the rebirth of a new world from out of the old. Such a new birth is marked by the institution of the eternal Sabbath of God, and the indwelling of God as the Shekinah. The Shekinah is in fact for Moltmann the completion of the Sabbath.[85]

---

83 Moltmann, *The Spirit of Life*, 231.
84 Moltmann, *The Coming of God*, 44ff.
85 Moltmann, *The Coming of God*, 266.

Moltmann sees the significance of this for an ethical outlook in the promise that God will be "all in all" (1 Cor. 15:28). As he interprets it, this implies a deeply ecological ethical responsibility on the part of Christians. The world is not simply the Lord's, but is in fact the "hidden presence of Christ."[86] This hidden presence is revealed eschatologically in God's indwelling presence and carries implications for how the nature of the world is to be conceived.

Once again, we need to consider the socio-political implications of this cosmological aspect. Moltmann writes that "the city of God [the New Jerusalem] is the center of a new creation."[87] This city is the true home of Christians, toward which they strive in the midst of the fallen characteristics of the world. Moltmann writes:

> Christians are citizens of the coming kingdom of God, which is symbolized in "the heavenly Jerusalem" and "the city to come." They are therefore refugees in all the kingdoms of the world. Because they wait for the redemption of this whole perverted world in the coming eternal kingdom, they feel that in this world, estranged from God as it is, they are strangers.[88]

As strangers in the world, Christians are set free from a responsibility to live as the world would have them live. They are called to ethical standards that are a reflection of the world that is coming to be, but is not yet apparent. In light of that, the messianic lifestyle that stands as the hallmark of Christian existence is the foretaste of the life that awaits all in the fulfillment of redemption.

Conclusion

In this chapter I have sought to understand Moltmann's emergent conception of public theology as a form of Christian social ethics, in critical conversation with modernity, while not being captive to its central claims. Rather, the ethics of the kingdom of God, for Moltmann, becomes the social ethic of Christians in the midst of a world that runs contrary to Christian expectations. It is precisely because Christians have both the capacity and the obligation to act in anticipatory fashion in light of their expectation of the coming kingdom that they can act without reservation within the social realm.

The point is not, as Walter Rauschenbusch might have had it, to "Christianize the social order." Rather, it is to live within the social order in light of the coming kingdom of God. This means that one need not attempt to shoehorn modern conceptualizations of social or political arrangements into a specifically Christian box, but one can bring the understanding of human relationships and their fulfillment into a secular setting.

At the same time, however, Christians are not alone in the world. Rather, they are members of a community, which forms and shapes them in light of their common hope and expectation. How the church offers resources for the participation of Christians in public life is the topic of the next chapter.

---

86 Moltmann, *The Coming of God*, 279.
87 Moltmann, *The Coming of God*, 308.
88 Moltmann, *The Coming of God*, 310.

Chapter 11

The Theological and Social Character of the Church

Introduction

The issues raised in the previous chapter lead to a difficult question for theological ethics: If the Christian community is at one and the same time a contrast society, and yet also a sign of the world as it is coming to be, how does that sign have an effect in the context of a pluralistic democracy? Earlier, I discussed the institutional and person-forming character of religious institutions (and particularly the church) within society. Yet, if that person-formation stands in total contrast to society as it exists, as Moltmann sometimes would seem to have it, on what basis can we derive a genuinely *social* ethic from it?

Moltmann's analysis has not delved into these questions except in the most general of terms. What is needed is a conception of the church in society that recognizes the unique calling of Christians to form and sustain civil society and institutional pluralism. Such an approach cannot be based solely on a set of theological claims that ignores the sociological dimension of ecclesial life. Yet, it cannot be reduced to a set of sociological categories that divest its Christian particularity from it.

In this chapter, I will examine further the nature of the church as both an institution within civil society and a theological entity, understood through the metaphor of the body of Christ. As a social institution, the church performs particular functions related to the broader role that institutions play in forming individuals for social participation. As a theological entity, however, the church offers a vision of the world that stands in contrast to many of the presuppositions of modern society. Christians, therefore, are in a sense "double-minded" with regard to the relationship of church to society. On the one hand, they develop resources for public participation, at the same time that the values they inherit create tensions with regard to how they enact that public participation. It is here that the idea of the exodus church is vitally important for understanding what role the church may prospectively play in the formation of society in light of its values and in anticipation of the coming kingdom of God.

The Church in Institutional Life

With regard to society, the twin dangers that the church faces are civil religion ad sectarianism. Yet, both civil religion and sectarianism are distortions of real virtues possessed by the church and civil society. As Robert Bellah notes, civil religion serves a vital social function in providing a set of symbols and myths that embody the values of society.[1] These values are then accessible within the public sphere for the purposes of both supporting society when it acknowledges those values, and critiquing society when it fails to give them due credence.[2]

Yet, to the degree that civil religion is the offspring of a marriage between theological ideas and social forces, it risks the associated mutations of such a pairing. Without an appropriate critical distance from which to approach its social context, civil religion may find itself without an adequate prophetic lens through which to view society, and from which to offer critique. At the same time, it may affirm as theologically appropriate or commendable, precisely those elements in society that are in most need of criticism.[3]

In Part III, I described four aspects of the church's responsibility within civil society, some of which dovetail with the social functions of civil religion. These aspects of the church were: integrative, meaning-making, participatory, and associative. Within civil society, the church assumes these roles regardless of its own theological disposition. Some churches may emphasize and execute these roles more effectively than others, but within institutional life, these are the roles filled by the church.[4]

Religious institutions may provide a symbolic mediation between the individual and the social setting that allows for a self-definition that is not governed by an overweening social hierarchy. They may also set up oppositional institutions. In either case, they demand personal decision about how to participate. They thus allow for the kind of individuation necessary for the development of persons within a democratic polity, capable of participation within a complex social order. To the degree that this self-definition is stunted through a malformed set of social institutions, individuals become less able to engage effectively in public participation. In this sense, the church's public role is most akin to the process of myth-making that takes place within civil religion.[5] It creates a standard by which its social setting may be understood, and the symbols associated with that standard provide a set of critical lenses through which individuals may effectively participate in public life.

Additionally, this symbolic mediation provides a sense of social purpose that extends beyond itself, and yet is not encompassed by society. Rather, it provides a set of mediating structures based upon which individuals may find life and participation to be meaningful. The question is not simply whether the symbolic mediation

---

1 Bellah, *The Broken Covenant*, xvi.

2 Bellah, *The Broken Covenant*, xv.

3 See Moltmann, "Christian Theology and Political Religion," in *Civil Religion and Political Theology*, 46–7

4 These roles can be filled in any meaning-making institutional structure within civil society, not just the church. Thus, a philosophical society, or a political party, or a network of social activists may fulfill these roles in ways akin to the church. Yet, it should be noted that the church's unique contribution to society is not to be found within a particular *functional* role, but precisely in its *substantive* claims about the nature of society and, moreover, reality. It is in uncovering the theological dimensions of lived existence that the church makes its best claim on a social role.

5 See Bellah, *The Broken Covenant*, passim.

provided by the religious institution gives the participant a set of critical lenses, but also whether it can inspire him or her to use them.

Within a pluralistic society, such a symbolic mediation needs to be fruitfully engaged with other such mediations in a socially constructive way. The church is an institution among many institutions (for example, the family, medical and educational institutions, corporations), and Christians must be aware of both of the ways in which other institutions in civil society function, and of their theological roots. Stackhouse and Skillen point out that institutional life cannot be separated from Christian discipleship.[6] As these institutions reflect (albeit often distortedly) the divine intention for a rightly ordered society, Christians have an obligation to support and participate in them. Simply providing for such standards is in itself insufficient to promote the kind of democratic polity of which I have been writing. There need to be within a religious tradition sufficient internal resources to be able to respond to external ways of thought in a socially viable manner. This implies that the substantive claims of the religious tradition are relevant to a proper understanding of its role. So it is important for us to ask then what resources the Christian theology we have been discussing up to this point offers for such a creative engagement. In order to comprehend this, we need to look at the metaphor of the body of Christ, and two corollaries of that metaphor – namely the practices of solidarity and reconciliation.

The Church as the Body of Christ

In order to understand how these two elements, solidarity and reconciliation, cohere within this metaphor of the Body of Christ, it is necessary to look briefly at Paul's exposition of the metaphor in 1 Corinthians 12:12–31 and relate it to his comments in 2 Corinthians 5:11ff.

The image of organic solidarity portrayed in Paul's image of the body is socially significant within civil society, for it speaks of unity with a differentiation of social roles. As he notes: "just as the body is one and has many members, and all the members of the body, though many, are one body, so it is with Christ" (12:12). The church as the earthly manifestation of this body does not create members who exist in a static unity with regard to one another, but that engage in multiple roles for the good of all. Within this community, no role is discounted as being unimportant: "If the foot would say, 'Because I am not a hand, I do not belong to the body,' that would not make it any less a part of the body" (12:15). Yet, any attempt to create uniformity within this unity is counter-productive, for "if the whole body were an eye, where

---

6 See Skillen, *Recharging the American Experiment*, 61ff., Stackhouse, *Public Theology and Political Economy*, 157ff. See Skillen, "Why Kuyper Now" in Lugo, ed., *Religion, Pluralism and Public Life*, 367ff., Max L. Stackhouse, "Social Theory and Christian Public Morality for the Common Life," in *Christianity and Civil Society*, Rodney Petersen, ed. (Maryknoll: Orbis/ BTI, 1995), Stackhouse, *God and Globalization*, vol. 2, 15ff. For discussions of the way in which the various institutions and authorities of society are understood theologically, see the individual essays in this and the other volumes of the series.

would the hearing be? If the whole body were hearing, where would the sense of smell be?" (12:17).[7]

The multiplicity of gifts within the church all aid in the creation of a community that reflects the love and grace of God. All individuals are members of the body of Christ, and contribute through their gifts to its life and sustenance. Paul's point in this metaphor is precisely to encourage cohesion in the midst of internal strife, and so he encourages the Corinthians to "strive for the greater gifts" of love (12:31), which would allow the community to cohere.

This relates to the questions of moral formation within the Christian community. As we saw in the section above, the integrative dimension of a religious community is key to its social function within society. Yet Paul does not write to the Corinthians in order to promote a social theory, but to articulate a theology with social implications. The church is to be a reflection of the being of Christ within the world in which it finds itself. It is therefore called to operate according to the standards that cohere to the nature of Christ. It is thus to be a community in which individuals may develop and use their gifts in communally productive ways.

This could be interpreted in an isolationist fashion – that is, that the church as body exists for its own sake and for God's, but that it is not called to make its reflection of God's being socially relevant. But the question must be asked whether the outworking of its beliefs in the realm of civil society may not have larger implications with regard to social structure. This relates back to questions of communicative rationality within a pluralistic society, for it raises the question of whether the theological foundation created by such a theology of organic solidarity extends beyond the boundaries of the church through its theological formation of persons within society.

Two authors who offer some analysis of the implications of this metaphor for a Christian understanding of society are Helmut Peukert and Gary Simpson. Peukert, in his *Science, Action, and Fundamental Theology* understands solidarity to be a central element in the theological interpretation of communicative action, though he does not offer an explicit ecclesiological framework for it. Yet it is possible to extrapolate the church as the universal communication community of which Peukert writes, which engages in a process of "anamnestic solidarity" through its intention to create an egalitarian and free community before God.[8]

By anamnestic solidarity, Peukert refers to an idea borrowed from Walter Benjamin. Benjamin had argued for an "empathic memory" which was capable of transforming foreclosed possibilities into open potentialities within history.[9] In other words, the past as a reality is not dead to those who are living in the present moment, but rather continues to exist as the result of the work done by those who have gone

---

7 However, as William Everett has argued, there is in this metaphor an implicit suggestion of hierarchy, particularly in the way in which it was used in the Catholic encyclical tradition. See William Everett, "Body Thinking in Ecclesiology and Cybernetics" (Ph.D. diss., Harvard University, 1970), 61ff.

8 See Helmut Peukert, *Science, Action, and Fundamental Theology* (Cambridge: MIT Press, 1986), 202ff.

9 Peukert, *Science, Action, and Fundamental Theology*, 207.

before. History as a human project cannot, as Horkheimer wished to argue, leave the dead behind, because human liberation is indebted to their suffering and sacrifices.[10] The human community thus cannot confine its work to the present liberative moment, but rather must create a society that is based upon "a solidarity which also includes the dead and the generations to come."[11]

This is a necessary element because otherwise the achievement of historical liberation would be a betrayal of those who struggled for it. Peukert writes:

> By definition, this generation is liberated; it has achieved the end state of happiness; its members can live with each other in perfect solidarity. But how is their relation to previous generations to be determined? They must live with the consciousness that they owe everything to the oppressed, the downtrodden, the victims of the prior process of liberation. This generation has inherited everything from the past generations and lives on what they have paid for.[12]

Through the possibility of a universal communication community of the kind described by Apel, such a debt to past generations might be paid if there were some way to make a connection to those who came before. It is this that is the fundamentally theological aspect of Benjamin's conception of "empathic memory," and which Peukert picks up and takes in both an ethical and in a theological dimension.

From an ethical perspective, solidarity is required for communicative action to take place. This is a practical solidarity which, by virtue of the nature of communication itself, in principle involves all potential participants in its circle: "to speak implies the creative projection of an interpretation of subjective, social, and objective reality on to my conversation partner in a way that both opens up an understanding to that person and invites my partner to share her or his own creative interpretation with me."[13] But this involves a risk, since "a person who orients herself or himself toward the freedom of the other as an end in itself, exposes herself or himself. That person becomes all the more vulnerable the more she or he is oriented to the freedom of the other and abandons without limitation any strategic-manipulative action directed toward the preservation of her or his own existence or social system."[14] But under such circumstances, can we treat the dead merely instrumentally, as tools for our liberation, or must we maintain trust with them as well? Peukert notes that indeed such trust is necessary, but it cannot be attained unless the theological implications

---

10 Horkheimer's response to Benjamin's proposal is intriguing, as he identifies Benjamin's insistence on the unclosed character of history as follows: "In the end, your statements are *theological*" (quoted in Peukert, *Science, Action, and Fundamental Theology*, 207. Italics in original). Benjamin's response was to acknowledge the theological dimension in his project, noting that "in empathic memory we have an experience that prohibits us from conceiving history completely non-theologically, as little as we may want to try to write about history in immediately theological concepts" (quoted in Peukert, *Science, Action, and Fundamental Theology*, 207).

11 Helmut Peukert, "Enlightenment and Theology as Unfinished Projects" in Browning and Fiorenza, eds, *Habermas, Modernity, and Public Theology*, 62.

12 Peukert, *Science, Action, and Fundamental Theology*, 209.

13 Peukert, "Enlightenment and Theology as Unfinished Projects," 59.

14 Peukert, "Enlightenment and Theology as Unfinished Projects," 59.

of Benjamin's proposal are seriously considered and placed in the context of the resurrection and of faith as concrete Christian praxis. "Faith itself is a practice that, as a practice, asserts God for others in communicative action and attempts to confirm this assertion in action."[15] This implies the acceptance of others as potential partners in the universal communication community, but, more importantly, asserts the reality of God both as salvation for ourselves and for others.

Relating this to the anticipatory character of the Christian community and the normativity of the kingdom of God, Peukert writes:

> In the understanding of the New Testament, the act of resurrection of Jesus makes possible faith in this resurrection and thus makes possible an existence that hopefully anticipates the completion of salvation for all. God's act of resurrection makes possible an existence that asserts God as the unconditionally saving reality for Jesus and – in anticipation of completion – for everyone. Faith is a remembering assertion of the saving reality of God for all others.[16]

Through the resurrection, the paradox embodied in anamnestic solidarity may be overcome between the living and the dead, and the possibility of a universal communication community may be opened up through the mirroring of Christ's life and action in our own lives.[17] The resurrection is an affirmation of God's stand on the side of the Other and against oppression.[18] It allows us to keep trust with the past and the future as aspects of the community of solidarity with which we are involved: "As anamnestic solidarity, it is universal solidarity in the horizon of all humanity and of one unified history; it constitutes one humanity in the unconditional solidarity of communicative action that anticipates the completion of salvation for all."[19]

For Peukert, writes Gary Simpson, "the category of solidarity [is] a version of 'trans-subjectivity.'"[20] Simpson notes that "anamnestic solidarity becomes a legitimate category for an emancipatory theory and thereby a legitimate moment of emancipatory practice only as it becomes a subsidiary category under the umbrella of communicative argumentation. Indeed, as a movement subsidiary to communicative argumentation, it is necessary!"[21] Yet Simpson recognizes that this category of solidarity as a version of trans-subjectivity is problematic on several fronts. First, following Benhabib, he observes that "because transsubjectivity (solidarity) remains tied to the philosophy of the subject and to the work model of activity, it undermines the fundamental plurality of communicative intersubjective action."[22]

---

15 Peukert, *Science, Action, and Fundamental Theology*, 226.
16 Peukert, *Science, Action, and Fundamental Theology*, 226.
17 Peukert, *Science, Action, and Fundamental Theology*, 227.
18 Peukert, *Science, Action, and Fundamental Theology*, 227.
19 Peukert, *Science, Action, and Fundamental Theology*, 227.
20 Gary Simpson, "*Theologia Crucis* and the Forensically Fraught World," in Browning and Fiorenza, eds, *Habermas, Modernity, and Public Theology*, 185.
21 Simpson, "*Theologia Crucis* and the Forensically Fraught World," 187.
22 Simpson, "*Theologia Crucis* and the Forensically Fraught World," 186.

Second, Simpson understands the idea of reconciliation to be central to a proper understanding of communicative action within society. The "forensically fraught" situation in which human beings find themselves in the world provides the context in which communicative action needs to be understood.[23] Peukert, according to Simpson, in his preference for an Apelian "universal communication community" rather than a more Habermasian understanding of the "ideal speech situation" ignores the implications of the theology of the cross and the problematic of human sin in his understanding of the intersection of theology and social theory. Simpson notes that "there ... can be no socio-political context which is or can be neutralized, immunized, or isolated from the forensically fraught world."[24] Simpson notes, as I have at a number of points, that Moltmann's approach to these questions also does not offer a sufficient link between theology and social analysis or an adequate approach to this issue of "forensic fraughtness." He proposes the idea of the "ministry of reconciliation" as an important linking concept in such a construction. "A practiced socio-political *Theologia Crucis* pursues the Christian hope *ultimately* as a ministry of reconciliation."[25]

In 2 Corinthians, Paul speaks of Christian life as a practice of the ministry of reconciliation, noting the eschatological implications of the concept: "From now on, therefore, we regard no one from a human point of view ... If anyone is in Christ, there is a new creation; everything old has passed away; see, everything has become new!" (2 Cor. 5:17). The reconciliation offered to human beings in Christ creates a context in which we can begin to see one another from the perspective of that reconciliation in a new way. The "message of reconciliation" (19) entrusted by Christ to his people extends beyond the view that persons have of themselves or the Christian community, but entails a new way of seeing the world. Christians are called, therefore, to be "ambassadors for Christ" (20) in the world.

Simpson argues that "the praxis of reconciliation aligns itself more closely to a forensically fraught political *theologia crucis* than does the praxis of solidarity" while at the same time insisting that solidarity remains a necessary element.[26] The ministry of reconciliation is more aware, according to Simpson, of the difficulties attending the making of the Christian message real within society. It recognizes and focuses more on the necessity of repentance in the midst of social circumstances and "more carefully counters the seductions of identity thinking and activity than does the praxis of solidarity."[27]

Apel's "universal communication community" operates without a full sense of its own utopian dimensions, as opposed to Habermas's ideal speech situation. Because Habermas recognizes the ideal speech situation as a limit principle against which actual communicative praxis may be evaluated, but which can never be achieved, there is more of an eschatological dimension to what Habermas is writing, and more of a recognition of human fallibility in the process of communication. The cross

---

23 Simpson, "*Theologia Crucis* and the Forensically Fraught World," 188.
24 Simpson, "*Theologia Crucis* and the Forensically Fraught World," 193.
25 Simpson, "*Theologia Crucis* and the Forensically Fraught World," 193.
26 Simpson, "*Theologia Crucis* and the Forensically Fraught World," 193.
27 Simpson, "*Theologia Crucis* and the Forensically Fraught World," 194.

thus looms more ominously over the society described in Habermas's approach to discourse ethics than Apel's:

> The ministry of reconciliation in the empirical, pragmatic circumstances of human sociopolitical life counters the cooptational and exploitative intensions of the powerful to the extent that this ministry and praxis is grounded and continually tested by the forensically fraught world of the cross. The constitutive interpenetration of the praxis of reconciliation with the forensically fraught world of critique and the cross is what delivers the promotion of reconciliation from being functionalized as a "cover-up, the sin of sins." ...
>
> It is only by grounding reconciliation forensically in critique and the cross that the ministry of reconciliation can be conceived *at all* in reference to murder and murderers.[28]

The moral resources for social transformation and critique can thus be drawn out of an appropriate understanding of the nature of solidarity and reconciliation, rooted in the being and action of Christ and the Christian community. But it is also necessary to understand the principles of communication and discursive praxis as rooted, not only in the practices of the community, but in the very Being of God. It is thus necessary to see how the church itself embodies a reflection of the Trinitarian Being of God.

The Church, the Trinity, and Communicative Rationality

The dual identity of the church as both an institution and as the body of Christ is reflective of a deeper reality that is echoed in both dimensions, namely, the innately relational character of human nature. As discussed in Chapter 3, a Trinitarian understanding of human identity allows one to see that human beings are created for community, and thus human nature is distorted through modern ideologies of autonomy and self-satisfaction.[29] What this means in terms of the social responsibility of the church encompasses multiple dimensions. First, it requires that we recognize that persons are communally constituted with regard to their ethical responsibilities. Second, it requires that we understand the church as reflective of the nature of God in both unity and plurality, and thus as reflective of a definite social model. Third, it requires that we understand communicative rationality in the Habermasian sense as being constitutive of the potential for human redemption within the context of, as Simpson would have it, a "forensically fraught" social setting.

Key to Moltmann's theology was an assertion that the *imago Dei* as reflective of the nature of the Trinity means that human beings are socially constituted, and that moral autonomy is in some sense parasitic on a basically communal human identity. From an ethical perspective, this implies that human beings are called to create social circumstances that are reflective of the communal image of God. There is no one social agenda that infallibly performs this task. However, it does provide us with a set of questions that are useful in the evaluation of social policy and ethical

---

28 Simpson, "*Theologia Crucis* and the Forensically Fraught World," 194. Italics in original.

29 See Cunningham, *These Three Are One*, 170ff.

decisions. We may ask, for example, if a particular course of action will enhance or diminish human possibilities for relationship. Thus, war may be evaluated on the basis of whether military action will, on the whole, allow for a greater possibility for human beings to exist in fruitful and rewarding interactions, or not. This is not the kind of question that can be answered in advance of circumstances with a "yes" or "no." Rather, it requires of Christians that they engage in moral reflection in dialogue with empirical social science.

Similarly, we can ask whether a course of action will degrade the actor's human nature or enrich it. We may also ask whether the social effects of a particular policy will lead to a greater alienation of human beings from one another or not. Again, one cannot answer these questions in advance of an examination of the facts at issue. Does abortion degrade human nature – is it murder? – and diminish possibilities for human relationality or not? In order to answer that question, all of the circumstances of abortion as an issue need to be taken into account and considered in reference to questions of Trinitarian relationality. Even if an examination of the issue allows us to formulate a general rule, however, it does not create an inviolable prescription. Particular circumstances may tilt the balance one way or another.

As socially constituted beings, humans also reflect the values of the communities in which they are formed, and here again the theological and institutional identities of the church mix. The kind of public person that I am is influenced by the theological formation that I encountered within the church. However, as a public person I am also formed by other institutional realities, and as such I am not determined by only one of them, but by the complex interaction within myself as a person in the light of competing considerations. The church may very well be the dominant formative influence for me, but it does not influence me to the exclusion of all else.

But to the degree that the church *does* form me, it does so through its own reflection of the Trinitarian Being of God. Again, the church is both a unity and a plurality. It is a complex organism in which many aspects come together to make a social whole. In many respects, the church is a shadow of the perichoretic unity of the persons of the Trinity. Within the Trinity, each person perfectly reflects the action and intention of the other two persons, so that there is no division within the Trinity with regard either to its activity or its ontology. In all things, the three persons are simultaneously and non-contradictorily one. To the extent that we are able to reflect one another's action and intention, it is always interlaced with egoism and self-service. But as the body of Christ, we recognize two things about our being-in-community. First, we recognize that our being as we perceive it is in fact part of a larger reality understood as the body of Christ, and thus as an echo of that perfect interpenetrating unity of the Trinity. Second, we recognize that the perfection of which the community of the church is a reflection is in fact a goal toward which human beings are called to strive. In this respect, the ethical demands of the kingdom of God and the ontological reality of the relational *imago Dei* are two sides of the same reality: the world as reflective of the Trinitarian Being of God. This idea is similar in at least one regard to Habermas's understanding of an ideal speech situation: It is a utopian limit principle against which we may judge our existing situation.

Helmut Peukert helpfully points out the underlying theological presuppositions of social theory in *Science, Action, and Fundamental Theology*.[30] To the degree that Habermas's theory of communicative action says something true about human beings, and human potentialities, it does so precisely because it reflects, although perhaps unknowingly, a basic theological truth, namely, that human beings are created in the *imago Dei* for relationship in community.[31]

Where Habermas fails to follow through is precisely in his lack of a theological explanation for the reasons why such communicative relations are impossible to achieve. In failing to deal with questions of human fallenness and sin, Habermas can offer no understanding of what prevents human beings from achieving precisely the kinds of ideal speech situations toward which he argues we strive. It is not *simply* that human beings are potentially capable of such openness in communication, but because that possibility is inscribed in the potential for human redemption from alienating personal and social failings. This entails both the ability to reflect on our own situation and recognize ourselves as being less than we ought to be, and an openness to that which may enable us to seek that goal.

In this sense, the idea of Simpson's "forensic fraughtness" again comes into play. Human circumstances are always laden with possibilities for failure, and the human character is always prone to corruption. A recognition that God is involved in the process of overcoming these tendencies through the creation of circumstances in which they may be overcome (for example, through the formation of persons in the recognition of their status as children of God, born of love and relationship with one another), and a recognition of the cost that entails (in the cross of Christ), offers a sobering realization of just what is at stake in the process of striving for the kind of communicative action of which Habermas writes. His social theory is not theologically indifferent. Rather, theology helps precisely in understanding both where his social theory is apt, and where it falls short of the mark.

---

30 Peukert, *Science, Action, and Fundamental Theology*, 143ff.

31 However, Habermas has become more attentive of the question of the interrelationship of religious and sociological concepts recently. See Jürgen Habermas, *Religion and Rationality: Essays on Reason, God, and Modernity* (Cambridge: MIT Press, 2002). Addressing the question of the translation of concepts between social science and theology, Habermas writes: "Theology for its assertions also aspires to a truth claim that is differentiated from the spectrum of the other validity claims. Yet, beyond the measure of uncertainty that all reflection brings as it intrudes upon practical knowledge, theology did not present a danger to the faith of the community as long as it used the basic concepts of metaphysics. ... Under the conditions of postmetaphysical thinking, whoever puts forth a truth claim today must, nevertheless translate experiences that have their home in religious discourse into the language of a scientific expert culture – and from this language retranslate them back into praxis." "Transcendence from Within, Translation from Without" in Browning and Fiorenza, eds, *Habermas, Modernity, and Public Theology*, 234, reprinted in *Religion and Rationality*.

Christian Resources for Public Discourse

Before ending this chapter, it is important to consider briefly some of the ways in which these reflections may provide resources for the encouragement of Christian participation in public discourse. These are in some sense a reiteration and summation of points that have been made elsewhere in this book, but that bear explication here.

Discourse Ethics and Substantive Moral Claims

The recurrent problem raised in speaking of Christian discourse in the public square, one that is addressed in public theology by Ronald Thiemann's articulation of a narrative approach to theological discourse, is that of the incommensurability of the "language-games" of moral universes to which we belong and which constitute the "sources" of our "selves."[32] Jeffery Stout speaks of this in terms of "normal" versus "abnormal" discourse.[33] The instrumental presumptions of modern society reduce moral language to private preference, which is then evaluated solely in terms of utility. Yet if we deny the arguments in favor of pure subjectivity in moral language we still need means of speaking of their objective truth in the context of a pluralistic society, in which the basis of moral decision-making varies from community of discourse to community of discourse.

A discourse ethic offers a means of providing translation across language games, while allowing participants to maintain a *prima facie* adherence to their own moral norms. This is what Karl-Otto Apel means when he refers to the idea of a "transcendental language game," one that overcomes the intransigence of different moral discourses:

> The *transcendental* conception of language-communication on the level of pragmatics or hermeneutics may show that, notwithstanding the indispensable mediation of meanings – and hence of all personal intentions – by the use of language, the ancient postulate of intersubjectively valid concepts of the essence of things may be fulfilled in the long run by the process of communication in the indefinite communication community of rational beings, which was intended and also brought along in all civilized language-communities by the invention of discussion by concepts.[34]

The open-ended character of communicative action directly implies certain formally necessary normative principles to govern the practice of discussion. These principles take up a similar place in discourse ethics to that taken in Kant's philosophy by the categorical imperative.[35]

---

32 See Taylor, *Sources of the Self*.

33 Stout, *Ethics After Babel* (Boston: Beacon Press, 1988), 294.

34 Karl-Otto Apel, "The Transcendental Conception of Language Communication and the Idea of a First Philosophy," in *The History of Linguistic Thought and Contemporary Linguistics*, ed. Herman Parret (New York: DeGruyter, 1976), 61. Italics in original. See also Apel, *Towards a Transformation of Philosophy* (London: Routledge & Kegan Paul, 1980), 136ff., 225ff.

35 See Jürgen Habermas, *Moral Consciousness and Communicative Action* (Cambridge, MA: MIT Press, 1990).

Habermas speaks of the rules of such discourse in the *Theory of Communicative Action*. He notes that it must include 1) a recognition on the part of the participants of the legitimacy of communicative acts, 2) that participants speak truthfully with regard to the facts of the matter, 3) that the participants speak truthfully with regard to their own orientation toward the facts as well.[36] He notes: "The fact that the inter-subjective commonality of a communicatively achieved agreement exists at the levels of normative accord, shared propositional knowledge, and mutual trust in subjective sincerity can be explained in turn through the functions of achieving understanding in language."[37]

Under such conditions, it may be possible to overcome the incommensurability of language games, at least in terms of our attempt to achieve understanding, if not in our ability to bring about agreement about moral norms. Under such conditions, however, it is necessary to note that what is being put into conversation and dispute *is* precisely an affirmation of moral norms as being objectively valid. The participants in such discourse, if they are following the rules of discourse as Habermas and Apel conceive of them, do not attempt to reduce moral discourse to matters of feeling, but recognize in the midst of moral differences a difference in the *perception of social and historical reality*.

Within a pluralistic society the moral universe formed by the affirmation of the person and work of Jesus Christ is an obligation to witness to the truth of that affirmation, not simply as a way of perceiving the world, or as a truth that is valid only within the context of that community, but as in fact a truth that reflects something true about reality itself. Such an assertion about the truth of the reality within discourse cannot be said to be "anti-liberal" in the way that John Rawls seems to argue at points. At the same time, it cannot be said to be "liberal" in the strictly modernist sense of the term. Rather, it acknowledges the reality and benefit of an open discursive society while at the same time not allowing its own sense of moral normativity to be abrogated.[38]

Covenantal Theology and Social Cohesion

If Christian participation in public life is based upon an affirmation about the truth of reality *per se*, then it needs to articulate an understanding of the world as reflective

---

36 Habermas, *The Theory of Communicative Action*, I:307–8.

37 Habermas, *The Theory of Communicative Action*, I:308. Recall that for Habermas, communication is the *natural* orientation of language. Language exists to bring about conditions of understanding, and so the proper result of a communicative act is precisely the kind of honest discourse of which he is writing here.

38 See Rescher, *Pluralism*; Schrag, *The Resources of Rationality*. Of particular interest on this score as well is S. Mark Heim's *Salvations* (Maryknoll, N.Y.: Orbis Books, 1995), in which he argues in favor of a type of "orientational pluralism" with regard to interfaith dialogue. The same thing can be said here vis-à-vis social discourse. Society interacts with many worldviews implicit in institutional pluralism. These worldviews are affirmed by their adherents as being true descriptions of the world, or true prescriptions for how it should be. At the same time, discourse demands a willingness to recognize the internal coherence of a worldview, even while rejecting its affirmations about reality *per se*.

of God's will. As I discussed in Chapter 4, the Reformed covenantal tradition offers one way in which society can be conceived as reflecting a truth about the relationship between human prospects and divine intentions. For the Reformed tradition, society is not simply a Hobbesian arrangement inaugurated by human beings to keep violence and self-service at bay, but is rather a good, and an aspect of the divine intention for the world. The organization of social life is a reflection of the intentions of God, and various institutions such as the family, political and economic structures, and cultural and religious systems, are in some way rooted in the divine will.[39] There is no original or eschatological anarchism, then. Government, even in its fallen forms in the world, is a reflection of the divine intention that human beings live in relationship with one another.

The vantage point that is gained through a covenantal interpretation of human society is precisely that it allows one to view society as meaningful despite the instrumental and self-serving dimensions that are so much a part of public life. One may very well acknowledge, in the face of corruption, that this is often the way the world is, and yet not be governed by it, in the realization that this is a distortion of a much more profound truth.[40]

In both the Catholic and Protestant interpretations of the institutional pluralism of civil society, diversity in the public realm is envisioned as a necessary and positive dimension of human development. In striving for a multitude of ends, some ultimate, many less than ultimate, human beings contribute to the health of the society in which they live. Yet, from a Christian perspective, the social good produced under such conditions is always penultimate, and in the service of the nurturing of a society in anticipation of the kingdom of God.

The great ambiguity of Christianity in public life is precisely the question of how such a pluralism of ends can mesh with a unitary interpretation of social life. Yet, the missionary purpose of the Christian community relies on a presumption that this purpose can only be made clear in the context of human activity.[41] When Moltmann speaks of the exodus community going into the world of vocation for the purpose of bringing about anticipations of God's reign, it is out of the presumption that the moral force employed by those who follow Christ in public life can shift the focus of social activity. And this then raises the question of how Christian norms can be understood as binding in such activities, lest the shift in focus move in the other direction, and Christians be converted by the world, rather than converting it. The link between the communicative rationality of Habermas and Apel on the one hand,

---

39 See Stackhouse, *Public Theology and Political Economy*, 163–4.

40 This perspective is often present in Augustine's reflections on the nature of political society in *The City of God*. For Augustine, Rome, for all of its flaws and corruptions, is a genuine reflection of God's intention for society. This intention was an outgrowth of human inability to follow God's will, although for later followers of Augustine, such as John Calvin and Heinrich Bullinger, the structure of governance itself reflected the divine ordering of society for the positive good of human beings. See Augustine, *The City of God* (New York: Cambridge University Press, 1998); John Calvin, *Institutes of the Christian Religion* (Philadelphia: Westminster Press, 1960), Heinrich Bullinger, "The One and Eternal Testament or Covenant of God," in *Fountainhead of Federalism*, 99ff.

41 Moltmann, *Theology of Hope*, 329ff.; *The Church in the Power of the Spirit*, 76ff.

and Moltmann and the covenantal tradition on the other may be found precisely in the possibilities for understanding within deep commitments that is engendered through communicative action. In such circumstances, the dialogical activity may itself become a reflection of covenantal dynamics.

The faith that leads out of the church and into the public realm is rooted in the affirmation that God indeed has a covenant that extends not, as Ronald Thiemann would have it, only to the interpreting community of the church, but that can be extended to the various institutions of pluralistic society, and furthermore, to the entire world. The conversion that Christians seek is a reorientation of society as a whole to become more reflective of God's intention. This need not mean a conversion of all persons in society to Christianity, but it does mean the structuring of a society in ways that differ from the instrumental rationality of modernity precisely by being oriented to horizons of value, broadly conceived. In fact, the religious pluralism within a diverse society may itself be seen as a reflection of God's will in a society where God has not yet become "all-in-all" but remains hidden behind the veil of the cross. Under such circumstances, the diversity of religious ideas and ends in society is a testament precisely to the idea that God does not compel belief, but seeks to persuade through the activity of the Holy Spirit. If we are indeed led by "bonds of love" toward God (Hosea 11:4), then a multitude of religious points of view provide the setting where such persuasion may take place in the context of open discursive practices.

The affirmation of a covenantal structure of human society also allows for the insistence that liberal society is rooted in something more than a procedural or formal way of relating to one another. Rather, it recognizes that what is good in liberal society is precisely a reflection of, and evolution of, the political principles deriving from covenantal theology. Human beings as created by God are constituted for relationship with one another in such a way that their fundamental humanity is respected and honored, and thus human beings are freed from external social compulsion to seek those ends that most correspond to their deepest aspirations, even under those circumstances where those aspirations may not correspond to the will of God. Under such circumstances, it is through persuasion and not compulsion that a renewal or recovery is possible. This emphasis on human dignity and persuasive polity is a dimension of liberal democracy only because it was first a dimension of covenantal theology.

But covenantal theology is itself in need of a grounding in that which is ultimate. What William Schweiker calls a "moral ontology" has itself to be rooted in a proper understanding of the Being of God.[42] This entails a recognition that covenantal theology, and derivatively liberal democracy, are themselves reflections of the triune nature of God.

---

42 William Schweiker, *Power, Value, and Conviction: Theological Ethics in the Postmodern Age* (Cleveland: Pilgrim Press, 1998), 5ff.

Trinitarian Theology, Democratization, and Human Dignity

A Trinitarian conception of God, as I have discussed both in this chapter and in earlier chapters, provides a basis for a relational moral theory, in which the *imago Dei* is reflected in the capacity in human beings for I/Thou relationships.[43] When Moltmann writes of the Trinity as "our social program,"[44] it is from this wellspring that he is drawing, yet he never adequately makes the theoretical links between the keystone implications of this concept of the *imago* and the practical questions of social organization that are necessary corollaries.[45] The question I would like to consider here is how the idea of the Trinity can translate into a social theory of democracy and human dignity. There are three dimensions to this: First, the connection between Trinity and covenant, second, the relation of covenant to democracy, and third, the rootedness of human dignity in the *imago Dei*.

As I discussed earlier, the covenantal dimension of the church as an element of the church's social identity offers a way of understanding the church as being neither bound within a system of civil religion, according to which it simply affirms its social setting, nor as a community set apart from the world, but rather as a community/association that is dynamically involved with its social setting in an effort to anticipate its final form within boundaries of human finitude. Yet, the very ability to engage in covenant is dependent upon the eternally covenantal relations among the persons of the Trinity, and is reflected in the way in which the *imago*

---

43 The literature on this is vast. For a partial set of perspectives on this issue, see the following: Martin Buber, *I and Thou* (New York: Scribner, 1958); Barth, *Church Dogmatics* (Edinburgh: T & T Clark, 1936–69), III:2, 222ff.; Karl Rahner, *The Foundations of the Christian Faith* (New York: Crossroad, 1982) and *The Trinity* (New York: Crossroad Pub., 1997); Volf, *After Our Likeness*; Jensen, *The Triune Identity* (Philadelphia: Fortress Press, 1982); LaCugna, *God for Us* (San Francisco: HarperCollins, 1991); Cunningham, *These Three Are One*; Douglas John Hall, *Thinking the Faith* (Minneapolis: Augsburg, 1989), idem., *Confessing the Faith* (Minneapolis: Fortress Press, 1996), and idem., *Professing the Faith* (Minneapolis: Fortress Press, 1996). Of course, the classical sources of much of this reflection can be found in the work of the Cappadocian Fathers, particularly *On the Holy Spirit* and *On Not Three Gods*.

44 Moltmann, *Experiences in Theology*, 332ff.

45 Which is not to say that he does not point to the importance of ideas of social freedom and human dignity in his explication of the doctrine of the Trinity. In particular, he writes in *The Trinity and the Kingdom*: "The Trinitarian doctrine of the kingdom is the theological doctrine of freedom. The theological concept of freedom is the concept of the Trinitarian history of God: God unceasingly desires the freedom of his creation. God is the inexhaustible freedom of those he has created" (218). Yet, helpful as this is in offering a critique of unfreedom, it does not aid in determining how freedom should be positively understood in the means of social organization. Miroslav Volf is more helpful in this regard, as he considers the complexity of viewing the relations of Trinity, church and society: "the church is not an aggregate of independent individuals, but rather a communion of ecclesially determined persons. On the other hand, the church cannot simply be a social organism, since a person is not simply born into it, but rather is *re*born. Christian rebirth presupposes personal faith with its cognitive and volitional dimensions" (180, italics in original). A central element of this is precisely in the recognition of the relational character of God and human beings created in the divine image, a recognition rooted in God's triune being.

is present in each human being. To be in covenant is to be in relationship, and our human relationality is precisely a reflection of the relational identity of the Trinity.

Just as within the Trinity the Father, the Son, and the Holy Spirit are in perfect harmony of accord with one another, so we human beings are called to be in accord with one another in the midst of our relationships. The covenantal framework that, within the Reformed tradition, reflects both God's relation to human beings and human beings' relations to one another sets the pattern according to which social agreements may be set down. Without recognizing the essential relationality that underlies covenantal agreements, covenant quickly becomes a matter of contract, and thus becomes less a matter of the relational aspect of the parties involved and more a matter of mutual convenience and utility. Yet, this divests the idea of covenant of its substantive form and its communicative presupposition, and reduces it once again to a question of strategic rationality. A recovery of the importance of relationality rooted in Trinity is essential for an understanding of the social implications of such agreements.

Paralleling the interpersonal interpretation of covenant, such as in marriage, is the large-scale organization of covenantal, pluralistic democracy. If the nature of the good society is based upon the kind of relationality that is reflected in the doctrine of the Trinity, then it must reflect the non-hierarchical and egalitarian nature of those relations. In this regard, the language of Father, Son, and Holy Spirit can hinder as well as it helps. While it emphasizes the relational dimension of the Trinity, it would also imply, as it often seemed to do for the Cappadocians, a paternalistic relationship between Father and Son, with a "hierarchy of office," if not of being.[46]

Yet a reflection on the oneness of God's Being-in-Trinity would lead to the conclusion that the Father/Son conception of the Trinity is analogical at this point rather than univocal.[47] It provides an image that aids us in understanding the intratrinitarian nature of God, but also leads us into the mystery of the immanent Trinity, which is beyond our comprehension. In the perichoretic unity of the three Persons of the Trinity, there is no genuine hierarchy, but a mutual indwelling in love and equality.[48] It is the love and equality reflected in these Trinitarian relations that defines the anthropological presupposition that lie behind both a covenantal theology of human relations and a covenantal view of social relations.[49]

The chief advantage a theory of civil society offers in this regard is a realm in which spheres of intimacy can develop among like-minded persons. This becomes a kind of "training ground" for social relations, in that as persons learn within

---

46 See Miroslav Volf, *After Our Likeness: The Church as the Image of the Trinity* (Grand Rapids: Eerdmans, 1998); Catherine LaCugna, *God for Us: The Trinity and the Christian Life* (San Francisco: HarperCollins, 1991).

47 See Thomas Aquinas, *Summa Contra Gentiles* Bk. 1, Chs. 28–34 in Sigmund, ed., *Thomas Aquinas on Politics and Ethics* (New York: W.W. Norton, 1987).

48 See Moltmann, *The Trinity and the Kingdom*; Leonardo Boff, "The Trinity," in *Mysterium Liberationis* (Maryknoll, N.Y.: 1993).

49 At the same time, and following a more Madisonian view of social pluralism, it is a happy coincidence that social relations in a pluralistic society not only foster such love and equality, but also serve to prevent the creation of overly-powerful factions that can undermine the social whole. See Madison, "Federalist 10," 14.

community the kind of respect and mutuality that is a reflection of the Trinitarian relations within the godhead, they may also extend that lesson beyond the smaller associations of civil society to reflect a broader view of human beings in society, and human being in general. For that reflection to take place, though, it is necessary to have the kind of plurality-in-unity among social institutions and relations that can truly manifest both the equality and the love that is rooted in the Trinity.

But neither a covenantal view nor a democratic view is possible without an understanding of the unique human person as a being of dignity before God. We are *imago Dei*, not only in our relationality, but also in our uniqueness.[50] As such, contrary to Rousseau, we cannot be "forced to be free" according to a prefabricated conception of freedom.[51] Rather it is through the communicative process of persuasion that honors the dignity of the person within the conversation that a conception of freedom can develop that leads into community. While within a fallen social setting such a conception of freedom and persuasion needs to be comprehended within a system of laws and mores that constrain the worst possibilities of human freedom gone awry, freedom as individuality-within-community is predicated precisely on the human dignity that presumes our capacity to come to God through an act of grace and the assent of the human will.[52]

Conclusion

The place of the Christian within society, as one on a pilgrimage within the matrix of social relations within which he or she is surrounded, and yet not fundamentally belonging to them, creates a tension within the Christian identity. This tension is reflected in the call of theologians like John Milbank and Arne Rasmussen to define the Christian identity apart from the claims of modern social science, and to understand the Christian as one set apart from the world. Yet, Christians are not truly "apart" from the world in a social sense. We exist within the world, as participants in the multiplicity of institutions to which we belong. Our identity, shaped and molded by each of those institutions, not solely by the church, reflects dimensions of the whole of the society to which we belong. The church exists as one, but not the only, institution engaged in our moral and social formation.

---

50 See Moltmann, *On Human Dignity*, 11ff.; Schweiker, *Power, Value and Conviction*, 142.

51 Rousseau, "On the Social Contract," in *Basic Political Writings*, 150.

52 Moltmann prefers a different language to describe what I am trying to say here. He argues that the term "person" is better than "individual" in this case. He writes: "A person, unlike an individual, is a human existence living in the resonant field of his social connections and his history. He has a name, with which he can identify himself. A person is a social being. The modern thrusts towards individualization in society prompt the suspicion that a modern individual is the product of that age-old Roman principle of dominance: *divide et impera* – divide and rule." *Experiences in Theology*, 333. In *On Human Dignity*, however, he did tie the Triune *imago Dei* with individual human rights, writing: "In fellowship before God and in covenant with others, the human being is capable of acting for God and being fully responsible to God. As a consequence of this, the social rights and duties of the human community are just as inalienable and indivisible as persons' individual rights and duties" (25).

At the same time, what the church forms us to be must inevitably come into conflict with much of what modernity asks us to be. The church calls us to be disciples, rather than consumers, to love one another, rather than treat one another instrumentally. How we understand the resources that the church gives us in attempting to negotiate the tensions within our identity depends on what contributions we believe the modern ethos can make to Christian life, as well as what contributions Christianity can make within the modern ethos.

The advantage of a communicative conception of rationality, such as the one offered by Habermas and Apel, is that it provides a secular analogue to the Christian conception of love and mutuality in human relationships, which are themselves a reflection of the intratrinitarian life of God. Such analogues, where we can find them, offer bridges between modernity and Christianity. Thus, the Christian conception of the exodus community, through which Christians participate anticipatorily in the institutional life of modernity, is enabled by the analogical interplay between particularly useful modern conceptions of self and society, and the Christian conception of personhood within the church and under God. As Christians traverse the rough and untamed pathways of modernity, they may, however incompletely, attempt to transform them in light of their conception of the destination, the journey toward which is the sum of the Christian moral life.

Chapter 12

Conclusions and Prospects

Introduction

This book has been wide-ranging, and I have attempted throughout to draw upon the various strands of reflection on the subjects of public theology, political theology, and civil society. At the same time, I have wanted to make clear the way in which Jürgen Moltmann's theology offers resources for a further development in public theological discourse – through his creative and critical use of philosophical and sociological categories, through his eschatological approach to ethics, through his doctrines of the Trinity and anthropology, and particularly through his understanding of the role of the church within a complex and pluralistic society.

In Chapter 1, we considered the various problems raised for Christian theology in a modernist social framework. Privatization, instrumentalism, and individualism are threats that theology must confront directly. Throughout this book, I have attempted to point toward those themes that may allow theology to more fully recognize and respond to the public obligations implied by life in modern society. For the next few pages, I would like to summarize the conclusions of this book and allude to possible directions for further development.

A Viable Public Theology Needs a Theory of Civil Society

Throughout this book, I have returned repeatedly to the question of how it is possible for Christians to have a credible voice in a modern social context. The approaches to public theology represented by Tracy, Thiemann, and Skillen each attempt to deal with that problem, either by rooting theology in a universal rational potential and common human experience, by asserting the identity of the church as a community over against the external world, or by turning to a reliance on the doctrine of creation. Alternatively, one can look to the "radical orthodoxy" of John Milbank and argue that the church's public role is found precisely in refusing to acknowledge a separate realm from that of the religious. All social theory is derived directly from theology. Accordingly, to this approach civil society is irrelevant because the only society of any theological or ethical importance is the society embodied and advocated in the church. Other institutions – economic, educational, political – are destined to be assimilated within the ecclesial superstructure, or pass to the dustbin of history.

Yet, what binds Tracy, Thiemann and Skillen together with Moltmann, despite their differences, is precisely their recognition that the church participates in a variegated public realm, in which organizational structures come into being and pass away, meld and merge, overcome and undermine one another. And Christians, for better or worse, are members not of one institution, but of many. The overlapping nature of social life demands that Christian theology take account of that pluralism. If Christians are not simply to detach themselves from all associational life, becoming truly alien and not very resident in the modern world, then there must be a theological understanding of what the parameters of that social life entail. What may be allowed from an ethical standpoint as Christians seek to make their way in the world? What forms of institutional life are mandated by the gospel (that is, in what way might family, economy, or political life be more truly oriented toward the divine will)? What forms of institutional life (organized crime? racial supremacist?) are beyond the pale of acceptable Christian involvement?

I have tried to begin to sketch a theory of Christian public involvement in civil society in describing the church's nature as dialectical – as always being *both* a social *and* a theological institution simultaneously. The church is indelibly the body of Christ. This is an aspect of its nature that cannot be separated from it. It is at the same time a formational social institution, which, like many other social institutions, gives women and men a social space in which to develop into public persons. The church is, to use William Everett's terminology once more, a "theaterola" of public life.[1]

Furthermore, if, as I have argued, public theology needs to deal with human social life in *all* of its dimensions, and not just the political, it needs to possess the intellectual resources to fruitfully engage in the broader social conversation. Through an engagement with the theory of civil society, public theology can, through dialogue, come to a greater understanding of the assorted worldviews that constitute the complexity of modern society. These are not only church and state that must be considered in the development of a theory of Christian public life. Church and state must each be understood within the grid of all approaches to human knowing and being – philosophical, scientific, aesthetic, and moral.

The advantage offered by an understanding of the theory of civil society is precisely that it gives us a framework on the basis of which we can comprehend the interrelationships of institutions in public life, and thus comprehend more clearly the multiple ways in which Christians see themselves within society. It is not as simple as saying that Christians are formed by the church. Christians are formed by a whole congeries of institutions, and in the context of a pluralistic society, these many institutions create a complex moral framework with which Christians must deal.

The Kingdom of God Provides the Normative Model for Christian Public Life

With the previous section in mind, it is nevertheless important to consider what Christians bring that is distinctive to public discourse. We are formed by institutions, but are we merely blown by every wind? Do we have something within the Christian moral tradition that can serve as an anchor? It is in answering this question that Moltmann's approach to public theology in particular is helpful.

---

1 Everett, *God's Federal Republic*, 155ff.

Within the pattern that Moltmann establishes in *Theology of Hope*, and which extends through his latest work, Moltmann navigates the difficulties of how the church is to respond to its society by engaging in both an affirmation and a critique. But both affirmation and critique need to be based on a substantial idea of what the existing conditions are to be compared with. By seeking, as he says in *Theology of Hope*, to see the whole of theology through the lens of eschatology,[2] he lays a foundation based upon which his critique of public life will be built. The promise, given by God to Abraham and his people, fulfilled and continued in the person of Jesus Christ, and expected in the eschatological fulfillment of that promise, sets the standard by which we can consider public life. In all of our moral and political judgments, we stand in the shadow of the kingdom of God.

But how does the kingdom of God serve as a governing symbol to lead Christians in their public lives? The kingdom sets up a set of normative dispositions and ideas that Christ's followers are required to take seriously in their public commitments. Moltmann's approach to these issues follows the Reformed tradition in its affirmation that there is no realm that is beyond the sovereignty of God, and no realm through which God's power cannot act for the sake of human redemption.[3]

It is that emphasis on the possibility of redemption that allows Christians to embrace their public responsibility. If the kingdom serves as a critical principle against which the present is judged, and toward which the present is tending, then it is the responsibility of Christians in public life to engage in that critique and to realize that tendency. They must awaken those latencies within the present that open up towards the possibility of the kingdom. This can be done through a recognition that Christians are not bound in their public lives to embrace a Machiavellian calculation of interest, but are freed in Jesus Christ to engage in politics for the sake of the common good.

This is by no means to imply that Christians can engage in public life free of the possibility of suffering and rejection. Such a possibility is always present in public action. Yet, in rejecting the idols of expediency and power, Christians are liberated from the deception that these things are ultimate, and are freed to hope in the possibility of the kingdom to which they are called.

It is in this, I believe, that the truth of Moltmann's reflections in *The Way of Jesus Christ* on the nature of "messianic ethics" can be found. A doctrinaire pacifism such as he sometimes seems to suggest may not be viable in the midst of the ambiguities of history. Yet a commitment to non-violence may be part and parcel of the way of life formed in the following of Jesus Christ and in a commitment to his kingdom.

---

2   Moltmann, *Theology of Hope*, 11.

3   On the Reformed tradition's affirmation of public life, see John Calvin, *Institutes of the Christian Religion*; Martin Bucer, "De Regno Christi" in Wilhelm Pauck, ed., *Melanchthon and Bucer* (Philadelphia: Westminster Press, 1969); Heinrich Bullinger, "A Brief Exposition on the One and Eternal Covenant of God," in *Fountainhead of Federalism*. Although Reinhold Niebuhr's position sometimes bears stronger resonance with the Lutheran viewpoint on this, his acknowledgement of the possibility of redemption even in the midst of the ambiguity of public life puts him squarely within the spectrum of the Reformed tradition on this question. See *Nature and Destiny of Man*, II:269ff.

However, as Moltmann recognized in *The Church in the Power of the Spirit*, there are limits to the possibilities we can expect to embrace within history:

> We are already freed from "the body of death" (Rom. 7) through justifying faith; and we walk in new obedience by virtue of newness of life (Rom. 6). But we are still living in the "body of death" and are still waiting with eager longing, together with the whole of creation, for "the redemption of our bodies" (Rom. 8). Otherwise the messianic action would no longer be action in history; it would already be free movement in the kingdom of God. As long as people are not redeemed from "the body of death" they can only practice their freedom from the body of sin in our mortal life. As long as the dead are dead, freedom is fighting freedom, but not yet freedom in its own world, in the kingdom of God. The "body of death" does not only mean physical death; it also means a deadly cohesion to which all life belongs. This cohesion has been broken in principle, but not yet in fact, through liberation from the power of sin.[4]

Christians are not governed by this reality, but nevertheless must pay heed to it. Moltmann correctly notes that Christian ethical life must "encourage everything in history which ministers to life, and strive against everything that disseminates death,"[5] but it cannot be told in advance what form that encouragement might take, or what tragic dimensions that striving might entail. But what can be said is that if the recognition of the kingdom as the norm toward which Christians are to strive in their public lives means anything, it means that the tragedy of the tragic will be fully acknowledged, and that even in the midst of unavoidable evil, Christians will endeavor to minister to life and struggle against death.[6]

The Church Within The World Remains an Exodus Church

In saying this we must return to the central theological contribution that Moltmann makes to an understanding of civil society, namely the church's identity as an exodus community. Insofar as persons are formed within the church according to a particular way of life – that is, the way that Moltmann identifies as messianic, it remains a "contrast society".[7] The contrast that the church offers to the world is a contrast that is represented by a community that anticipates society's own possibilities better than society itself. The church remains an exodus church because the church is on the move toward the kingdom of God, and beckons society to follow.

Yet, because of this, if Christians take seriously the values that their faith entails, they will not be able to sit comfortably within a world that offers different moral

---

4 Moltmann, *The Church in the Power of the Spirit*, 195.
5 Moltmann, *The Church in the Power of the Spirit*, 196.
6 Thus, I believe, one can agree with Moltmann in terms of both his theological and ethical ideals here, while also recognizing, as he himself did at an earlier stage, that violence may at some points be necessary, not as a positive good, but as a consequence of that "body of death" in which we still dwell, which may limit the possibility of non-violence in the achievement of some historical good. That any such historical good will inevitably be tainted is an implication of the limits that history, sin, and mortality place on our possibilities.
7 See Arne Rasmussen, *The Church as Polis*, 76ff.

standards. In a modern world in which religious life is privatized, such a faith will publicly proclaim itself and its social relevance. In a secular world where religion is deemed irrational, such a faith will point to the rationality and moral force of its values. And in a society in which instrumental rationality is triumphant, it will constantly refer back to its Trinitarian source, and declare that humans are made, not to be commodities for one another, but to be in a genuinely open relationality.

The church is called to be the exemplary moral community in society. Insofar as it is motivated to a praxis rooted in the anticipation of the kingdom of God, it will always experience the exodus within modern society to which Moltmann refers.

What distinguishes this sense of "contrast society" from the various narrativist approaches, is that Moltmann's understanding of the exodus church is self-consciously rooted in a critical dialogue with modernity. Moltmann does not begin with the presumption that modernity is suitable only for rejection. On the contrary, the dialectical dimension of Moltmann's theology leads him to both affirm and to critique the social system of modernity. At the same time that he regards the privatization of religious life as a failure of modernity, he recognizes with it the significance of human rights. But again, whereas a modernist conception of human rights is rooted in rational autonomy, Moltmann seeks to root it in the covenantal relationship between God and humans. This leads to my next point, namely:

The Idea of Covenant Provides the Bridge Between Church and Society

The conception of covenant, which is a kind of a golden thread connecting the three major aspects of this study, serves as the theological medium through which the particularities of the church's identity-forming vocation can come into contact with the residual covenantal aspects of modern society. The emergence, as we explored earlier, of the concept of the social contract from the earlier covenantal models of society elaborated by Althusius, Bullinger and Grotius, has often obscured the deeply religious underpinnings of modern society.[8]

Within American public theology, this link is often made explicitly and articulated as a justification for Christian public involvement.[9] A version of covenantalism resides within David Tracy's critical correlationism. It is a central feature in the work of James Skillen, and Max Stackhouse's arguments in favor of human rights

---

8   On the other hand, I should note the objection that, even if this is true, the pedigree of an idea does not lay any obligation on the inheritors of its progeny. A social contract may be a valid way of organizing society, whether or not it has a religious underpinning, and the religious underpinning could be viewed as an optional or even an embarrassing hold-over from a less enlightened era, akin to an ideological residual tail. This may or may not be true, although I am inclined to say that such links are neither determinative nor irrelevant. Yet the family line of modern liberal democracy heaves so closely to Christian covenantal theology that it virtually screams out for acknowledgement as a piece of common ground between religiously motivated proponents of modern democratic society and those who find a secular social contract more convincing.

9   Although, as we have seen, Ronald Thiemann stands in contrast to this trend, standing by his own more Barthian interpretation of covenant and Christian social responsibility.

are dependent on the linkage between covenantal theory and the articulation of these basic aspects of human dignity deriving from the *imago Dei*.

Moltmann, too, develops this insight through the lens of his own theological project, emphasizing in particular the principle of the *imago Dei* in human beings that lends them the divine dignity that stands at the foundation of their rights. Human beings are created to live in community with one another, and on the basis of that community, to acknowledge one another's dignity before God. But the implications of the *imago Dei* are spelled out for Moltmann in the covenant and most explicitly in the eschatological promise that exists between God and humanity, sealed in the life, death, and resurrection of Jesus Christ.

This covenantal basis for human rights is finally rooted in Moltmann's Trinitarian understanding of human nature as it relates to the inbreaking of the future, and thus from the social vision that he develops from it. These together can serve as a moral palliative against the degradation of human values in an instrumentalized society. In attempting to orient social values toward something reflective of the kingdom of God, a baseline insistence that human beings be recognized and honored in their humanity is a principle that can certainly be formed within the church, and which also links to the broader assumptions of liberal democracy about the inalienability of human rights.

The covenantal model, reshaped in the idea of the social contract, serves as a basis for understanding the dynamics of institutional pluralism in the theory of civil society. Particularly in its Tocquevillian form, the idea that society is held together through the relatively loose associations of persons within institutions, and not through authoritarian coercion, provides a strong justification for the importance that covenantal agreements play within diverse social systems. As institutions within civil society shape their members in accord with commonly accepted social values, persons learn the civic virtues that provide the basis for public involvement. This is as true of the church as of other social institutions. The church, however, brings the subterranean theological elements to the surface, and understands its vocation, both in its affirmative and critical modes, in light of God's covenantal relationship with the Christian community.

Also centrally important for understanding the link between covenant and civil society is the way in which the kind of discourse ethics of which we have been speaking is itself rooted in a set of covenantal expectations that dialogue partners entertain in encounter with one another. Conversation is predicated on agreement with regard to such issues as honesty, fairness, and full-disclosure. Genuine dialogue depends on the good will of each agreeing party to the conditions for communicative action.[10] There is underlying this a pledge that takes place, not simply between autonomous communication partners, but between human beings. This is a pledge to recognize one another's inviolable dignity in the process of communication. Such an agreement runs deeper than a merely contractual relationship, but assumes the kind of trust best conveyed through a covenantal theological framework.

---

10 Habermas, *Theory of Communicative Action*, I:117.

A Deliberative Democracy Is Essential for Life in Liberal Society

A corollary to this emphasis on the inviolable dignity assured to us in the covenantal relationships of which we are a part is that we must strive to create in our social institutions, relations that reflect the respect and reciprocity that are implied in the covenantal structure of human being. It is here that the work of Habermas and Apel becomes most compelling. The covenantal structure of our created being and the relational foundation of our identity as *imago Dei* are echoed in the communicative action and discourse ethics elaborated within their theories. This implies that human social relationships are unalterably pluralistic, and that pluralism extends throughout the organization of society.

A society that recognizes the importance of such pluralistic relations will strive to create conditions under which that pluralism can thrive within the context of binding covenantal relationships. How those relationships are bound together must, furthermore, be rooted in that respect for persons of which I have been writing. In theological terminology, this can be understood as an ethic of love, and an anticipation of the kingdom of God.[11] In sociological terminology, this can be seen as an ethic of discourse, rooted in democratic and egalitarian presuppositions.[12]

This brings us back once again to the issue of civil society. As it has developed in the Anglo-American tradition, civil society has an expanded view of the realm of free association and person formation, and of the informal ties forged by such associations, which aid in the maintenance of a substantially democratic and pluralistic society. Within the European tradition of civil society, the situation is more complex, due to the association of civil and political institutions. Certainly, Hegel did not place primacy on the freedom of associative relationships within civil society, although he did recognize its importance in mediating between the realms of family and state.[13] As developed in Gramsci's analysis, it provides a realm that has the potential for both liberation and repression.

---

11 See Anders Nygren, *Eros and Agape* (New York: Harper & Row, 1969), Gene Outka, *Agape* (New Haven: Yale University Press, 1972); Reinhold Niebuhr, *The Nature and Destiny of Man*, particularly volume II, and *Moral Man and Immoral Society*; Paul Tillich, *Love, Power, and Justice* (New York: Oxford University Press, 1954); Paul Ramsey, *Deeds and Rules in Christian Ethics* (New York: Scribner, 1967).

12 Gary Simpson's theological analysis of Habermas's relationship to the theory of civil society roots these presuppositions in the search for the common good. He notes: "A prime moral claim of the communicative imagination is that the search for the common good ought to proceed as a common search for the good. In this way, common searching – communicatively imagined – becomes a comprehensive moral good that serves the well-being of other moral goods ... A communicative civil society frequently shares argumentatively tested moral wisdom with the everyday lifeworld. Further, a communicative civil society often spots the colonizing consequences of instrumental and functional rationalities operating within the economy's medium of money and the state's medium of administrative power." Simpson, *Critical Social Theory*, 107.

13 See Peter G. Stillman, "Hegel's Critique of Liberal Theories of Rights," *American Political Science Review* (68 no. 3, Sept. 1974), 1086–92; Irving Louis Horowitz, "The Hegelian Concept of Political Freedom," *The Journal of Politics* (20 no. 1, Feb, 1966), 3–28; Steven B. Smith, "What is 'Right' in Hegel's Philosophy of Right?" *The American Political Science*

The question of the fundamental nature and prospects of civil society is certainly far from resolved, although it is increasingly recognized across the political spectrum as of central importance in securing a respect for democracy and an acknowledgement of human rights.[14] As I argued in Chapter 9, however, the central theological significance embodied in the idea of civil society is its capacity for the formation of persons according to a set of principles that are, to use Paul Tillich's terminology, neither autonomous nor heteronomous, but have at least the capacity to become carriers of a validly theonomous spiritual and ethical life.[15]

As an exodus community, the church exists as an institution within civil society that engages in just such a practice of moral and spiritual formation. Were it the goal of the church to form persons for its own sake, then this would have no larger social implications. Yet the church exists for the sake of the world, and the persons that are formed within the walls of the church are formed for the purpose of walking through the doors of the church and engaging in their Christian vocation through their myriad worldly vocations within the larger social context in which they live.[16]

The possibility that the church may have a significant social impact is related to the degree of deliberative democracy that exists in the social setting in which the church finds itself. As a participant with other traditions, movements, and institutions in the formation of a liberal democratic context, with a highly developed and differentiated civil society, the prospects for the church having a significant impact are great. But this is not to imply that the church as an exodus community is only viable within such societies. The church is an exodus church in whatever setting it finds itself, but its task of creating persons equipped to anticipate the kingdom of God in their own societies is complicated and rendered more difficult when civil society is trampled through institutions of repression.

At the same time, the church within society is always at risk of cooptation in the name of civil religion. The virtue of civil religion is that it may offer Christians a moral basis for critique of the existing society, as Robert Bellah has argued.[17] Yet that virtue must be weighed against the very real possibility that the task of anticipating the coming kingdom through the lenses of the tendencies and latencies within the world will be twisted against the aspirations of Christian ethics, and toward the aims of the society within which the church is engaged.

This risk, however, cannot be considered sufficient for the church to retreat to an enclave of safety in the midst of strife. A set of judgments informed by the formation of persons within the community of the church make taking that risk, in recognition of its own fallibility in the midst of a missionary situation, necessary.

Review (83 no. 1, March 1989), 3–18; G.A. Kelly, "Hegel's America," *Philosophy and Public Affairs* (2 no. 1, Aug. 1972), 3–36.

14 See Cohen and Arato, *Civil Society and Political Theory*, 29ff.

15 See Paul Tillich, *Systematic Theology,* 3 vols. (Chicago: University of Chicago Press, 1951), I:84ff.; *Political Expectation* (New York: Harper & Row, 1971), passim.

16 See Stackhouse, ed., *God and Globalization*, 2:18ff. See also Stackhouse, *Public Theology and Political Economy*, 24ff.

17 Bellah, *The Broken Covenant*, xv.

Utopia, Liberal Democracy, and the Kingdom of God

Liberal democracy is not the kingdom of God, and it is not the fulfillment of the utopian vision of human society of which Moltmann so often writes. To idealize, and perhaps romanticize, liberal democracy and capitalism, declaring them to be the hallmarks of the "end of history" is to preempt the anticipatory consciousness of a society that does not rest on the fulfillment of human aspirations.

But within the boundaries of a liberal democratic society, there exist signs that point toward that utopia. There are tendencies and latencies that, in conversation with, and under the critique of, socially committed Christians, may be nurtured into the kind of anticipations of the kingdom that may lead to a more just and equitable society.

Constitutional democracy, whether in its more or less direct forms, is not discursive democracy according to the guidelines indicated in the work of Habermas and Apel. Instrumental rationality continues to predominate in political life, and communicative action is seldom the basis for public discourse. Yet, the recognition of the distance between our ideals and our realities provides, as does the symbol of the kingdom of God, a basis upon which we may strive to approximate that wide reflective equilibrium[18] through which communication in the midst of diversity may take place. For this to happen, however, men and women in civil society must insist on their innate dignity as persons. Furthermore, the social and economic predilection for viewing the calculation of means and ends as the only publicly valid rationality must be overcome, and a broader realm for recognition of rationality's complexity must be recognized.

The importance of the idea of civil society to this project resides both in the social pluralism that it encourages and embraces and in the formation of persons within the institutional life of the church that creates Christians committed to the life of faith in public. It has been recognized more in the realm of American public theology than in the work of political theologians such as Moltmann that such social pluralism is vital to the life of society. It is here that Tracy, Stackhouse, and Skillen are most instructive, as they each provide us with a theological analysis of society that incorporates that social pluralism, and seek to show how that pluralism either encourages or is necessary for the development of an idea of both the public relevance of theology and the importance of a respect for persons in their distinctiveness within society.

The institutions of civil society offer a venue for individuals to develop a sense of self governed by neither a focus on individual autonomy, nor on an ideology of devotion to the state. This is a potentiality, and not an actuality, of society, and not all civil institutions are equal to this task. Yet, as the church functions within civil society, it has an obligation to make the gospel a practical reality for its members. Insofar as it is able to do this, it can provide the basis for a social ethic motivated by a real practical idealism in the public realm, and a real sense that the public good in modern society is not merely instrumental, but based on values that are at one and the same time concrete and particular to a particular community, and yet universal in their aspiration for all of humanity.

---

18 See Schrag, *The Resources of Rationality*, 176ff.; van Huyssteen, *The Shaping of Rationality*, 277ff.; Fiorenza, "The Church as a Community of Interpretation," in Browning and Fiorenza, eds, *Habermas, Modernity and Public Theology*, 81.

Bibliography

Adams, J.L. *Voluntary Associations: Socio-cultural Analyses and Theological Interpretation.* Edited by J. Ronald Engel. Chicago: Exploration Press, 1986.

Adorno, Theodore. *Negative Dialectics.* New York: Continuum, 1973.

Althusius, Johannes. *Politica; An abridged translation of Politics methodically set forth, and illustrated with sacred and profane examples.* Edited and translated by Frederick S. Carney. Indianapolis: Liberty Fund, 1995.

Apel, Karl-Otto. "The Transcendental Conception of Language Communication and the Idea of a First Philosophy," in *The History of Linguistic Thought and Contemporary Linguistics.* Edited by Herman Parret New York: DeGruyter, 1976.

———. *Towards a Transformation of Philosophy.* Translated by Glyn Adey and David Frisby. London: Routledge & Kegan Paul, 1980.

Aristotle. *The Politics of Aristotle.* Edited by Ernest Barker. New York: Oxford University Press, 1958.

Augustine, *The City of God Against the Pagans.* Edited and Translated by R.W. Dyson. New York: Cambridge University Press, 1998.

Barber, Benjamin. *Jihad vs. McWorld: How Globalism and Tribalism Are Reshaping the World.* Revised edition. New York: Ballantine Books, 2001.

Barth, Karl. *Church Dogmatics.* 4 vols. Edited by G.W. Bromily and T.F. Torrance. Edinburgh: T. & T. Clark, 1936–69.

Bartley, W.W. *The Retreat to Commitment.* La Salle, IL: Open Court Publishers, 2003.

Bauckham, Richard. *The Theology of Jürgen Moltmann.* Edinburgh: T&T Clark, 1995.

———.ed. *God Will Be All In All: The Eschatology of Jurgen Moltmann.* Edinburgh: T&T Clark, 1999.

Beckley, Harlan. *Passion for Justice: Retrieving the Legacies of Walter Rauschenbusch, John A. Ryan, and Reinhold Niebuhr.* Louisville, KY: Westminster/John Knox Press, 1992.

Bedford-Strohm, Heinrich. *Vorrang für die Armen: Auf dem Weg zu Einer Theologischen Theorie der Gerechtigkeit.* Gütersloh: Chr. Kaiser, 1993.

———. *Gemeinschaft aus Kommunikativer Freiheit: Sozialer Zusammenhalt in der Modernen Gesellschaft: Ein Theologischer Beitrag.* Gütersloh: Chr. Kaiser, 1999.

Bellah, Robert. *The Broken Covenant: American Civil Religion in Time of Trouble.* Chicago: University of Chicago Press, 1992.

Bellah, Robert, Richard Madsen, and William Sullivan. *The Good Society.* New York: Vintage Books, 1991.

Bellah, Robert, Richard Madsen, William Sullivan, Ann Swidler, Stephen Tipton. *Habits of the Heart: Individualism and Commitment in American Life*. Updated edn. Berkeley: University of California Press, 1996.

Benhabib, Seyla. *Situating the Self: Gender Community and Postmodernism in Contemporary Ethics*. New York: Routledge, 1992.

Benne, Robert. *The Paradoxical Vision: A Public Theology for the Twenty-First Century*. Philadelphia: Fortress Press, 1995.

Berger, Peter L.. *The Sacred Canopy*. Garden City, NY: Anchor Books, 1969.

——— ed. *The Desecularization of the World: Resurgent Religion and World Politics*. Grand Rapids: Eerdmans, 1999.

———. "Sectarianism and Religious Sociation." *American Journal of Sociology*. 64 no. 1 (July, 1958): 41–4.

Bloch, Ernst. *The Principle of Hope*. Translated by Paul Knight, Neville Plaice, Stephen Plaice. Cambridge: MIT Press, 1986.

Boff, Leonardo. "The Trinity," in *Mysterium Liberationis: Fundamental Concepts of Liberation Theology*. Edited by Ignacio Ellacuria and Jon Sobrino. (Maryknoll, N.Y.: 1993).

Breitenberg, E. Harold Jr. "To Tell the Truth." *The Journal of the Society of Christian Ethics*. 23. no. 2 (fall/winter, 2003): 70.

Brown, Charles C. *Niebuhr and His Age: Reinhold Niebuhr's Prophetic Role in the Twentieth Century*. Philadelphia: Trinity Press International, 1992.

Browning, Don and Francis Schüssler Fiorenza, eds. *Habermas, Modernity, and Public Theology*. New York: Crossroad, 1992.

Buber, Martin. *I and Thou*. Translated by Ronald Gregor Smith. New York, Scribner, 1958.

Bucer, Martin. "De Regno Christi" in *Melanchthon and Bucer*. Edited by Wilhelm Pauck. Philadelphia: Westminster Press, 1969.

Bullinger, Heinrich. Trans. *Fountainhead of Federalism: Heinrich Bullinger and the Covenantal Tradition*. Louisville: Westminster/John Knox Press, 1991.

Calvin, John. *Institutes of the Christian Religion*. Edited by John T. McNeill. Translated by Ford Lewis Battles. Philadelphia: Westminster Press, 1960.

Carlson-Thies, Stanley W. and James Skillen, eds. *Welfare in America: Christian Perspectives on a Policy in Crisis*. Grand Rapids: Eerdmans, 1996.

Carter, Stephen L. *The Culture of Disbelief: How American Law and Politics Trivialize Religious Devotion*. New York: Basic Books, 1993.

———. *God's Name in Vain* (New York: Basic Books, 2000).

Cicero, Marcus Tullius. *De Republica*. Cambridge: Harvard University Press, 1928.

Cohen, Jean L., and Andrew Arato. *Civil Society and Political Theory*. Cambridge: MIT Press, 1992.

Craig, Gordon A. *The Germans*. New York: G.P. Putnam's Sons, 1982.

Cunningham, David S. *These Three Are One: The Practice of Trinitarian Theology*. Oxford: Blackwell Publishers, 1998.

Diggins, John Patrick. *Max Weber: Politics and the Spirit of Tragedy*. New York: Basic Books, 1996.

Durkheim, Emile. *Suicide: A Study in Sociology.* Edited by, George Simpson. Translated by John A. Spaulding and George Simpson. Glencoe, IL: Free Press, 1951.

——. *Selected Writings.* Edited and translated by Anthony Giddens. Cambridge: Cambridge University Press, 1972.

——. *The Division of Labor in Society.* Translated by W.D. Halls. New York: Free Press, 1984.

——. *Durkheim on Religion.* Edited by W.S.F. Pickering. Atlanta: Scholars Press, 1994.

——. *The Elementary Forms of Religious Life.* Translated by Karen E. Fields. New York: Free Press, 1995.

Eck, Diana. *A New Religious America.* San Francisco: Harper & Row, 2001.

Elazar, Daniel. *Covenant & Polity in Biblical Israel: Biblical Foundations & Jewish Expressions.* New Brunswick, N.J., U.S.A.: Transaction Publishers, 1995.

——. *Covenant and Commonwealth: From Christian Separation through the Protestant Reformation.* New Brunswick, N.J.: Transaction Publishers, 1996.

——. *Covenant and Civil Society: The Constitutional Matrix of Modern Democracy.* New Brunswick, N.J.: Transaction Publishers, 1998.

——. *Covenant & Constitutionalism: The Great Frontier and the Matrix of Federal Democracy.* New Brunswick, N.J., U.S.A.: Transaction Publishers, 1998.

——. "Althusius' Grand Design for a Federal Commonwealth" in Johannes Althusius, *Politica.* Indianapolis: Liberty Fund, 1995.

Everett, William Johnson. "Body Thinking in Ecclesiology and Cybernetics." Ph.D. diss., Harvard University, 1970.

——. *God's Federal Republic: Reconstructing Our Governing Symbol.* New York: Paulist Press, 1988.

——. *The Politics of Worship: Reforming the Language and Symbols of Liturgy.* Cleveland: United Church Press, 1999.

Fox, Richard Whiteman. *Reinhold Niebuhr: A Biography.* San Francisco: Harper & Row, 1987.

Frei, Hans. *The Eclipse of Biblical Narrative.* New Haven: Yale University Press, 1974.

——. "Eberhard Busch's Biography of Karl Barth" in *Karl Barth in Review.* Edited by H. Martin Rumscheidt. Pittsburgh: Pickwick Press, 1981.

Fukuyama, Francis. *The End of History and the Last Man.* New York: Avon Books, 1992.

Gathje, Peter R. "A Contested Classic." *The Christian Century.* (June 19–26, 2002): 28–31.

Gilkey, Langdon. *On Niebuhr: A Theological Study.* Chicago: University of Chicago Press, 2001.

Goode, Erich. "Social Class and Church Participation." *American Journal of Sociology.* 72 no. 1 (July, 1966): 102–11.

Gramsci, Antonio. *Prison Notebooks.* Edited by Joseph A. Buttigieg. Translated by Joseph A. Buttigieg and Antonio Callari. New York: International Publishers, 1971.

Gustafson, James. "Introduction" in Richard H. Neibuhr, *Christ and Culture*. San Francisco: Harper & Row, 2001.

Habermas, Jürgen. *The Theory of Communicative Action*. Translated by Thomas McCarthy. 2 vols. Boston: Beacon Press, 1984–87.

———. *Moral Consciousness and Communicative Action*. Translated by Christian Lenhardt and Shierry Weber Nicholsen. Cambridge, MA: MIT Press, 1990.

———. *Religion and Rationality: Essays on Reason, God, and Modernity*. Edited by Eduardo Mendieta. Cambridge: MIT Press, 2002.

Hall, Douglas John. *Thinking the Faith: Christian Theology in a North American Context*. Minneapolis: Augsburg, 1989

———. *Confessing the Faith: Christian Theology in a North American Context*. Minneapolis: Fortress Press, 1996.

———. *Professing the Faith: Christian Theology in a North American Context*. Minneapolis: Fortress Press, 1996.

Hauerwas, Stanley. *Vision and Virtue: Essays in Christian Ethical Reflection*. Notre Dame: Notre Dame University Press, 1974.

———. *Truthfulness and Tragedy: Further Investigations in Christian Ethics*. Notre Dame: University of Notre Dame Press, 1977.

———. *The Peaceable Kingdom*: *A Primer in Christian Ethics*. Notre Dame: Notre Dame University Press, 1983.

———. *Unleashing the Scripture: Freeing the Bible from Captivity to America*. Nashville: Abingdon, 1993.

———. *Dispatches from the Front: Theological Engagements With the Secular*. Durham, NC: Duke University Press, 1994.

———. *Christian Existence Today: Essays on Church, World, and Living in Between*. Grand Rapids: Baker Books, 1995.

Hauerwas, Stanley and William Willimon. *Resident Aliens: Life in the Christian Colony*. Nashville: Abingdon, 1989.

———. *Where Resident Aliens Live: Exercises for Christian Practice*. Nashville: Abingdon Press, 1996.

Hegel, Georg Wilhelm Freidrich. *Elements of the Philosophy of Right*. Edited by Allen W. Wood. Translated by H.B. Nisbet. Cambridge: Cambridge University Press, 1991.

Heim, S. Mark. *Salvations: Truth and Difference in Religion*. Maryknoll, NY: Orbis Books, 1995.

———. *The Depth of the Riches: A Trinitarian Theology of Religious Ends*. Grand Rapids: Eerdmans, 2001.

Held, David and Anthony McGrew. *Globalization/Anti-Globalization*. Oxford: Blackwell, 2002.

Heslam, Peter S. *Creating a Christian Worldview: Abraham Kuyper's Lectures on Calvinism*. Grand Rapids: Eerdmans, 1998.

Hessel, Deiter L. ed. *Theology for Earth Community: A Field Guide*. Maryknoll, NY: Orbis Books, 1996.

Hobbes, Thomas. *Leviathan*. Baltimore: Penguin, 1968.

Hollenbach, David. *The Common Good and Christian Ethics*. New York: Cambridge University Press, 2002.

Horkheimer, Max. *Critical Theory: Selected Essays*. Translated by Matthew J. O'Connell and others. New York: Continuum, 1972.

———. *Critique of Instrumental Reason: Lecures and Essays Since the End of World War II*. Translated by Matthew J. O'Connell and others. New York: Continuum, 1974.

———. *Eclipse of Reason*. New York: Continuum, 1974.

———. *Between Philosophy and Social Science: Selected Early Writings*. Translated by G. Frederick Hunter, Matthew S. Kramer, and John Torpey. Cambridge, MA: MIT Press, 1993.

Horkheimer, Max and Theodore Adorno. *Dialectic of Enlightenment*. Translated by John Cumming. New York: Continuum, 1972.

Horowitz, Irving Louis. "The Hegelian Concept of Political Freedom." *The Journal of Politics*. 20 no. 1 (Feb, 1966): 3–28.

Huber, Wolfgang. *Protestanten in Der Demokratie: Positionen Und Profile Im Nachkriegsdeutschland*. München: Kaiser, 1990.

———. *Die Tägliche Gewalt: Gegen Den Ausverkauf Der Menschenwürde*. Freiburg: Herder, 1993.

———. *Gerechtigkeit Und Recht: Grundlinien Christlicher Rechtsethik*. Gütersloh: Chr. Kaiser, 1996

———. *Kirche in der Zeitenwende: Gesellschaftlicher Wandel und Erneuerung der Kirche*. Gütersloh: Gütersloher Verlaghaus, 1998.

Huber, Wolfgang, ed. *Öffentliche Theologie*. 12 vols. Gütersloh: Chr. Kaiser, 1991-2000.

Huber, Wolfgang and Hans-Richard Reuter. *Friedensethik*. Stuttgart: W. Kohlhammer, 1990.

Huber, Wolfgang and Stefan Berg. *Meine Hoffnung Ist Grösser Als Meine Angst: Ein Bischof Zu Glauben, Kirche Und Gesellschaft*. Berlin: Wichern-Verlag, 1996.

Jenkins, Philip. *The Next Christendom: The Coming of Global Christianity*. London: Oxford University Press, 2002.

Jensen, Robert. *The Triune Identity*. Philadelphia: Fortress Press, 1982.

John Paul II. *Centismus Annus*. Boston: St. Paul Editions. Originally promulgated, 1991.

Johnson, Benton. "On Church and Sect." *American Sociological Review*. 28 no. 4 (Aug. 1963): 539–49

Kegley, Charles W. and Robert W. Bretall. *Reinhold Niebuhr: His Religious, Social, and Political Thought*. New York: Macmillan, 1956.

Kelly, G.A. "Hegel's America." *Philosophy and Public Affairs*. 2 no. 1 (Aug. 1972): 3–36.

Kim, Hyun-Sook. *Christian Education for Postconventionality: Modernization, Trinitarian Ethics, and Christian Identity*. Seoul: Kangnam Publishers, 2002.

Krut, Riva. *Globalization and Civil Society: NGO Influence in International Decision-Making*. UN Research Institute for Social Development, 1997.

Küng, Hans. *Global Responsibility: In Search of a New World Ethic*. New York: Continuum, 1993.

———. *A Global Ethic for Global Politics and Economics*. New York: Oxford University Press, 1998.

Kuyper, Abraham. *Lectures on Calvinism*. Grand Rapids: Eerdmans, 1931.
———. *The Problem of Poverty*. Edited by James W. Skillen. Grand Rapids: Baker, 1991.
LaCugna, Catherine Mowry. *God For Us: The Trinity and the Christian Life*. San Francisco: HarperCollins, 1991.
Lakeland, Paul. *Postmodernity: Christian Identity in a Fragmented Age*. Philadelphia: Fortress Press, 1997.
Leo XIII. *Rerum Novarum*. Boston: St. Paul Editions. Originally promulgated, 1891.
Leonard, Stephen T. *Critical Theory in Political Practice*. Princeton: Princeton University Press, 1990.
Lindbeck, George. *The Nature of Doctrine*. Philadelphia: Westminster Press, 1984.
Locke, John. *A Letter Concerning Toleration*. Indianapolis: Hackett, 1983.
———. *Second Treatise of Government*. Indianapolis: Hackett, 1980.
Long, D. Stephen. *Divine Economy: Theology and the Market*. New York: Routledge, 2000.
Lovin, Robin. *Reinhold Niebuhr and Christian Realism*. New York: Cambridge University Press, 1995.
Lugo, Luis E. ed. *Religion, Pluralism, and Public Life: Abraham Kuyper's Legacy for the Twenty-First Century*. Grand Rapids, Michigan: W.B. Eerdmans, 2000.
Lukács, Georg. *History and Class Consciousness: Studies in Marxist Dialects*. Cambridge: MIT Press, 1971.
Madison, James. "Federalist 10." in *The Federalist Papers*. Edited by Roy P. Fairfield. New York: New American Library, 1961.
Marcuse, Herbert. *One Dimensional Man: Studies in the Ideology of Advanced Industrial Society*. Boston: Beacon Press, 1991.
Marty, Martin. "Reinhold Niebuhr: Public Theology and the American Experience." *Journal of Religion*. 54, no. 4 (Oct. 1974): 332–59
Marx, Karl. "On the Jewish Question" in *The Marx–Engels Reader*. Edited by Robert C. Tucker. New York: Norton, 1978.
Maughan, Steven S. "Civic Culture, Women's Foreign Missions, and the British Imperial Imagination, 1860–1914," in Frank Trentman, ed., *Paradoxes of Civil Society: New Perspectives in German and British History*. New York: Berghan Books, 2000.
Maurer, Heinrich H. "Studies in the Sociology of Religion I: The Sociology of Protestantism." *American Journal of Sociology*. 30 no. 3 (Nov. 1924): 257–86
McCoy, Charles S. and J. Wayne Baker. "Heinrich Bullinger and the Origins of the Federal Tradition," in *Fountainhead of Federalism: Heinrich Bullinger and the Covenantal Tradition*. Translated by Heinrich Bullinger. Louisville: Westminster/ John Knox Press, 1991.
McDermott, Gerald R. *One Holy and Happy Society: The Public Theology of Jonathan Edwards*. University Park, PA: Pennsylvania State University, 1992.
McFague, Sallie. *The Body of God: An Ecological Theology*. Minneapolis: Fortress Press, 1993.
Meeks, Douglas. *The Origins of the Theology of Hope*. Philadelphia: Fortress Press, 1974.

Meier, Heinrich. *Carl Schmitt and Leo Strauss: The Hidden Dialogue*. Chicago: University of Chicago Press, 1995.

Metz, Johann Baptist. *Theology of the World*. Translated by William Glen-Doepel. New York: The Seabury Press, 1973.

———. *A Passion for God: The Mystical-Political Dimension of Christianity*. Edited and translated by J. Matthew Ashley. New York: Paulist Press, 1998.

———. "Politische Theologie" in *Evangelische Kirchenlexicon* IV, 3rd edition. Göttingen: Verdenhoek & Raprecht, 1986.

Metz, Johann Baptist. ed. *Christianity and the Bourgeoisie*. New York: Seabury Press, 1979.

———. *Faith and the World of Politics*. New York: The Paulist Press, 1968.

Metz, Johann Baptist and Jean-Pierre Jossua. eds. *Theology of Joy*. New York: Herder & Herder, 1974.

———. *Christianity and Socialism*. New York: Seabury Press, 1977.

Metz, J.B., Jürgen Moltmann, and Willi Olemüller. *Kirche im Prozess der Aufkarlung*. Munchen: C. Kaiser, 1970.

Meyer, Donald. *The Protestant Search for Political Realism: 1919–1941*, 2nd edition. Middletown CT: Wesleyan University Press, 1988.

Miguez-Boniño, José. *Doing Theology in a Revolutionary Situation*. Philadelphia: Fortress, 1975.

Milbank, John. *Theology and Social Theory: Beyond Secular Reason*. Cambridge, MA: Blackwell, 1991.

———. *The Word Made Strange: Theology, Language, Culture*. Cambridge, MA: Blackwell, 1997

Milbank, John, Graham Ward and Catherine Pickstock. eds. *Radical Orthodoxy: Ontology and Pardon*. New York: Routledge, 1999.

Miller, Richard B. *War in the Twentieth Century: Sources in Theological Ethics*. Louisville: Westminster/John Knox Press, 1992.

Moltmann, Jürgen. *Theology of Hope: On the Ground and Implications of a Christian Eschatology*. Translation of *Theologie der Hoffnung: Untersuchungen zur Begründung und zu den Konsequenzen einer christlichen Eschatologie*. München: Chr. Kaiser, 1965. New York: Harper & Row, 1967.

———. *Religion, Revolution, and the Future*. Translated by M. Douglas Meeks. New York: Charles Scribner's Sons, 1969.

———. "Political Theology." *Theology Today*. 28 no. 1 (April 1971): 6–23.

———. *Hope and Planning*. New York: Harper & Row, 1971.

———. *Religion and Political Society*. Edited and translated in the Institute of Christian Thought. New York: Harper & Row, 1972.

———. *The Crucified God: The Cross of Christ as the Foundation and Criticism of Christian Theology*. Translation of *Der gekreuzigte Gott; Das Kreuz Christi als Grund und Kritik christlicher Theologie*. München: Chr. Kaiser, 1972. New York: Harper & Row, 1974.

———. *The Experiment Hope*. Edited and translated by M. Douglas Meeks. Philadelphia: Fortress Press, 1975.

———. "A Theological Declaration on Human Rights," in World Alliance of Reformed Churches, *Theological Basis for Human Rights*. Geneva: W.A.R.C., 1976.

———. *The Church in the Power of the Spirit: A Contribution of Messianic Ecclesiology.* New York: Harper & Row, 1977.
———. *The Open Church.* London: SCM Press, 1978.
———. *On Human Dignity: Political Theology and Ethics.* Translated by M. Douglas Meeks. Philadelphia: Fortress Press, 1984.
———. *Politische Theologie – Politische Ethik.* München: Kaiser/Grünewald, 1984.
———. *God in Creation: A New Theology of Creation and the Spirit of God.* Translated by Margaret Kohl. Philadelphia: Fortress Press, 1985.
———. "Christian Theology and Political Religion," in *Civil Religion and Political Theology.* Edited by Leroy Rouner. Notre Dame: University of Notre Dame Press, 1986.
———. "Open Letter to José Miguez-Boniño." *Christianity and Crisis.* March 29, 1976. In *Liberation Theology: A Documentary History.* Maryknoll: Orbis Books, 1992.
———. *The Spirit of Life: A Universal Affirmation.* Minneapolis: Fortress Press, 1992.
———. *History and the Triune God: Contributions to Trinitarian Theology.* New York: Crossroads Publishing Co., 1992.
———. *The Trinity and the Kingdom: The Doctrine of God.* Translated by Margaret Kohl. Minneapolis, MN: Fortress Press, 1993.
———. *The Way of Jesus Christ: Christology in Messianic Dimensions.* Minneapolis, MN: Fortress Press, 1993.
———. "Ist der Markt das Ende aller Dinge?" in *Die Flügel nicht stuzen: Warum wir Utopien brauchen.* Edited byTeicher and von Wedel. Dusseldorf, 1994.
———. *The Coming of God: Christian Eschatology.* Philadelphia: Fortress, 1996.
———. *God for a Secular Society: The Public Relevence of Theology.* Philadelphia: Fortress Press, 1999.
———. *Experiences in Theology: Ways and Forms of Christian Theology.* Translated by Margaret Kohl. Philadelphia: Fortress Press, 2000.
———. *Science and Wisdom.* Translated by Margaret Kohl. Philadelphia: Fortress Press, 2003.
Montesquieu, Charles de Secondat. *The Spirit of the Laws.* New York: Hafner Publishing Company, 1949.
Morse, Christopher. *The Logic of Promise in Moltmann's Theology.* Philadelphia: Fortress Press, 1979.
Müller-Fahrenholz, Geiko. *The Kingdom and the Power: The Theology of Jurgen Moltmann.* Philadelphia: Fortress Press, 2000.
National Conference of Catholic Bishops, *Economic Justice for All* (Washington, D.C.: United States Catholic Conference, 1986).
Neuhaus, Richard John. *The Naked Public Square: Religion and Democracy in America.* 2nd edition. Grand Rapids: Eerdmans, 1984.
Niebuhr, H. Richard. *Christ and Culture.* New York: Harper & Row, 1951.
———. *The Social Sources of Denominationalism.* New York: Meridian Books, 1957.
———. *The Responsible Self: An Essay in Christian Moral Philosophy.* New York: HarperCollins, 1963.

———. *The Kingdom of God in America.* Middletown, CT: Wesleyan University Press, 1988.

———. *H. Richard Niebuhr: Theology, History, and Culture: Major Unpublished Writings.* Edited by William Stacy Johnson. New Haven: Yale University Press, 1996.

Niebuhr, Reinhold. *The Irony of American History.* New York: Scribner, 1952.

———. *Moral Man and Immoral Society: A Study in Ethics and Politics.* New York: Charles Scribner's Sons, 1960.

———. *An Interpretation of Christian Ethics.* New York: Harper & Row, 1963.

———. *The Nature and Destiny of Man: A Christian Interpretation.* 2 vols. New York: Macmillan, 1964.

———. "The Christian Church in a Secular Age." in *The Essential Reinhold Niebuhr: Selected Essays and Addresses.* Edited by Robert McAfee Brown. New Haven: Yale University Press, 1986.

Nygren, Anders. *Eros and Agape.* Translated by Philip S. Watson. New York: Harper & Row, 1969.

Outka, Gene. *Agape: An Ethical Analysis.* New Haven: Yale University Press, 1972.

Pannenberg, Wolfhart. ed. *Revelation as History.* Translated by David Granskou. New York: Macmillan, 1968.

———. *Theology and the Kingdom of God.* Philadelphia: Westminster Press, 1969.

———. *Systematic Theology.* Translated by Geoffrey W. Bromiley. 3 vols. Grand Rapids: Eerdmans, 1991.

Paolini, Albert. *Between Sovereignty and Global Governance: The United Nations, The State, and Civil Society.* London: Macmillan, 1998.

Parsons, Talcott. *The Social System.* London: The Free Press, 1951.

———. *The System of Modern Societies.* Englewood Cliffs, NJ: Prentice-Hall, 1971.

Peukert, Helmut. *Science, Action, and Fundamental Theology: Toward a Theology of Communicative Action.* Translated by James Bohman. Cambridge: MIT Press, 1986.

Pius XI. "Quadragesimo Anno." in Skillen and McCarthy, eds. *Political Order and the Plural Structure of Society.* Originally promulgated, 1931.

Polányi, Karl. *The Great Transformation: The Political and Economic Origins of Our Time.* Boston: Beacon Press, 1957.

Putnam, Robert D. *Bowling Alone: The Collapse and Revival of American Community.* New York: Simon & Schuster, 2000.

Putnam, Robert D. and Lewis M. Feldstein. *Better Together.* New York: Simon & Schuster, 2003.

Rahner, Karl. *The Foundations of the Christian Faith.* New York: Crossroad, 1982.

———. *The Trinity.* New York: Crossroad Pub., 1997.

Ramsey, Paul. *Deeds and Rules in Christian Ethics.* New York: Scribner, 1967.

Rasmussen, Arne. *The Church as Polis: From Political Theology to Theological Politics as Exemplified by Jürgen Moltmann and Stanley Hauerwas.* Notre Dame: University of Notre Dame Press, 1995.

Rauschenbusch, Walter. *Christianizing the Social Order.* New York: Macmillan Company, 1926.

———. *A Theology for the Social Gospel.* Nashville: Abingdon Press, 1978.

———. *Christianity and the Social Crisis.* Louisville, KY: Westminster/John Knox, 1991.

———. *The Righteousness of the Kingdom.* Lewiston: Edward Mellen Press, 1999.

Rawls, John. *A Theory of Justice.* Cambridge, MA: Harvard University Press, 1971.

———. *Political Liberalism.* New York: Columbia University Press, 1996.

Rescher, Nicholas. *Pluralism: Against the Demand for Consensus.* New York: Oxford University Press, 1993.

Reuther, Rosemary Radford. *God and Gaia.* San Francisco: HarperSanFrancisco, 1992.

Rouner, Leroy, ed. *Civil Religion and Political Theology.* Notre Dame: Notre Dame University Press, 1986.

Rousseau, Jean Jacques. *Basic Political Writings.* Indianapolis: Hackett, 1987.

Schmitt, Carl. *Der Begriff des Politischen.* Berlin: Duncker & Humblot, 1963.

———. *Der Leviathan in der Staatslehre des Thomas Hobbes.* Koln: Hoenheim, 1982 [English Edition: *The Leviathan in the State Theory of Thomas Hobbes*. Translated by George Schwab. Greenwood Press, 1996].

———. *Politische Theologie: Vier Kapitel zur Lehre von der Soveranität.* München and Leipzig: Verlag von Dunker & Humbolt, 1934.

Schrag, Calvin O. *The Resources of Rationality: A Response to the Postmodern Problem.* Bloomington: Indiana University Press, 1992.

Schultz, William F. *In Our Own Best Interest: How Defending Human Rights Benefits Us All.* Boston: Beacon Press, 2001.

Schweiker, William. *Power, Value, and Conviction: Theological Ethics in the Postmodern Age.* Cleveland: Pilgrim Press, 1998.

Sigmund, Paul. ed. *Thomas Aquinas on Politics and Ethics.* New York: W.W. Norton, 1987.

Simpson, Gary. *Critical Social Theory: Prophetic Reason, Civil Society, and Christian Imagination.* Philadelphia: Fortress, 2002.

Simon, Derek. "The *New* Political Theology of Johann Baptist Metz: Confronting Schmitt's Decisionist Political Theology of Exclusion." *Horizons.* 30, no. 2 (Fall, 2003): 227–54.

Skillen, James. *Recharging the American Experiment: Principled Pluralism for Genuine Civic Community.* Grand Rapids: Baker Books, 1994.

———. *The Scattered Voice: Christians at Odds in the Public Square.* Edmonton: Canadian Institute for Law, Theology, and Public Policy, 1996.

Skillen, James and Rockne M. McCarthy. eds. *Political Order and the Plural Structure of Society.* Atlanta, GA: Scholars Press, 1991.

Smidt, Corwin. ed. *Religion as Social Capital: Producing the Common Good.* Waco, TX: Baylor University Press, 2003.

Smith, Adam. *The Wealth of Nations.* Edited by Edwin Cannan. New York: The Modern Library, 1994.

Smith, Steven B. "What is 'Right' in Hegel's Philosophy of Right?" *The American Political Science Review.* 83 no. 1 (March 1989): 3–18.

Stackhouse, Max L. *Creeds, Society, and Human Rights*. Grand Rapids: Eerdmans, 1984.

———. *Public Theology and Political Economy: Christian Stewardship in Modern Society*. Lanham, MD: University Press of America, 1991.

———. "Social Theory and Christian Public Morality for the Common Life." in *Christianity and Civil Society*, Edited by Rodney Petersen. Maryknoll: Orbis/BTI, 1995.

———. "Public Theology" in *The Dictionary of the Ecumenical Movement*. Edited by Nicholas Lossky, *et al*. Geneva: World Council of Churches, 2002.

Stackhouse, Max L., Peter Berger, Dennis McCann, and Douglas Meeks. *Christian Social Ethics in a Global Era*. Nashville: Abingdon Press, 1995.

Stackhouse, Max L. ed. *God and Globalization*. 4 vols. Trinity Press International, 2000–2007.

Stassen, Glen. ed. *Authentic Transformation: A New Vision of Christ and Culture*. Nashville: Abingdon, 1996.

Stenmark, Michael. *Rationality in Science, Religion, and Everyday Life*. Notre Dame: University of Notre Dame Press, 1995.

Stillman, Peter G. "Hegel's Critique of Liberal Theories of Rights." *American Political Science Review*. 68 no. 3 (Sept. 1974): 1086–92.

Stone, Ronald. *Professor Reinhold Niebuhr: A Mentor to the Twentieth Century*. Louisville, KY: Westminster/John Knox Press, 1992.

Stout, Jeffrey. *Ethics After Babel*. Boston: Beacon Press, 1988.

Taylor, Charles. *Hegel*. New York: Cambridge University Press, 1975.

———. *Sources of the Self* Cambridge, MA: Harvard University Press, 1989.

———. *Philosophical Arguments*. Cambridge, MA: Harvard University Press, 1995.

Taylor, Mark L. *The Executed God: The Way of the Cross in Lockdown America*. Minneapolis: Fortress Press, 2001.

Thiemann, Ronald. *Revelation and Theology: The Gospel as Narrated Promise*. Notre Dame: University of Notre Dame Press, 1985.

———. *Constructing a Public Theology*. Louisville, KY: Westminster/John Knox Press, 1991.

———. *Religion in Public Life: A Dilemma for Democracy*. Washington, DC: Georgetown University Press, 1996.

Thompson, Thomas. *Imitatio Trinitatis*. Princeton Theological Seminary. Diss. 1994.

Tillich, Paul. *Systematic Theology*. 3 vols. Chicago: University of Chicago Press, 1951.

———. *Love, Power, and Justice*. New York: Oxford University Press, 1954.

———. *Political Expectation*. New York: Harper & Row, 1971.

Tönnies, Ferdinand. *Community and Society*. New York: Harper & Row, 1957.

Tocqueville, Alexis de. *Democracy in America*. New York: Alfred Knopf, 1972.

Tracy, David. *Blessed Rage for Order*. Chicago: University of Chicago Press, 1975.

———. *The Analogical Imagination: Christian Theology and the Culture of Pluralism*. New York: Crossroad, 1981.

Troeltsch, Ernst. *Religion in History*. Translated by James Luther Adams and Walter E. Bense. Minneapolis: Fortress Press, 1991.

———. *The Social Teaching of the Christian Churches.* 2 vols. Louisville, KY: Westminster/John Knox Press, 1992.

Van Huyssteen, J. Wentzel. *The Shaping of Rationality: Toward Interdisciplinarity in Theology and Science.* Grand Rapids: Eerdmans, 1999.

Volf, Miroslav. *After Our Likeness: The Church as the Image of the Trinity.* Grand Rapids: Eerdmans, 1998.

Walzer, Michael. *Toward a Global Civil Society.* Providence: Berghahn Books, 1995.

Weber, Max. "Politics as a Vocation" in *From Max Weber: Essays in Sociology.* Translated and edited, by H.H. Gerth and C. Wright Mills. New York: Oxford University Press, 1946.

———. *The Protestant Ethic and the Spirit of Capitalism.* New York: Charles Scribner's Sons, 1958.

———. *Economy and Society: An Outline of Interpretive Sociology.* Edited by Guenther Roth and Claus Wittich. Translated by Ephraim Fischoff *et al.* Berkeley: University of California Press, 1978.

Welker, Michael. *Theologie und funktionale Systemtheorie: Luhmanns Religionssoziologie in theologischer Diskussion.* Frankfurt am Main: Suhrkamp, 1985.

Werpehowski, Paul. "*Ad Hoc* Apologetics." *Journal of Religion.* 66 (1986): 202–301.

Wiggershaus, Rolf. *The Frankfurt School: Its History, Theories, and Political Significance.* Translated by Michael Robertson. Cambridge: MIT Press, 1994.

Woi, Amatus. *Trinitatslehre und Monotheismus: Die Problematik der Gottesrede und ihre social- politische Relevanz bei Jürgen Moltmann.* Frankfurt am Main: Peter Lang, 1998.

Woodhouse, A.S.P. ed. *Puritanism and Liberty: Being the Army Debates.* London: J.M. Dent & Sons, 1992.

Wuthnow, Robert. *Christianity and Civil Society.* Valley Forge: Trinity Press International, 1996.

Index

abortion 181
academic theology 93-4
academy, 'public' of 78, 80, 82
action 96, 102, 110, 129, 130, 167, 169
    see also communicative action
actors 102, 144, 155, 181
ad hoc 83, 84, 86
Adams, James Luther 145
Adorno, T. 101, 107
affirmation 52, 136, 155, 184, 193
agency 108, 110, 115
agreement 108, 118, 137, 138, 154, 184, 196
alien 28; *see also* enemies; others
alienation 20, 30, 181
Althusius, J. 116, 137-8, 195
analogy 28, 45, 46, 188, 190
analysis 62-4, 67, 94
anomy 143, 144n.
anthropology 45, 65, 191
anticipation 24, 25, 30-31, 43, 47, 49,
    54, 56, 92, 95, 96, 97, 149, 168,
    169,173, 178, 185, 195, 197
    and ethical norms 161ff., 164
    and modern society 166
Apel, Karl-Otto 177, 179, 180, 183, 184,
    185, 197, 199
apocalyptic 39
Aristotle 28, 40, 62, 114-5, 147n.
art 79
articulation 160
association 137, 197
associations 115, 119, 121, 122, 123, 128,
    129, 138, 142-3
associative needs 50, 174, 197
atheism 20, 21
    'protest' 31, 32, 33
Augustine 185n.
authoritarianism 19, 111
authority 18, 30, 51, 52, 89, 90, 91, 116,
    122, 134, 135, 137
autonomy 9, 10, 47, 124, 180, 195, 199

Barth, Karl 20, 44, 54, 84
Bauckham, Richard 5
beatitudes 163
being 181
Being of God 180, 181, 186
    in Trinity 188
belief 50, 86, 104, 117, 120, 121, 186
Bellah, Robert 130n., 148, 173, 198
Benhabib, S. 155, 178
Benjamin, Walter 176-7, 178
Berger, Peter 143
Bible 23
    historicity of 22
    see also Old Testament
binding moral principles 102, 185, 197
Black church 77, 130
Bloch, Ernst 3, 18, 20-21, 25n., 50, 95, 166
Breitenberg, Harold 75
Bullinger, Heinrich 136-7, 185n., 195
Bultmann, Rudolf 22, 30
bureaucracy 101, 103, 110, 119

calculation 4, 13, 78, 102, 103, 104, 109,
    193, 199
'calling' 49, 55, 140
Calvinism 89, 139
capitalism 13, 20, 68, 69, 103, 107, 133, 199
Centismus Annus 133
Christian community 83-4, 96, 176, 178
Christian ethics 4, 176
Christian-Marxist dialogue 5, 7, 13
Christian theology 17
    and modernity 11
    see also theology
Christianity
    and church 167
    and culture 74, 83
    and education 141-2
    and politics 33
    self-description of 83-4, 85
    social dialectic of 17ff.
    social ethics 159-60

and social pluralism 27
  uniqueness of 65
  see also church; Christians
'Christianization' 68, 69-70
Christians 12, 15, 16
  and critique 193
  and institutional life 192
  and new creation 172
  responsibilities of 21, 23-4, 37, 54-5, 69, 143, 172, 175, 185
Christology 29
church 27, 28, 34, 44-5, 69, 96, 142
  as body of Christ 173, 175-80, 192
  and civil society 113, 125, 127ff., 142-8, 198
  communicative role 176
  and covenant 187, 196
  discursive process 157, 158
  dual identity 49, 51, 52, 173, 180, 181, 192
  early 29
  as 'generalized other' 81, 93
  institutional role 51, 56, 173-5, 181
  integrative role 143-4, 174, 176
  international aspect 132
  interpretative role 157
  meaning-making 143, 174
  mission 49-50, 54, 96, 185
  and modernity 47, 66, 190
  nature of 66
  openness of 45
  and participation 129, 144-5, 174
  and pluralism 146-7
  and politics 6, 7, 24, 33, 129
  as 'public' 78, 80-82, 83
  social dangers for 147-8, 173-4
  and social discourse 82-8
  social divisions in 73
  and society 5, 6, 14, 27-8, 34, 47, 50-52ff., 66, 81-2, 142, 189
  and state 33, 120
  and Trinity 44-5, 180-81
  voluntarism 145-6
  and world 166, 167
  see also 'contrast society'; 'exodus church'; 'exodus community'
Church in the Power of the Spirit, The 194
Cicero 115n.
civic institutions 130, 142
civil religion 52-4, 113, 173-4
civil rights movement 77, 130

civil society 12, 13, 14, 111, 199
  American tradition 121-2, 197
  associations 115, 119, 121ff., 128, 129
  and 'body' metaphor 175ff.
  church and 125, 127ff., 142-8, 198
  diversity of 134, 138
  European tradition 122-4, 197
  exodus church and 54-5
  global 131-2
  Hegelian concept 118-21
  integrative role 129-30, 131, 143
  and meaning-making 129-30, 143
  mediating role 127-8, 131, 132
  models 132-42
  modern synthesis 122-4
  participation in 128-9, 144-5
  and pluralism 115ff., 120ff., 124, 125, 130-31, 134, 146-7, 185
  and society 131-2
  state and 116ff., 122-4, 125, 127ff., 132
  theory of 3, 8, 92, 114-18ff., 191-2, 196, 197, 198
  voluntarism 125, 131, 145-6
class 106, 107, 171
coercion 109, 128, 130
  see also violence
Cohen, Jean L. and Arato, Andrew 115n., 118, 123, 129
commitment, ethical 23
commodities 15, 195
common good 119, 134, 136, 139, 193
communal responsibility 141
communication 84, 111, 132, 176, 177, 183
  between living and dead 178
  see also communicative action; communicative rationality
communicative action 108, 111, 112, 176ff., 182, 184, 186, 196
communicative rationality 108-9, 155, 176, 185-6, 190
  and Trinity 180-82
'communion' 45
communism 6, 20, 69, 103, 105, 122
communities 12, 28, 42, 45, 114-5, 132, 167, 171, 176, 181, 183
  see also human community; religious communities
community 96, 97, 124, 180, 189
  concept of 51, 56, 115
  discourse about 78

complexity 17, 73, 91, 94, 95, 110, 115, 131, 137, 142, 181, 192, 199
conscience 117, 131, 143
consciousness 106, 107
consensus 86, 156, 157
construction 67, 109, 179
contradiction 26, 28, 29, 47, 56
'contrast society' 47, 96, 162, 163, 165, 171, 194, 195
    problems of 173
conversion 170, 185, 186
cooperation 109
cooptation 147, 148, 149, 198
Corinthians 176
corporations 119-20
'correspondence' model 33-4
corruption 182, 185
cosmic horizon 39, 170, 171-2
covenant 9, 37, 38, 40, 83, 149, 185, 186
    concept 137, 195-6
    and pluralism 136-7, 196, 197
    social consequences of 142
    and Trinitarian social ethic 187-8
    see also covenantal model
covenantal model 127, 133, 136-42, 149, 185-6, 196
creation 39, 41, 43, 44, 133, 140, 158, 176
    doctrine of 41, 65, 66, 90- 92, 95, 191
    new 25, 95, 170, 171-2, 179
creativity 20, 55
'critical correlation' 63-4, 81, 84, 85
critical modernism 154-60ff.
critical theory 32-3, 105-6
    see also critical modernism
criticism 81, 85, 86, 130, 155, 174, 180, 195
    see also critical modernism; critical theory; social criticism
cross 13-14, 21, 22, 23, 54, 71, 93, 165
    as critical social theory 31-3
    and political theology 33-4, 35
    and resurrection 24-7, 29, 30
    theology of 179-80
Crucified God, The 5, 25, 27, 31, 33, 37, 167
crucifixion *see* cross
cruelty 31
cultural liberation 35
culture 73, 74, 78, 79, 83, 94, 110, 141

data 63, 64, 85
dead, the 177, 178
death 25, 26, 30, 39, 40, 41, 165, 194

decentralization 14
decision, call to 22
dehumanization 42
democracy 4, 8, 15, 16, 18, 19, 35, 42, 69, 75, 78, 135, 136, 198
    American 121, 174-5
    and Christianity 74, 75
    and public discourse 86-7
    and Trinitarianism 187, 188
    see also liberal democracy
denominationalism 72
description 83, 96
    'thick' 84
dialectic of critique and transformation 17, 24ff., 28, 35, 37, 47, 64, 153, 154, 166, 180, 193, 195
dialectical thought 28, 56, 105n., 118, 156, 157, 165, 192, 195
dialogue 62, 63, 64, 85, 157-8, 186, 192, 195, 196
dictator 19
difference 28
Dilthey 22
disclosure 160
disenchantment 10, 50, 105
disciplines 62, 63-4, 67, 80, 84, 85
discourse 62, 63, 78-9, 159
    ethic of 183-4, 196
    modernist 155-6ff.
    see also public discourse
dispossessed 28
diversity 92, 134, 138, 142, 146, 185, 186
domination 10, 19, 109, 111, 123
Dooyeweerd, H. 90, 91
Dostoevsky 32
Durkheim, E. 51, 52, 66, 124, 128n., 130n.
duties 42, 102

East Germany 5, 6
ecclesiology 66
Eck, Diana 146n.
ecology 66, 162, 168, 172
    see also environment
economic institutions 141
economic justice 168
Economic Justice for All 133, 136
economics 61, 62, 64, 103
economy 3, 12, 78, 102, 124n., 129, 157,192; *see also* market economy
educational institutions 69, 70, 91, 141-2
Edwards, Jonathan 68

efficiency 50, 103
Elazar, Daniel 53, 65n., 115, 137
emancipation 106, 108, 178
empiricism 4, 63, 85, 108, 122, 180, 181
   see also data
employers 133, 134
ends 78, 101, 102, 103, 104, 105, 108, 118, 185
enemies 19, 53, 75, 164, 165
enlightenment 107, 110, 112, 115, 160
environment 6, 12, 35, 171; *see also* ecology
epiphany 38
equality 11, 46, 69, 70, 71, 72, 89, 115, 188, 189
eschatology 3, 5, 21, 22, 23, 24, 25-7, 29, 30, 34n., 37, 38, 39, 40, 50, 54, 75, 95, 161, 165, 183, 185, 191, 193, 196
   and reconciliation 179
   and social diversity 92, 93
   and universality 170, 171, 172
ethics 8, 12, 23, 24, 41, 47, 66, 88-9, 148, 156, 158, 197
   of discourse 183-4, 197
   and instrumental reason 103-5, 155
   messianic 161-6
   see also social ethics
evaluation 168
evangelism 143
Everett, William 144, 192
evil 13, 26, 30, 32, 33, 39, 164, 165
'exodus church' 14, 49, 51, 52, 95, 149
   and civil society 54-5, 198
   social ethic of 165, 173, 194-5
   see also 'contrast society'; 'exodus community'
'exodus community' 47, 49, 56, 158, 165, 166, 169, 185, 190, 194
   see also 'exodus church'
expectation 21, 25, 37, 38, 54, 55, 161
Experiences in Theology 44, 167

facts 63, 64, 67, 181, 184
   see also data
faith 5, 21, 25, 27-8, 33, 38, 86, 96
   commitments 80, 85, 86
   and practice 178
false consciousness 106, 107
family 12, 69, 70, 90, 91, 118, 127, 138, 140, 141, 171
fantasy 166, 169

fascism 15n., 107, 122, 123, 134
Father 32, 33, 43, 46, 188
federalism 138, 139
fellowship 9, 21n., 35, 42, 44, 138, 170, 171
fideism 86
Fiorenza 156, 157
forgiveness 23, 30, 75
formal rationality 4n., 102-3
foundationalism 84, 86
Frankfurt School 3, 4, 21, 101, 105, 106
freedom 107, 117, 118, 124, 189
freedom of association 121, 128, 129, 131, 135, 197
freedom of choice 115, 121, 124, 128, 145
freedom of conscience 42
Frei, Hans 83
friends 19, 53, 165
Fukuyama, Francis 15n.
fulfilment 39, 171
future 20, 23, 25, 26, 37, 95, 166, 169
   and God's promise 38, 40, 171, 178

Geertz, Clifford 79
'generalized others' 81, 93, 160
Germany 5, 6, 17n., 18, 52, 120, 121, 130n.
gifts 80, 176
'global marketing of everything' *see* marketing, global
globalization 6, 8, 13, 63, 131-2
God 9, 10, 16, 28, 80, 90ff., 138, 186
   authoritarian concept 19
   claim of 41-3
   and evil 32
   existence of 31
   and future hope 23, 25, 171
   involvement of 21
   Marxism and 20
   promise of 37ff.
   and social order 133, 134, 185
   and sovereign spheres 139-40
   suffering of 31-2, 33
   see also Being of God
'God-abandonment' 28, 30, 33, 56
good/goods 4, 10, 78, 87, 88, 89, 91, 93, 96, 98, 119, 134, 136, 138, 139, 142, 164n., 185, 186, 188, 193, 199
   and evil 39
   'thin' and 'thick' conceptions 156-7
gospel 167
   messianic interpretation 163
   political hermeneutic of 55-6

government 74, 85, 89, 117, 118, 185
grace 25, 28, 80, 176
Gramsci, A. 122-3, 129, 197

Habermas, Jürgen 108-12, 149, 155, 160, 161, 179, 180, 181, 182, 184, 185, 197, 199
Hauerwas, Stanley 83, 87, 154
Hebrews 167
Hegel, G.W.F. 118-21, 122, 125, 130n., 142, 197
Heim, Mark S. 184n.
Held, David and McGrew, Anthony 132
hermeneutic 11-12, 17, 18, 23, 64, 157
    eschatological 21, 22
    existentialist 22
    political 12, 21-4, 34, 55, 56
    Trinitarian 21n.
    see also interpretation
hierarchy 134, 135, 144, 145, 188
history 21, 22, 31, 41, 71, 72, 91, 97, 165, 166, 170, 177, 194
    'end of' 15, 199
    and God's promise 37, 38, 40, 171
Hobbes, Thomas 18, 115-16, 118, 128
Holy Spirit 43, 44, 46, 170, 171, 172, 186, 188
hope 11, 12, 15, 16, 17, 20, 21ff., 29, 31, 33, 40, 47, 50, 52, 56, 71, 92, 97, 179, 193
    and messianic ethics 161, 164
    and suffering 168
    utopian 166
Horkheimer, Max 32, 101, 105-8, 112, 177
human beings 9, 11, 41, 43, 182, 189, 196
    relational nature of 44, 180, 181, 186
human community 37, 42, 45, 76, 95, 114, 177
human dignity 8, 11, 23, 35, 41, 43, 160, 186, 187, 189, 196
human freedom 12, 43, 107, 160, 189
human life 41, 42, 44, 61, 69, 110, 139, 140, 163, 170, 194
human nature 95, 115, 180
human relationality 66, 95, 180, 186, 188
human rights 6, 8, 11, 12, 15, 23, 24, 35, 136, 165, 168, 196
    fundamental 41, 136
    and God's claim on humanity 41-3

'ideal speech situation' 160, 179, 181, 182

identity 9, 90, 107, 110, 130, 141, 144, 188
    of Christ 29
    Christian 27-8, 37, 83, 84, 96, 179, 189, 190, 197
    of church 14, 49, 52, 56, 113, 125, 157, 158, 180, 187, 191, 194, 195
    crisis of 62
    human 107, 141n., 180
    see also institutional identity
ideology 9, 15, 54, 123, 129, 199
imago Dei 41-2, 46, 95, 180, 181, 182, 187, 189, 196
incarnation 29, 41, 65
individual 22 *see also* self, autonomous
individualism 88, 89, 128, 148, 155
individuals 9, 42, 44, 50, 51, 85, 106, 170, 174, 176, 189
    and civil society 116, 119, 121, 124, 127, 128, 130, 131, 143, 199
    and meaning 130
    see also persons
injustice 23
institutional forms 51, 91, 141
institutional identity 56, 167, 181
institutional life 3, 13, 47, 55, 56, 67, 134, 136, 141, 142, 148, 190, 192
    church in 173-5
institutional pluralism 98, 115, 116, 124, 142, 173, 185, 196
institutions 51, 55, 56, 69, 90, 91, 113, 115, 118, 185, 191, 192, 196
    meaning-making role 129-30
    mediating 122, 175
    rights and responsibilities 134
instrumental rationality 4, 101-5, 109, 112, 155, 186, 195, 199
    critique of 105ff., 156ff.
instrumentalism 78, 183
    critique of 5, 8, 11, 106, 191
integrity 55, 76, 86, 91, 98, 138, 142, 154
intellectual activities 130, 131
intelligentsia 106
international law 165
interpretation 22, 23, 64-7, 157, 159
    see also hermeneutic
inter-subjectivity 183, 184
irrationality 102, 108
'is' and 'ought' 72, 91
isolation 10, 11, 128, 129
Israel *see* Jews
Italy 122

Jesus Christ 13, 14, 15, 21, 22, 25, 29ff., 54, 65, 71, 74, 95, 97, 172, 193
    'body' of 173, 175-80, 181
    Jewishness of 40
    messianic hope 161
    and social ethics 68, 69, 161ff.
Jews 38, 39, 40, 65n., 163, 167
Jubilee, year of 162
justice 119, 120
    'thin' conception 158

Kant 67, 161, 183
kenosis 28
kingdom of God 14, 16, 17-18, 20, 23, 24, 25-7, 34, 47, 52, 54, 92-3, 95, 97, 147-8, 185, 193, 199
    pre-apprehension of 166-7
    social ethics of 68-70, 161-6, 170
Kingdom of God in America, The 73, 148
knowledge 39, 46, 63
Küng, Hans 67n.
Kuyper, Abraham 89-90, 139-40

labor organizations 12, 129, 135, 140
language 45, 78, 108-9, 111, 183, 184
'language games' 7, 159, 183, 184
Latin America 12, 13
law 30, 89, 92, 120, 134, 137, 138
    messianic 162-3, 164
Left 6, 21, 34, 88n., 106n., 128, 168n.
liberal democracy 8, 86, 95, 154, 157, 186, 195n., 196, 198, 199
liberalism 4, 8, 9, 18, 42, 72, 87, 134, 135, 154, 184, 186
    see also liberal democracy
liberation theology 12-14, 35, 135
'lifeworld' 109-11, 112, 161
limit principle 179, 181
Lindbeck, George 83
Locke, John 116-18, 120, 130n.
longing 20
love 24, 32, 33, 45, 70, 71, 164, 169, 188, 190, 197

McCarthy, R.M. *see* Skillen, James and McCarthy, R.M.
McGrew, Anthony *see* Held, David and McGrew, Anthony
marginalized people 169
market economy 15, 94, 119, 124n.
marketing, global 8, 10, 15n., 94, 146, 153, 160, 167n., 170
'marketplace of ideas' 98, 121, 130, 146n. 156, 158
martyrdom 165
Marx, Karl 22, 106, 107, 119, 123
Marxism 5, 7, 13, 20, 105, 106n., 108, 119, 121, 123
meaning 4, 22, 52, 74, 82, 105, 112, 129, 159, 166, 174, 185
    making of 97, 129, 130, 143, 174
'means-ends' rationality 78, 101-2, 103, 104, 108, 199
mediation 110, 127-8, 131, 132, 158, 175, 183
    symbolic 174-5
Meeks, Douglas 6n.
memory, empathic 176, 177
messianic lifestyle 95, 161, 162, 163, 172, 194
Metz, J.B. 6, 7, 18, 19, 21
Miguez-Boniño, Jose 13, 91n.
Milbank, John 4, 87, 189, 191
mirror image 31, 34
misery 7, 13, 14, 22, 68, 69, 92
modernity 4, 5, 8, 10, 11, 13, 23, 98, 124, 153, 154, 155, 156, 158, 166, 169, 172, 186, 190, 195
    church and 47, 66, 190
    and civil society 122-4
    contradictions of 101, 105, 109
    dangers of 96, 155
    and ethics 155
    good of 11, 96
    instrumental rationality 101-5
    and religion 50-51
    social structures 110
    see also critical modernism
Moltmann, Jürgen 3, 153, 154, 186, 189n., 193-4, 199
    and American public theology 75, 76, 93ff.
    and Bloch 21, 95, 166
    dialectic of 165
    and discursive process 157-8
    eschatology of 95, 193
    and Frankfurt School 106, 112
    and kingdom of God 167, 170
    and liberation theology 12-13
    messianic ethics 161-6
    methodology 96, 97

and modernity 8, 160
political hermeneutic of 55-6
political theology 6-7, 11, 17ff., 54, 93-4ff., 98
  problems for 113, 149, 168, 173, 187
  public theology 7, 56, 57, 61, 98, 113
  and Skillen 94-5, 96, 98
  and 'society' 8
  theological aims of 5
  and Thiemann 96-7, 98
  and Tracy 93-4, 98
Montesquieu 116, 122
moral action 96
moral differences 184
moral formation 3, 128n., 129, 130n., 176
moral values, substantive 3, 157, 158, 159
mutuality 45, 85, 86, 138, 189, 190
myths 166, 173, 174

narrative theology 4, 82, 84ff., 96, 144, 158, 159, 169n., 183
National Socialism 18, 19n., 52
natural world 10, 35, 50, 119
nature 115, 118, 119
needs 13, 14, 35, 50, 119
negation 27, 29, 31, 40, 41, 166
NGOs 132
  see also non-governmental agencies
Niebuhr, H. Richard 63, 72-6, 145, 148
Niebuhr, Reinhold 70-72, 74, 76, 193n.
non-governmental agencies 129
non-identity 27, 28
non-violence 42n., 163, 164, 193, 194n.
norms 105, 108, 124, 157, 178
  ethical 68, 164, 165, 169, 171, 183, 184, 185, 193
nuclear weapons 12, 72, 165

objectification 10, 107, 109
objectivity 80, 177, 183, 184
obligations 8, 9, 42, 88, 102, 117, 139, 141, 191
Old Testament 40, 41, 167
  promise of God 38, 39
ontology 90, 91, 181, 186
openness 97, 158, 167, 182
oppression 12, 13, 21, 28, 30, 31, 33, 35, 168, 178
optimism 26, 31, 70, 165, 166
order 115, 116
others 144, 147, 160, 177, 178

outcast 13, 14, 23, 28, 33, 52, 169, 170
outsiders 19, 53; see also others

pacifism 193; see also non-violence
Pannenberg, W. 25n.
parousia 167
Parsons, Talcott 123-4
participation 72, 85, 128-9, 136, 143, 144-5, 174
past 176, 177, 178
Paul, St 144, 175-6, 179
peace 12, 14, 24, 25, 27, 52, 163, 167, 168, 171
peace movements 168
per se 11, 41, 49, 94, 132, 157, 171, 184
perfection 181
perichoresis 44, 45, 181, 188
person-formation 173, 197, 198, 199
persons 44, 45, 118, 119, 124, 144, 174, 177, 181, 188, 197
persuasion 160, 186, 189
pessimism 101, 107
Peukert, Helmut 176, 177, 182
philosophy 21, 67, 80, 84, 115, 178, 183
Pius XI 133, 135
pledge 24, 25, 43, 137, 196
pluralism 3, 8, 14, 18, 19, 27, 66, 70, 86, 88, 92, 95, 98, 153, 184n., 192, 196, 197, 199
  Aristotelian view 115
  church and 146-7, 180
  and civil society 115ff., 120ff., 124, 125, 130-31, 134, 138ff., 146-7
  and covenant 136-7, 185, 196, 197
  democratic 16, 136, 173, 188
  and public discourse 79
  social 139, 140
police 119, 120
policy 78, 85, 180
policy studies 85
polis 114-15, 127, 128n., 147n.
political hermeneutic 12, 21-4, 34, 55, 56
political institutions 69, 122, 129, 141
Political Liberalism 87
political parties 122, 129
political theology, 5, 6-7, 11, 15, 94
  changing idea of 18-21
  and civil religion 53-4
  and cross 30-31, 33-4, 35
  social dialectic of 17-18
  and suffering of God 33-4, 35

see also political hermeneutic
political theory 128
politics 5, 12, 15, 30, 33, 54, 74
   and covenant 137
   communicative action in 109
   global crises 14
   and instrumental rationality, 103-4
   participation in 129
   and social differentiation 92
   see also political hermeneutic; political theology
polity, realm of 78-9, 94, 95
poor, the 13, 14, 23, 24, 52, 68, 85, 170
possibilities, human 11, 15, 16, 19, 20, 56, 71, 82, 95, 166, 170, 176, 181, 194
   see also 'tendencies and latencies'
postmodernism 154-5
potentialities 12, 47, 99n., 176, 182, 199
   see also possibilities, human
poverty 23, 35, 70, 148, 163
power 18, 19, 103, 104, 110
praxis 13, 21, 22, 23, 55, 112, 178, 179, 180, 195
present 26, 95, 167, 168, 176, 177, 193
principle 104, 164, 165
private sphere 4, 7, 19, 50, 53, 127n., 138, 154, 155, 156, 162, 183
process 164
proclamation 22, 23, 29, 51, 54, 162
professions 141-2
prolepsis 30, 168; *see also* anticipation
promise 9, 26, 37, 38ff., 49, 52, 55, 87, 95, 168, 171
   fulfilment of 39-41
property 69, 117, 133
prophetic role 39, 82, 85, 97, 130, 174
protection 18, 19, 52
Protestantism 127, 133, 142, 185
   see also Reformed tradition
public discourse 75, 78, 156-9
   democratic 86
   Christian resources for 183-9
public life 66, 72-3, 76, 94, 95, 192, 193
   ethics of 103-5
public responsibility 3, 5, 12, 54, 74, 76, 98, 139, 164, 193
public space 87, 154, 159, 160
public sphere 7, 8, 14, 53, 54, 111, 147n., 156, 162, 174
public theology 7-8, 11, 14, 15, 16, 17, 56, 57
   American 68-76, 77, 78ff., 87, 97-8, 149, 199
   analytical 62-4, 67 'Christianization' 69-70
   and civil society 113, 191-2
   constructive task 67
   and critical modernism 154-60
   as discursive practice 156-9
   interpretation 64-7
   and Jesus Christ 161ff.
   meaning of 3, 75
   'publics' of 78-82
   purpose of 61-2
   and social responsibility 72-6
   see also political theology
publicity 144, 145
'publics' 78-82, 83
Puritans 139, 148
Putnam, H. 148

Quadragesimo Anno 133, 134-5
quantitative values 4, 102

Rad, Gerhard von 38
Rahner, Karl 44
Rasmussen, Arne 87, 168n., 189
rationality 3-4, 7, 8, 10, 50, 78, 82, 86, 101-5, 156, 195
   communicative 108-9, 155
   formal 102-3
   substantive 103
   see also instrumental rationality
Rauschenbusch, Walter 68-70, 74, 76, 172
Rawls, John 86, 87, 155, 156ff., 161, 184
realism 70, 165
reality 171, 177, 181, 184
reason, instrumental *see* instrumental rationality
rebellion, metaphysical 33
rebirth 11, 170, 171
reconciliation 31, 66, 170, 175, 179, 180
redemption 40, 165, 171, 193
re-description 83, 96
reflection 83, 84, 181, 182, 189
Reformed tradition 132, 133, 136, 139, 149, 185, 188, 193
   see also covenantal model
reification 91, 106, 112
relationships 9, 10, 37, 43ff., 180, 181, 182, 188, 197
   see also human relationality

relevance 3, 4, 6, 7, 23, 27, 28, 61, 62, 66, 79, 142, 146, 155, 156, 161, 176, 195, 199
religion 22, 30, 79, 117, 120, 121
 as institutional form 141
 and modernity 50-51, 125
 privatisation of 50
 public relevance of 142
 veneration of 66
 see also civil religion
religious communities 12, 27, 49ff., 77, 120, 146, 147, 157, 176
religious freedom 117, 120, 121, 125
religious institutions 143, 174-5
religious studies 80
remembrance 24, 37, 38
repentance 37, 170, 179
Rerum Novum 133-4
Rescher, Nicholas 157n., 184n.
respect 44, 46, 86, 160, 189, 197, 199
responsibility 103, 104, 134, 139, 141
 crisis of 62
 see also social responsibility
resurrection 13, 22, 43, 50, 52, 93, 95, 178
 and cross 24-7, 29, 30
 and God's promise 39-41, 171
revelation 22
 and promise 37-9
revolution 13, 23, 42n., 51, 68, 74, 107, 132
rights 118, 119, 134
Right-wing 21, 34, 88
Roman Catholic Church 127, 132, 133ff., 142, 145n.
Romans 194
romanticism 50, 51
Rouner, L. 54
Rousseau 52, 53, 116, 128, 189
rules 9, 74, 133, 147, 164, 181

Sabbath, messianic 162, 167, 168
salvation 44
sanctification 169, 170
Schmitt, Carl 14, 18-19, 21, 53, 54
Schrag, C. 155, 184n.
Schweiker, William 186
science 10, 61, 64, 66, 74, 80, 85, 105
 see also social science
sectarianism 88, 113, 114n., 144, 173
secularism 50, 53, 73, 88, 112, 168
self 10, 50, 104, 129, 183, 190, 199
self, autonomous 8-10, 129

self-definition 174
self-description 83, 84, 85
self-determination 9, 15, 42
self-interest 54, 75n.
self-righteousness 73, 74
self-understanding 82, 84, 142
separatism 113
Sermon on the Mount 163, 164
service 54, 55
sharing 69, 170
Shekinah 171
sickness 52
Sigmund, Paul 133, 135-6
Simpson, Gary 107, 110, 176, 178-80, 182, 197n.
sin 14, 19, 26, 30, 70, 163, 182
Skillen, James 88-93, 94-5, 98, 149, 175, 191, 195, 199
Skillen, James and McCarthy, R.M. 136
social change 12, 13, 15, 129
social cohesion 120, 128, 129, 131, 148, 184ff.
social contract 116, 117, 139, 195, 196
social criticism 52, 82, 130
 dialectic of 17, 24, 32, 35, 37, 47, 64, 153, 154, 180, 193
 purpose of 105, 106
social differentiation 88-92, 106, 110, 115, 124, 127, 133, 142, 149, 175
social ethics 4, 12, 16, 118, 155, 158, 172, 173, 180, 199
 and covenant 140
 and kingdom of God 68-70
 public theology as 159-60
 'thick' conception 159, 160
 and Trinity, 187-9
social forms 91, 95, 96, 148
social good 13, 78, 87, 89, 149, 157, 185
social gospel 72, 74
social institutions 91, 138, 141, 173
social integration 121, 124, 129, 129-30, 131, 143, 174, 176
social justice 12, 13, 14, 15, 24, 35, 55, 70, 72, 133, 160, 168
social life 7, 8, 14, 43, 47, 52, 53, 56, 69, 90, 92, 95, 117, 131, 135, 137ff., 154, 164, 167, 171
 and God's covenant 185
 institutional forms of 141
 new mode of 170
 theology and 142, 192

social movements 27, 28, 33, 167, 168, 169, 171
social order 17, 19, 27, 69, 76, 133, 134, 172, 174
social policy 180-81
social problems 72, 129
social reform 14, 33, 69, 70, 77
social responsibility 66, 141, 143, 180
　public theology and 72-6, 148
social roles 51, 55, 111, 122, 144
social science 80, 105, 181, 182n., 189
social services 129, 131
social status 73
social structure 110
social system 75, 110-11, 165
social theory 11, 30, 31, 87, 95, 176, 179, 182, 187, 188, 191
　and cross 31-3
social whole 81, 128, 135, 137, 181
socialism 34, 51, 69, 71, 72, 103, 123, 133, 134
society 4, 5, 8, 14, 19, 53, 66, 110, 174, 189
　and covenant 139, 184-6
　'estates of' 119
　and government 117-18
　pluralistic 3, 138ff.
　as 'public' 78-9, 82
　relationships in 46
　and state 90, 91
　transformation of 162
　utopian hope for 20
　see also civil society
sociology 13, 61, 64, 67, 98, 101, 104, 105, 108, 111, 112, 121, 124, 142, 144, 150, 182n., 191, 197
　and church 80ff., 148, 149, 153, 173
solidarity 24, 32, 52, 124, 128, 136, 164, 169, 175
　anamnestic 176-80
Son 32, 34, 43, 46, 188
sovereign 19, 116
sovereignty 19, 30, 44, 90, 91, 96, 128, 139, 140
speech 160, 179, 181
'spheres of society' 19, 54, 83, 88-93, 124, 129, 140, 159
'spheres of sovereignty' 89-90, 93, 139-40
Stackhouse, Max 68, 140-41, 149, 175, 195, 199

state 6n., 11, 12, 14, 15, 30, 33, 42, 53, 89, 103, 104, 110, 111, 115n., 135, 137, 139n., 140, 142, 192, 197, 199
　authority of 134
　and civil society 116ff., 122-4, 125, 127ff., 129, 132
　Hegelian concept 118-19, 120
　society and 90, 91
　as sovereign protector 18-19
Stoics 115
Stout, Jeffery 183
struggle 7, 26, 27, 39, 164, 166
student movements 13, 167
subjectivity 44, 50, 108, 177, 178, 183
subsidiarity 91, 149
　model of 133-6, 142
substantive rationality 4n., 102, 103
subsystems 110, 124
suffering 13, 19, 26, 30, 56, 97, 168, 169, 193
　of God 31-2, 33
suicide 32
symbols 53, 66, 73, 78, 79, 110, 129, 173-4

Taylor, Charles 119
teaching 141
technoeconomic realm 78, 94
teleology 161
'tendencies and latencies' 96, 166-9, 171, 198, 199
theism 33
theologians 7, 11, 63, 67, 76, 77, 80ff., 93, 96, 113
theology 3, 5, 47, 148, 173, 175, 181, 182
　academic 93-4
　and civil society 127ff., 142, 149
　and cross 179-80
　and culture 79-80
　and disciplines 61-2, 63-4, 67, 80, 84
　discursive process 157
　and modernity 11, 154ff.
　political changes in 18ff.
　purpose of 79
　social context 73, 93, 94, 176
　and social theory 191
　see also liberation theology; narrative theology; political theology; public theology
Theology of Hope 5, 24, 37, 51, 55, 193
'thick' concepts 156-7, 159, 160

Thiemann, Ronald 82-8, 96-7, 98, 149, 183, 186, 191
Tillich, Paul 20, 198
Tocqueville, Alexis de 116, 121-2, 125, 130n.
toleration 117, 120, 146
Tönnies, F. 124
Torah, messianic 162-3, 167, 168
totalitarianism 123
Toulmin, Stephen 80
Tracy, David 63-4, 68, 78-82, 85, 93, 98, 149, 160, 191, 195, 199
tradition 5, 46, 63, 64, 81, 82, 83, 84, 96, 121, 146, 158, 159, 175
tragedy 71, 72, 164n., 168, 171, 194
training 85
transformation 14, 22, 55, 69, 70, 95, 149, 158, 162, 166, 170
    dialectic of 17, 24, 35, 37, 47, 64, 153, 154, 180
translation 159-60, 183
trans-subjectivity 178
Trinity 65
    and communicative rationality 180-82
    and covenant 187-8
    and human relationships 43-6, 66
    and social ethics 187-9
trust 177, 196
truth 82, 147, 160, 183, 184, 185

'unburdening' model 33
understanding 63, 109, 160
United States 7, 57, 116, 130, 136, 142
    civil society 121-2
    congregationalism 73
    participation 129
    pluralism 146
    public theology 68-76, 77, 78ff., 87, 195, 199
    religious choice in 145-6
    social differentiation 88-9ff.
unity 44, 53, 121, 175, 180, 181, 188
universality 118, 169-72, 178, 199
utopianism 4, 11, 15, 56, 161, 166, 179, 199
    limit principle 181
    religious 20

value-rationality 102, 103, 108
values 4, 8, 10, 11, 55, 63, 86, 103, 143, 155
    and civil religion 174, 199
    communal discourse 78-9
    substantive 108
van Huyssteen, W. 86, 87
violence 18, 42n., 103-4, 105, 109, 111, 163-5, 185
vocation 54, 55, 140, 141, 142, 149, 185, 195
Volf, Miroslav 45
voluntarism 125, 131, 145-6
voluntary associations 81, 121, 129, 138, 145

war 11, 52, 72, 75, 115, 181
Way of Jesus Christ, The 161n., 193
weakness 52
Weber, Max 3, 10, 50n., 72n., 101-5, 108, 109, 112
West, Cornel 68
workers 68, 69, 106, 107, 123, 133, 134, 135
world 181, 186
    Christian action in 167
    cosmic destiny 171, 172
    pre-apprehension of 166-7

Yahweh 40